STOREY'S
CURIOUS COMPENDIUM
OF PRACTICAL AND OBSCURE
SKILLS

214 Things You Can Actually Learn How to Do

**From the How-To Experts at
Storey Publishing**

Storey Publishing

The mission of Storey Publishing is to serve our customers by
publishing practical information that encourages
personal independence in harmony with the environment.

Edited by Carleen Madigan, Sarah Guare, and Hannah Fries
Art direction and book design by Alethea Morrison
Text production by Erin Dawson
Indexed by Christine R. Lindemer, Boston Road Communications
Photography and illustration credits appear on page 342

Storey books are available at special discounts when purchased in bulk for premiums and sales promotions as well as for fund-raising or educational use. Special editions or book excerpts can also be created to specification. For details, please call 800-827-8673, or send an email to sales@storey.com.

Be sure to read all of the instructions thoroughly before undertaking any of the projects or techniques in this book. Follow all manufacturer's safety guidelines. Take proper safety precautions before using potentially dangerous tools and equipment or undertaking potentially dangerous activities.

Storey Publishing
210 MASS MoCA Way
North Adams, MA 01247
storey.com

Printed in China by Shenzhen Reliance Printing Co. Ltd.
10 9 8 7 6 5 4 3 2 1

Library of Congress Cataloging-in-Publication Data on file

CONTENTS

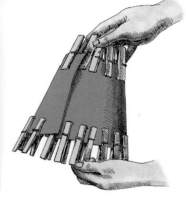

WELCOME!

Are you curious about how things work? Do you like to roll up your sleeves and make stuff? Then this book is for you! Since we published our first book catalog in 1983, Storey Publishing has been teaching people how to garden, farm, cook, craft, build, fix, and heal. Our authors — who include renowned herbalist Rosemary Gladstar, award-winning butcher Adam Danforth, and best-selling fermentistas Kirsten and Christopher Shockey — are all experts in their field. They live their passions, tinkering, researching, teaching, and exploring, and their books are the distillation of their vast sea of knowledge.

We have sifted through this treasure trove of expertise to find the most compelling, useful, interesting, and enjoyable projects and information from the hundreds of Storey titles on our office shelves. As you flip through these pages, we hope you are delightfully surprised by what you find. Like to garden and bake? Maybe you should try baking bread in a flowerpot (page 52)! Ever wonder how to milk a goat? You'll find the easiest and most reliable method here (page 55). And if you are hungry for more, be assured that there's a Storey book to guide you deeper into the topic of your choice. May the passion and enthusiasm of our authors be contagious, and may your life be enriched by the satisfaction and joy of having done it yourself.

— The Makers and Doers of Storey Publishing

BUILD A FIRE PIT
FOR OUTDOOR ROASTING

There's nothing quite like crisp, juicy meat cooked over a fire. An efficient and pleasant roasting hearth can be as simple as a saucer-shaped depression neatly lined with like-sized stones. Egg-shaped or oblong rocks about the size of a grapefruit or large orange are ideal. Some sand, for bedding the stones, is helpful if your soil is very heavy.

1. A rough, lumpy depression in the lawn is the perfect site for a new fire pit. Eyeball the size of the hearth you'll need, based on your cooking plans, and scratch it on the ground.

2. Remove any turf and dig out a shallow, shapely pit a few inches deeper than your intention for the finished specimen. Rough it out with a shovel and use a trowel or your hand to smooth out the saucer. If your soil is heavy clay, you might want to spread about an inch of sand in the pit to make it easier to nestle the stones.

3. Line the pit with stone, starting from the center and working outward in a spiral. Tap the stones down with the butt of your trowel, another stone, or a rubber mallet. After the center of the hearth is established, work against the slope at the rear to build a subtle fire-back, intended to bounce heat back at future roasting projects.

4. Sprinkle sand or light soil over the whole thing and use a small broom or hand brush to sweep it around, allowing it settle into the cracks. Your pit is ready for roasting! It can be easily enlarged or modified with spit supports or a tripod to support a great range of cooking projects.

Step 2

Step 3

Step 4a

Step 4b

[Adapted from *Cooking with Fire* by Paula Marcoux]

SMOKE MEAT
ON THE STOVE

Stove-top smokers are a great way to start playing around with smoking without investing a lot of time, energy, or money. It's more than likely that you already have everything you need to put together a stove-top smoker: a pot, a steamer basket, aluminum foil, and wood shavings or sawdust. You'll need a good range hood fan or an otherwise very well-ventilated kitchen, or do it on a hot plate outside. Stove-top smoking is best suited for hot smoking smaller cuts of meat that only need a short smoking time — foods like fish, poultry, steaks, pork chops, and tenderloins.

1. Line the bottom of the pot with aluminum foil to protect it, and spread a thin, even layer (about ¼ inch) of wood shavings or sawdust on it.

2. Place the steamer insert in the pot, making sure there is room between the steamer basket and the pot for smoke to flow. Place your food in the steamer basket.

3. Place the pot over high heat until it starts smoking, about 5 minutes.

4. Place a tight-fitting lid on the pot. Scrunch extra foil around the edges of the lid to ensure that no smoke can escape.

5. Lower the heat to medium-low and cook until the meat reaches the desired temperature (using a wireless thermometer is helpful in this process). Turn off the heat and let the food rest in the smoker for about 10 minutes. Remove the foil and lid. If the meat is cooked through, it's ready to eat right now. If not, transfer it to a sheet pan and finish it in the oven.

Step 1

Step 2

Step 3

Step 4

[Adapted from *Smokehouse Handbook* by Jake Levin and *Home Cheese Making* by Ricki Carroll]

Smoke Cheese on the Grill

Smoking cheese is a way to add flavor. The smoke evaporates moisture, bringing butterfat to the surface of the cheese; when combined with the smoke, which contains antimicrobial substances, the butterfat has a preservative effect, provided the cheese is kept dry.

Put some dampened hardwood sawdust into a metal pan and place it on a few warm coals that have been allowed to burn down on the bottom of your outdoor grill. Set the cheese on a rack well above the smoking material. Cover the grill and allow the smoke to escape through the vent in the cover. Keep a close eye on your cheese to make sure it doesn't get too warm (above 40°F/4°C). Smoke the cheese until the exterior is golden brown.

MAKE MORE HOUSEPLANTS FOR FREE

It's quite easy to take cuttings from your favorite houseplants to make more plants. Most plants can be propagated by rooting 3- to 4-inch-long cuttings taken from the tips of the stems. The places that will develop new roots and leaves are the nodes — the places where the leaves attach to the stems.

It's a good idea to root more cuttings than you need, just in case some don't take. Most plants with soft, fleshy stems root best when the cutting is set to root immediately after being taken from the parent plant, but succulents and semi-succulent plants sometimes root better if the cut surface is allowed to callus for a day — or up to to several days — before it is set to root.

1. Cleanliness counts when handling cuttings. Wash your hands before filling small, clean containers with your growing medium of choice (see the box at right). Dampen the medium well and use a chopstick or skewer to make holes for the cuttings.

2. Sterilize a sharp knife or pair of scissors by dipping it in boiling water for several seconds. Allow your cutting instrument to cool before using it to sever a healthy stem just below a node.

3. Remove all but the topmost leaves from the cutting. If you are using rooting powder, pour out the amount you'll need onto a piece of paper or into a small dish to avoid contaminating the powder in its original container. Dip the cut end in water, then dip it in rooting powder, tap off the excess, and poke it into its prepared hole. Dispose of any leftover rooting powder in the dish when you're done.

The Best Growing Mediums for Rooting Houseplants

To ensure rooting success, be sure to use a medium that does not support the growth of fungi, which can promote root rot. Three good mediums to use are:

* Seed-starting mix, which is usually composed of vermiculite and peat moss
* Plain perlite
* A half-and-half mixture of peat moss and sand

A few plants prefer one medium over another, but most plants root equally well in any of the three.

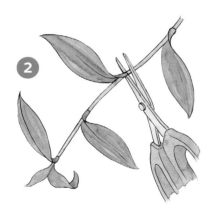

[Adapted from *The Complete Houseplant Survival Manual* by Barbara Pleasant]

4. Use your fingers to gently pack the medium around the stem.

5. For the first 2 weeks after setting any type of cuttings to root, enclose them in plastic, container and all, and place them where they will receive no direct sunlight. This plastic humidity chamber is needed because, until they develop roots, the cuttings have no way to replenish moisture lost through their leaves. A translucent plastic bag, held aloft with sticks, works great for individual containers, or you can place several containers together in a small box and cover the top with a piece of plastic.

6. Each morning, remove the plastic and lightly mist the cuttings. In warm weather, check them again in the afternoon. Add water to the containers only if the medium appears to be drying out. Try to keep it lightly moist but not extremely wet.

7. In the third week, take off the plastic cover, but continue to mist the cuttings daily and keep them out of bright light. Remove and dispose of any cuttings that have obviously died (the stems will be black or shriveled). By the third week, you may see signs of new growth in some of the cuttings. If so, move them to a place where they will get a little more light, and begin mixing a small amount of fertilizer into the water used to replenish the moisture in the containers.

Most stem cuttings will begin to root in 3 to 4 weeks, but some plants may need 2 months or more before they are ready to be potted into regular potting soil. Use the appearance of new growth as your guide. You can also test for the presence of roots by gently pulling on a cutting. A bit of resistance means that roots have anchored the cutting in the rooting medium.

BUILD A SELF-WATERING CONTAINER FOR HOUSEPLANTS

Buried clay pots have been used for irrigation for thousands of years. This system adapted for houseplants works by the same basic principle. Not only does your plant get watered while you are away, but its roots will grow better and it will be less prone to disease.

A porous capsule made out of a terra-cotta pot (and matching base) is buried in the soil of a larger pot. Water seeps out of the capsule gradually, at exactly the rate the plant needs, and is replenished by way of a plastic reservoir above the soil. The reservoir, made out of a recycled plastic container, can be connected directly to the capsule with a single fitting, or, to let the capsule sit deeper inside a larger pot, use a second fitting and a short piece of tubing to lengthen the connection.

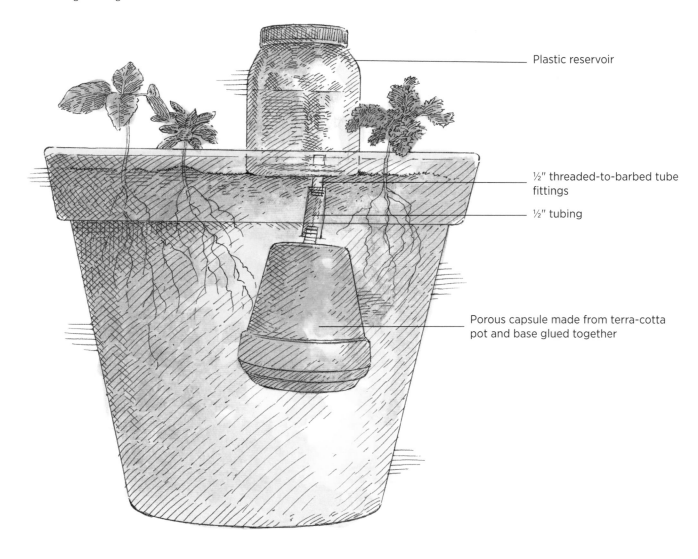

Plastic reservoir

½" threaded-to-barbed tube fittings

½" tubing

Porous capsule made from terra-cotta pot and base glued together

[Adapted from *Gardening with Less Water* by David A. Bainbridge]

This terrarium in a jar is a mini-ecosystem, with plants, soil, and water all working in harmony, and a pretty addition to your desk or windowsill. Keep your "jar-rarium" somewhere where it can get just enough light, and it can last for years.

MAKE A TERRARIUM

TOOLS AND MATERIALS

- Widemouthed quart-size (or larger) mason jar with two-piece lid
- Pebbles
- Activated charcoal (sold at pet stores)
- Coffee filter
- Scissors
- Potting mix
- Spray mister filled with water
- Fork or other long-handled tool
- Paper towel
- Moss and other low-growing woodland plants that will fit in a jar

1. Before you go out to gather plants, collect all the other materials you'll need and put them in your workspace.

2. Collect your plants. Look for moss and other low-growing plants that will fit in the jar. If you prefer to buy plants, ask at your local garden center or nursery for varieties that won't outgrow your terrarium.

3. Cover the bottom of the jar with an inch or so of pebbles. This creates an area where excess water can drain.

4. Spoon a ½-inch layer of activated charcoal on top of the pebbles.

5. Using the jar lid as a template, cut a circle from the coffee filter that is a little smaller than the diameter of the jar. Lay it over the charcoal. This prevents the soil from mixing with the pebbles and charcoal, keeping the drainage area clear.

6. Carefully spoon in about 2 inches of potting mix, or enough to fill the jar one-third of the way. Mist the soil with the sprayer until thoroughly dampened but not soggy.

7. If needed, lightly trim the roots and branches so the plants fit in the jar. Working with a fork or other long-handled tool, dig into the soil and press the moss and plants into place. Add any other decorations.

8. Mist the plants lightly, taking care to moisten the soil near the plants' roots. Use a paper towel to carefully wipe the inside walls of the jar. Screw on the two-piece cap and place the jar in a bright place, but not directly in the sun.

[Adapted from *Mason Jar Science* by Jonathan Adolph]

STITCH LEATHER

In leatherworking, what effect you want to achieve will guide the technique you use. For example, fine linen thread looks much more finished than a rugged leather lace, although both can be correctly used in the proper context. These illustrations show several options for machine- and hand-sewn stitches and seams with both thread and lace.

SEAMS

Thin leather can be sewn on a good sewing machine using a number 16 to number 19 leather needle, seven to nine stitches to the inch, with silk, cotton, or linen thread. Baste the seams together first with all-purpose cement.

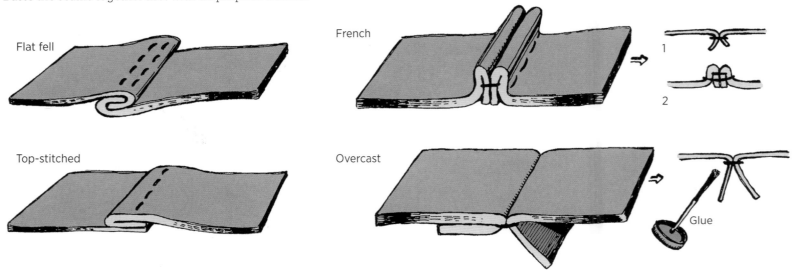

Flat fell

Top-stitched

French

1

2

Overcast

Glue

STITCHES WITH THREAD

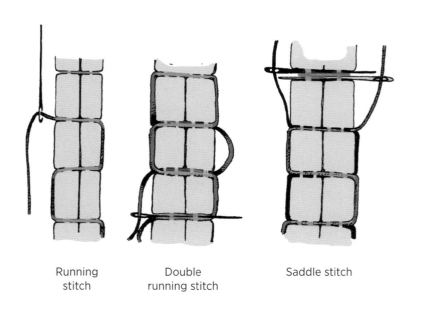

Running stitch

Double running stitch

Saddle stitch

STITCHES WITH LEATHER LACE

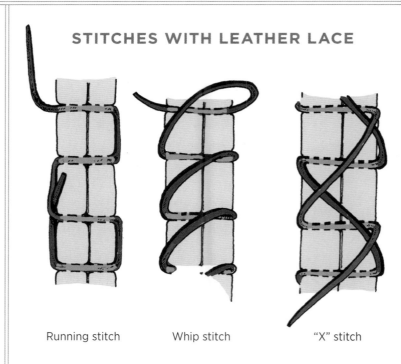

Running stitch

Whip stitch

"X" stitch

[Adapted from *Tan Your Hide!* by Phyllis Hobson]

ENDS WITH LACE

Tuck the lace ends under the stitches.

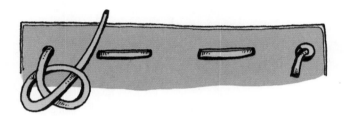

Knot and cut the lace ends.

ENDS WITH THREAD

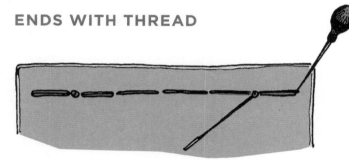

Tie thread ends and push the ends into the nearest hole.

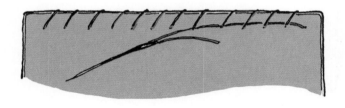

Tuck the thread under the last few stitches.

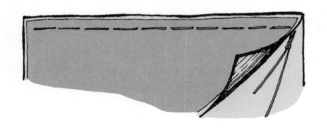

Tie a concealed knot inside.

MAKE A LEATHER BELT

This is a simple leatherworking project that can be done with either a home-tanned hide or commercial leather. Customize your belt with tooling, dye, and patterns of carved leather or rivets.

MATERIALS

- Buckle of your choice
- Heavy (6- to 8-ounce) leather with little stretch
- Rivets
- Aniline leather dye (optional)
- Saddle soap (optional)
- Paste wax

TOOLS

- Yardstick or long, straight board
- Utility knife
- Wooden or metal straightedge
- Revolving punch
- Edge beveler
- Edge creaser

1. Buy or make your buckle first. Of the three basic sorts, these instructions deal with a stud tongue buckle. If you wish to use another type, the difference is that the others require an oval slot to accommodate the buckle tongue.

2. Above all else, belt straps must be straight. Establish a straight edge on your leather with a yardstick or a long, straight board. Draw and cut along it.

3. Measure the interior width of the loop on your buckle. Standard sizes are in ¼-inch increments from 1 to 2 inches. Mark this measurement (minus ⅛ inch) in several places parallel to the straight edge of the leather. Connect the marks with your wooden or metal straightedge and carefully cut out a perfectly straight strap.

4. Add 7 inches to your waist measurement to find the actual strap length. This allows 2 inches to turn through the belt loop and 5 inches at the other end for adjustability holes.

5. Cut the strap to the proper length. Trim both ends to give a more finished look. Simply cut the corners from the buckle end. The loose end may be cut at an angle, rounded, or tapered.

6. Punch medium-sized holes for rivets to hold the buckle. Make two evenly spaced holes in the end first, then run it through the buckle loop. Fold it over and mark through the already punched holes with an awl. Punch them out.

7. Bevel and crease the edges of the strap.

Stud

Adjustability holes

Buckle

Strap

Buckle loop

[Adapted from *Tan Your Hide!* by Phyllis Hobson]

8. Tool the belt in sections, or with one pattern running the length. Or decorate with rivets or studs. Or leave it plain.

9. To dye the belt, dye the face first, then stand it on its side and dye the edges a darker color to accent them.

10. Mount the buckle, and rivet it down carefully to avoid cutting or marring the leather.

11. Finish the strap with saddle soap or paste wax.

12. Put the belt on and hold it so that it is tight enough to do its intended task. Press the buckle stud into the leather behind it. Remove the belt, center that mark within the width of the belt, and punch it out using a tube large enough to accommodate the stud. This hole becomes the center one of five adjustability holes.

Measure so that each one is 1 inch from the next, and punch them as well.

13. Finish the strap with paste wax.

Buckle Styles

Single bar

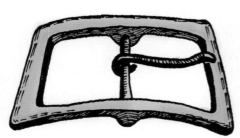

Double bar

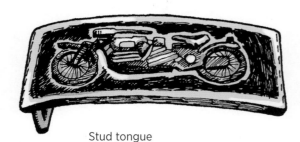

Stud tongue

Strap End Options

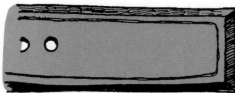

Squared

Tapered

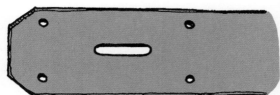

For stud tongue buckle

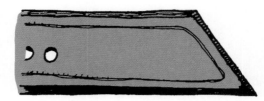

Angled

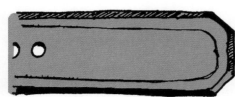

Trimmed

For single or double bar buckle

MOUNT A HORSE

It's fairly easy to mount a calm horse. Always check the cinch that holds the saddle in place before mounting to make sure it is tight enough. For both English and Western riding, using a mounting block is easier for the rider and puts less strain on the horse's back.

Step 1

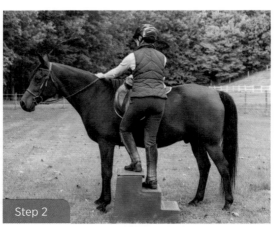
Step 2

Step 3

Step 4

1. Lead the horse to the mounting block, positioning it on his left side just at the girth.

2. Standing on the mounting block, slide your left hand up the reins so that the reins are short enough to stop the horse if he moves. With your right hand, hold the front of the saddle (or the horn, if using Western tack).

3. Holding the reins and the mane with your left hand, put your left foot in the left stirrup. Put your weight in the stirrup and in one smooth movement, swing your right leg over the horse's back and sit gently in the saddle.

   Tip: Some Western riders prefer to face the front of the horse, grab the reins in the left hand and the horn in the right hand, then put their left foot in the stirrup and swing on.

4. Place your right foot in your right stirrup and take the reins in two hands.

Mount from the Ground

To mount from the ground, face the horse on his left side. Grasp the reins in your left hand. Put your left foot in the left stirrup while steadying the stirrup with your right hand. Put your right hand on the seat or the horn and spring lightly up into the stirrup, swinging your leg over in one movement.

If the horse you are riding is spooked or excited for any reason and you feel that you will be safer on the ground than on him, you need to know how to do an emergency dismount. Once you are on the ground, it will be easier to calm your horse. After you dismount, remember to keep hold of the reins, so you will still have your horse, unless he's traveling through terrain where it would be unsafe to pull him around too quickly. Sometimes it's best to just bail off and let him keep going. Practice this while your horse is standing.

DISMOUNT
A HORSE
IN AN EMERGENCY

For the emergency dismount, slip both feet out of the stirrups, lean forward, swing a leg over the horse's back, then slide or jump off. Land with your knees bent, and move in the same direction as the horse to minimize the risk of injury.

How to Stop a Bolting Horse

To control a horse who gets up speed before you can stop him, quickly shorten your reins, brace a hand against his neck, grab the other rein close to the bit, and give a strong, quick pull to bring his head around by your knee, thus pulling him in a tight circle. If the terrain is such that you can't circle (for example, if it's slippery or rocky) or if you would put yourself at risk by circling (on a road with traffic, on a trail through trees, in a group of horses), pull strongly up and back with one rein while bracing with the other hand.

[Adapted from *Storey's Guide to Training Horses* by Heather Smith Thomas]

PREDICT THE WEATHER
BY THE CLOUDS

When you're outdoors, remind yourself to look up and observe how cloud patterns shift and change. Different cloud types indicate different kinds of weather. The better you get at watching the clouds, the better you will get at predicting the weather.

HIGH

CIRRUS
(fair weather)

CIRROCUMULUS
(a front, unsettled, possible storm)

CIRROSTRATUS
(often appear 12–24 hours before rain or snow)

MIDLEVEL

ALTOCUMULUS
(fair, with thunderstorms possible in the afternoon)

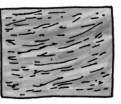

ALTOSTRATUS
(often form ahead of storms)

LOW

CUMULUS
(fair weather)

CUMULONIMBUS
(possible thunderstorms and severe weather)

STRATOCUMULUS
(dry weather)

STRATUS
(drizzle, fine snow, fog)

NIMBOSTRATUS
(long-lasting rain or snow)

[Adapted from *The Curious Nature Guide* by Clare Walker Leslie]

Any of these celestial bodies can point you in the right direction, if you know how to read them! You can use an analog watch and the position of the sun to find approximate north and south. At night, all you need are the stars or moon to lead the way.

NAVIGATE
BY THE SUN, MOON, AND STARS

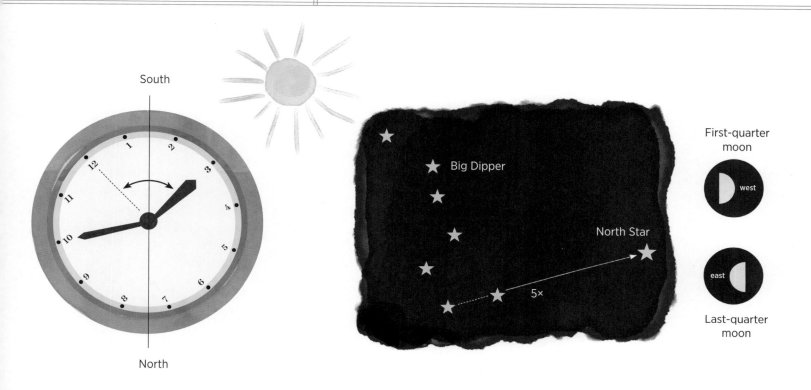

FINDING YOUR WAY BY SUN

NORTHERN HEMISPHERE: Holding the watch flat, point the hour hand in the sun's direction. South is halfway between the hour hand and 12:00 (or 1:00 during daylight saving time, from spring to fall).

SOUTHERN HEMISPHERE: Point the numeral 12 at the sun. North is halfway between the hour hand and the 12.

FINDING YOUR WAY BY STARS

Follow the Big Dipper's "pointer stars" to find the North Star, due north.

FINDING YOUR WAY BY MOON

A FIRST-QUARTER MOON rises in the east at about noon and sets in the west at about midnight. Its bright side points toward the west, because it is trailing the sun.

A LAST-QUARTER MOON rises in the east at about midnight and sets in the west at about noon. Its bright side points toward the east, because it is leading the sun.

[Adapted from *100 Skills You'll Need for the End of the World (as We Know It)* by Ana Maria Spagna]

MAKE
PROBIOTIC
PICKLES

Most people think of pickles as chunks of vegetables floating in vinegar, which is one type of pickle, but it's not the only kind. When vegetables are suspended in salt water and begin to interact with the brine in the process of osmosis, lactic-acid fermentation begins, and the result is a tasty probiotic pickle that your gut will love. This spice and vegetable combination was inspired by the pickled carrots and jalapeños served in many Mexican restaurants.

MAKES 1 GALLON

INGREDIENTS

- ½ cup unrefined sea salt
- 1 gallon unchlorinated water
- 1 head cauliflower, cut into florets
- 5 or more garlic cloves, whole or halved
- 2 pounds carrots, peeled and sliced
- 1 onion, cut into wedges
- 1 pound jalapeños, cored and cut into rounds (or 2 tablespoons chile pepper flakes and a few more carrots and cauliflower florets)
- 1–2 tablespoons dried oregano, crumbled
- 1–2 grape leaves (optional)

Step 1

1. Combine the sea salt and water to make the brine.

2. Combine the veggies and spices in a large bowl and mix to distribute the ingredients.

3. Pack the veggie and spice mixture into a glass jar, wedging the vegetables under the shoulder of the jar.

4. Pour in enough brine to cover the vegetables completely. Remember this mantra: *Submerge in brine and all will be fine.* Reserve any leftover brine in the fridge. (It will keep for 1 week; discard thereafter and make a new batch, if needed.)

5. Place a grape leaf or a piece of plastic wrap over the top to keep the spices and vegetables from floating.

6. Cover the jar with a lid but do not tighten. You want CO_2 to be able to escape.

7. Cover the jar with a cloth and set aside on a baking sheet to ferment, somewhere nearby, out of direct sunlight, and cool, for 7 to 21 days. During the fermentation period, monitor the brine level and top off with the reserved brine solution, if needed, to cover. You may see scum on top; it's generally harmless.

8. As the vegetables ferment, they begin to lose their vibrant color and the brine will get cloudy; this is when you can start to test your pickles. In the summertime this may be as soon as 1 week; in a cooler environment it will be closer to 2 weeks. They're ready when they're pleasingly sour and pickle-y tasting, without the strong acidity of vinegar; the flavors have mingled; and the vegetables are softer than they were when fresh but retain some crispness.

9. When the vegetables are ready, transfer them to smaller jars, add enough brine to submerge them, screw on lids, and store in the fridge.

10. After about 1 day, check to be sure the pickles are still submerged, topping off with more brine if necessary. These pickles will keep, refrigerated, for 1 year.

[Adapted from *Fermented Vegetables* by Kirsten K. Shockey and Christopher Shockey]

Step 2

Step 3

Step 4

Step 5

Step 6

Step 7

Step 8

Step 9

Step 10

MAKE SAUERKRAUT

Homemade sauerkraut is a world apart from the stuff that comes from the grocery store. Not only is it chock-full of probiotics and nutrient-dense, but it also has unimaginably complex, deep flavors. And the only ingredients you need are cabbage and salt.

You want firm heads of cabbage with crispy, shiny leaves. (They look dull as they lose vitality.) Unrefined sea salt is best, and start off with a small amount of salt, tasting and adding as you go. You should be able to taste the salt, but the kraut should not be "briny," "salty," or in any way unpalatable. If it is good fresh, it will be excellent fermented.

1. Remove the coarse outer leaves from 1 to 2 heads of cabbage (3½ pounds total). Rinse a few unblemished ones and set them aside. Rinse the rest of the cabbage in cold water. With a stainless steel knife, quarter and core the cabbage. Thinly slice with the same knife or a mandoline, then transfer the cabbage to a large bowl.

2. Add 1 tablespoon of salt and, with your hands, massage it into the leaves, then taste. You should be able to taste the salt without it being overwhelming. Add more salt if necessary.

3. The cabbage will soon look wet and limp, and liquid will begin to pool. If you've put in a good effort and don't see much brine in the bowl, let it stand, covered, for 45 minutes, then massage again.

4. Transfer the cabbage to a crock or 2-quart jar, a few handfuls at a time, pressing down on the cabbage with your fist or a tamper to work out air pockets. You should see some brine on top of the cabbage when you press.

5. Leave 4 inches of headspace for a crock, or 2 to 3 inches for a jar.

6. Top the cabbage with one or two of the reserved outer leaves.

7. For a crock, top the leaves with a plate that fits the opening of the container and covers as much of the vegetables as possible; weight it down with a sealed, water-filled jar. For a jar, use a sealed, water-filled jar or ziplock bag as a follower-weight combination.

8. Cover the jar or crock with a cloth and set aside on a baking sheet to ferment, somewhere nearby, out of direct sunlight, and cool, for 4 to 14 days.

9. Check daily to make sure the cabbage is submerged, pressing down as needed to release CO_2 and maintain brine coverage.

10. You can start to test the kraut on day 4. You'll know it's ready when it's pleasingly sour and pickle-y tasting, without the strong acidity of vinegar; the cabbage has softened a bit but retains some crunch; and the cabbage is more yellow than green and slightly translucent, as if it's been cooked.

11. Ladle the kraut into smaller jars and tamp down. Pour in any brine that's left. Tighten the lids, then store in the refrigerator. This kraut will keep, refrigerated, for 1 year.

The Bacteria with a Buttery Flavor

Pediococcus cerevisiae is one of the members of the Lactobacillaceae team and is the bacterium that gives lacto-fermented sauerkraut its buttery flavor. This occurs because *Pediococcus* produces diacetyl, a compound that tastes, well, buttery. The creamy flavor profile of this bacterium makes it a good influence on cheeses and yogurt; wine and beer makers, however, view the little guy as a contaminant.

[Adapted from *Fermented Vegetables* by Kirsten K. Shockey and Christopher Shockey]

Step 1

Step 2

Step 3

Step 4

Step 5

Step 6

Step 7

Step 8

Step 9

Step 10

Step 11

MAKE TEMPEH

Put simply, tempeh is a cake made of legumes (typically soybeans), grains, or seeds that is covered in white mold (the resulting growth of rhizopus spores). It has a savory flavor and satisfying texture that can easily double for meat in many dishes. You'll need tempeh starter (available online) and a dehydrator or sous vide setup.

**MAKES 2 TEMPEH CAKES,
1 POUND EACH**

INGREDIENTS

- 3 cups soybeans
- 2 tablespoons vinegar
- 1 teaspoon tempeh starter

1. Sanitize your tools and work surface before getting started.

2. Rinse the soybeans, transfer them to a large bowl, and cover by at least 4 inches of water. Leave on the counter for 8 to 24 hours. After 12 hours, change out the water.

3. Drain the beans, put them back in the bowl, and cover with fresh water. Massage the soybeans between your hands to slip the hulls off. The hulls will accumulate in the water on top of the soybeans; skim them off. Alternatively, drain and roughly chop the beans in a food processor. If you do this, you will need to boil the beans in the next step, instead of steaming them, and skim the hulls off the water as the beans boil.

4. Steam the soybeans for 10 minutes in a pressure cooker. Or bring a pot of water to a boil, add the beans, and simmer until al dente, about 45 minutes.

5. Pour the cooked beans into a colander to drain. Place them in a casserole dish and add the vinegar, mixing to disperse the vinegar and release steam. A lot of moisture will dissipate with the steam. Using a hair dryer on high heat, dry the beans until they are damp dry, stirring them gently as you work.

6. Add the tempeh starter and stir with a spoon or clean hands until it is well incorporated. Now you can ferment the beans. The steps that follow are for fermenting the beans in plastic bags in a dehydrator, but you can also use a water bath setup (see the box).

7. Using a large needle, perforate both sides of two quart-size ziplock bags in a grid with holes spaced apart about the width of a U.S. quarter. There is no specific pattern, so you can get creative if you like; just stay fairly uniform.

8. Fill each bag about three-quarters full with the beans so that when you lay it flat it is about 1 inch thick (and no more than 1½ inches). Squeeze out the excess air, seal, then lay flat on a cutting board and spread the beans in the bags with your hands so that they are evenly distributed. If either bag is not completely full, fold over the unused portion of the bag.

9. Place the bags in the center of a dehydrator and set the temperature to 88°F/31°C and the timer to 24 hours. Begin checking the temperature after 12 hours, and reduce the dehdyrator heat as needed to keep the tempeh at 88°F/31°C.

10. After 18 to 24 hours, white spores will begin to knit everything together. Keep the tempeh in the dehydrator, with the heat turned off, for another 6 to 12 hours.

11. When the tempeh is done, it will be a firm white cake. To serve, lightly boil or steam tempeh in a mixture of water and soy sauce (or other aminos), then slice and drop into hot oil for a few minutes.

Fermentation Alternative: Sous Vide

Instead of using a dehydrator, you could ferment your beans using a sous vide setup. Spread the beans in a high-sided stainless steel steamer pan (like the kind used for buffet setups) about ¾ inch thick. Fill a large plastic tub with water, attach an immersion circulator to the tub, and set the temperature to 88°F/31°C. Let the tempeh sit in the bath until firm, about 24 hours.

[Adapted from *Miso, Tempeh, Natto & Other Tasty Ferments* by Kirsten K. Shockey & Christopher Shockey]

Step 1

Step 2

Step 3

Step 4

Step 5

Step 6

Step 7

Step 8

Step 9

Step 10

Step 11

GROW A STRAW BALE GARDEN

Here's the simple concept of straw bale gardening: the straw in a bale breaks down over the course of the garden season to provide an effective substrate for the roots of the plants growing in it. A bale of straw is like a clean, blank slate. It may be mostly free of plant nutrients, but it is also free of diseases. It acts like a sponge, absorbing water and awaiting the application of materials that help the straw break down and produce a perfect environment for plant roots.

MATERIALS

- Thermometer
- Pesticide-free straw bale
- Granular blood meal (12-0-0)
- Balanced granular plant food (3-4-4)
- Compost-rich planting medium
- High-quality soilless planting medium
- Seedlings or seeds

PREPARING A BALE

DAY 1: Check and record the internal temperature of the bale; it will likely be around 80°F/27°C. Add 3 cups of 12-0-0 granular blood meal, sprinkling it evenly over the top of the bale. Using a hose with no connector and a moderate water flow, pour water evenly over the top of the bale for about 1 minute; you will see water emerging from the bottom of the bale. Note that the water will visibly dissolve the granular material but will begin to push that material down into the structure of the bale.

DAY 2: Check and record the internal temperature of the bale. Water the bale thoroughly from the top.

It is easy to check the internal temperature of the bales during the preparation process by inserting a thermometer into the interior of the bale.

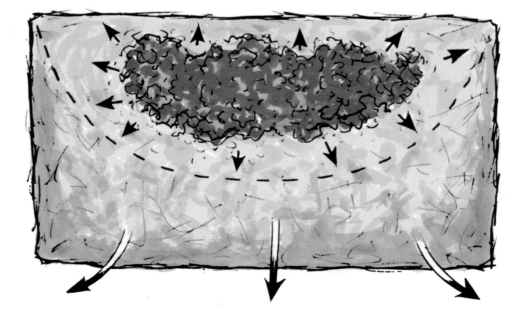

As you water and fertilize the bale, microbial activity generates heat that moves through the bale and breaks down the straw to provide an ideal habitat for plant roots.

[Adapted from *Growing Vegetables in Straw Bales* by Craig LeHoullier]

DAY 3: Repeat the day 1 activity. At this point, you should see the internal bale temperature begin to rise. The temperature should peak at approximately 120°F/49°C, which indicates the action of the nutrients on the bale components, breaking them down to provide a suitable environment for the plants. Over the course of treatment, the internal temperature will drift slowly downward, landing below 80°F/27°C, a safe temperature for the roots of your plants.

DAY 4: Repeat the day 2 activity.

DAY 5: Repeat the day 1 activity.

DAY 6: Repeat the day 2 activity.

DAYS 7–9: Repeat the day 1 activity but use only ¾ cup of blood meal.

DAY 10: Check and record the internal temperature of the bale. Sprinkle 2 cups of balanced (3-4-4) granular plant food across the top of the bale. Thoroughly water, as you have been doing daily.

DAYS 11–14: Check and record the internal temperature of the bale. Water thoroughly. If, on day 14, the temperature has fallen below 80°F/27°C, the bale is ready to plant.

TRANSPLANTING SEEDLINGS

If possible, plant seedlings on a cloudy day to minimize transplant stress. If you must plant when it's sunny, work later in the day to avoid setting out seedlings in the hot sun.

Using a trowel or another cultivating tool, create a hollow in the bale that is sufficient to contain the rootball, tuber, clove, or slip. Even when the bale is ready to plant, the straw will likely still be quite stiff; it will take some effort with your tool to create the depression, and you many need to plunge the tool into the bale and pull out some of the straw. Insert the plant into the hole and fill in around it with a compost-rich planting medium, leveling it with the top of the bale, and water it well. If you removed some of the straw when creating the hollow, you can use it as mulch around the newly planted seedling.

DIRECT SEEDING

After the bale is prepared, apply a level, 2-inch layer of high-quality soilless mix to the top of the bale and firm it down gently. Carefully water the medium and the top of the bale so that both are well moistened. Create holes or rows and sow the seeds, using the spacing indicated for the crop. After sowing, cover the seeds with planting medium at the appropriate depth indicated for that crop; then firm the planting mix gently and water lightly.

Cutaway view of a partially planted bale

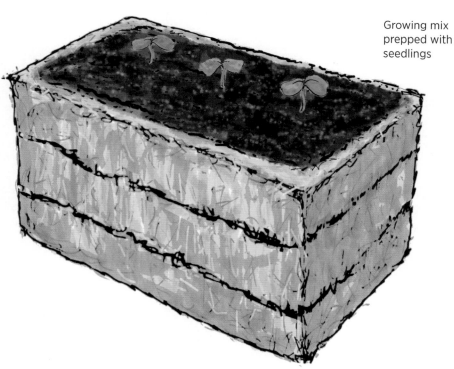

Growing mix prepped with seedlings

GROW VEGETABLES IN BAGS

Turning a patch of sun-drenched lawn into an edible garden may be one of the best things you will ever do in your life, and here we begin in the easiest way imaginable — by arranging 40-pound bags of topsoil over the new garden site and planting right into them. This method is almost too easy to believe, but it really works! And one of the nicest things is that there is no need to dig up and remove the grass. In the course of a season, the bags will smother the grass beneath them. In late fall, gather up the fragile bags and dig their contents into your new permanent beds.

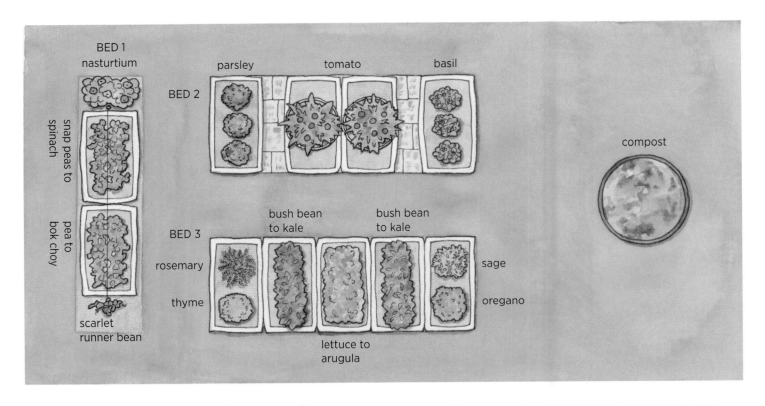

1. **PREPARE YOUR SITE.** Select a site and arrange bags as shown in the garden plan. Before positioning the bags in Bed 2, cover the ground between the tomato and herb bags with four to six sheets of damp newspaper or a single thickness of well-dampened cardboard to deter weeds. The bags will hold the covering in place. Set up your composter or assemble your composting enclosure. The following year, plant vegetables into your compost area.

2. **DO A LITTLE DIGGING.** Use a spade or shovel and digging fork to remove grass and weeds from the ends of Bed 1. Toss all plant debris into the compost. The same tools work well for breaking up the stripped soil; loosen it to a depth of at least 8 inches. Mix two handfuls of organic fertilizer into the soil at each end of the bed. Then install posts for the pea trellis by pounding them into the ground at the ends of the bags.

3. **PREPARE BAGS FOR PLANTING.** Use a utility knife to cut out a large rectangular window on the upper surface of each bag in Bed 1, leaving the sides and 2 inches of each top edge intact, like a picture frame. Lightly dust the surface of the soil inside the bags with organic fertilizer and mix it in with a trowel. Stab through each bag about a dozen times with a knife or screwdriver to pierce drainage holes in the bottoms. Plant roots will also use these holes to grow down into the soil below the bags.

[Adapted from *Starter Vegetable Gardens* by Barbara Pleasant]

4. **WEAVE THE TRELLIS.** Install the trellis netting or string between the posts. If you're using string, start by tying a horizontal line between the posts, no more than 6 inches above the soil's surface. Then tie more horizontal lines at least 6 inches apart (so there's room to reach through the trellis when harvesting) until the top string is 4 feet from the ground.

Create a trellis grid by weaving more string vertically in and out through the horizonal strings.

MIDSPRING

5. **SOW PEAS.** One month before your last spring frost date, plant pea seeds in the soil in the bags in Bed 1, sowing one row on either side of the trellis. Poke the seeds into the soil 1 inch deep and 2 to 3 inches apart.

6. **SOW PARSLEY.** In Bed 2, cut away the upper surface on three sides of the bag that will be planted with parsley, leaving the plastic attached along one short edge. Apply fertilizer and make drainage holes as you did in step 3. Plant about 25 parsley seeds ¼ inch deep and ½ inch apart (fewer than half will germinate). Lay the plastic flap over the seeded area to keep the soil moist, and hold the flap in place with a stone or small board. As soon as seeds germinate, in 1 to 2 weeks, lift and cut away the plastic flap. (If you buy parsley seedlings rather than seeds, see step 8; plant them at the same time that you plant the other herb seedlings.)

Continued on next page

A 2-inch rim of plastic on the surface of each bag prevents soil spillage and helps retain moisture.

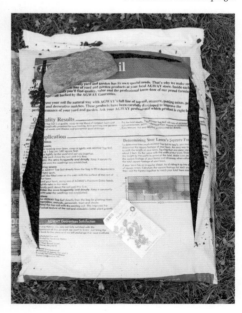

A flap of plastic helps keep the soil moist for slow-sprouting parsley seeds.

7. **SOW LETTUCE.** In Bed 3, cut out a window in the center bag (lettuce), as you did in step 3. Lettuce seeds sprout faster than parsley, so they don't need to be covered with a plastic flap. After applying fertilizer and making drainage holes, scatter lettuce seeds over the soil's surface so that they are about 1 inch apart. Two to three weeks later, fill any gaps in the planting with small pinches of seeds.

8. **PLANT HERBS.** As soon as they're available at garden centers, buy rosemary, thyme, sage, and oregano plants for Bed 3. Prepare the end bags in the bed as you did in step 3. Keep the plants watered until you're ready to set them out. Plant them at even spacing, with each plant about 10 inches in from the edge of the bag. Position each herb in its planting hole so that the base of the main stem is no deeper than it grew in the container.

Plant roots have no trouble growing through drainage holes into the soil below.

LATE SPRING

9. **SOW BEANS AND MORE.** After the last frost passes, cut away the tops of the remaining bags, sprinkle on fertilizer, and make drainage holes. In Bed 3, poke 10 to 15 bush bean seeds into each of the two bags, 1 inch deep and 6 inches apart. Sow pinches of basil seeds ½ inch deep and 10 inches apart in Bed 2, or plant basil seedlings. In Bed 1, plant five or so nasturtium seeds 1 inch deep and 2 inches apart at one end of the trellis; plant five scarlet runner bean seeds 1 inch deep and 2 inches apart at the other end.

10. **PLANT TOMATOES.** Water your tomato seedlings, and try to handle them by the roots rather than the stem as you transplant them into Bed 2. Place the plants at an angle so the bottom part of the stem is buried. Water well. Install tomato cages soon after you set out the plants.

THROUGHOUT SUMMER

11. **WATER WHEN NEEDED.** Since plastic helps retain moisture, your bag garden may not need as much watering as plants growing in the ground would. But even so, be sure to water your plants during periods of warm, dry weather.

12. **ENJOY THE HARVEST OFTEN.** Visit your garden at least every other day to harvest what's ready for your table. Be sure to gather peas every other day, because they quickly go from perfect to starchy.

LATE SUMMER

13. **SOW FALL CROPS.** Pull up and compost tattered peas, bush beans, and lettuce. In those beds, scatter a dusting of organic fertilizer over the soil's surface, and lightly mix it in with a hand trowel. Sow bok choy and spinach in Bed 1, and kale and arugula in Bed 3. Plant the seeds ¼ inch deep and 3 to 4 inches apart, in rows at least 8 inches apart. Keep the soil moist until the seeds germinate.

FALL

14. **START GARDEN CLEANUP.** A heavy frost will end the season for the runner beans, tomatoes, basil, and nasturtiums, but cold nights actually improve the flavor of leafy greens. As exposure to cold damages more and more crops, pull up old plant debris and throw it into the compost. Once a bag is vacant, gather up the plastic and dispose of it in the garbage, leaving the topsoil or planting mix in place. Don't try to remove bags where perennial herbs are growing, though! Leave them in place through the winter.

EARLY WINTER

15. **PUT THE GARDEN TO BED.** As time and weather permit, dig the topsoil into the beds, cultivating the soil at least 12 inches deep. Then mulch over the beds with any organic mulch you can get your hands on, from shredded leaves to dry grass clippings. Spread the mulch 3 to 4 inches deep, and leave it in place until the soil begins to warm in spring.

Why grow plants upside down? Why not! You will see some interesting plant shapes and will never have to weed. The upside-down growing system works best for tomatoes and strawberries but is doable for other plants that naturally trail, such as cucumbers, beans, and peas. Peppers and eggplant also do acceptably well with this method.

GROW UPSIDE-DOWN VEGETABLES IN A 5-GALLON BUCKET

Put the open top end of the bucket to work growing microgreens, small root crops (radishes, baby carrots, small beets), and herbs, or even trailing nasturtiums and other edible flowers to add visual appeal.

Tip: Plants instinctively grow upward, and some interesting shapes will occur as they do. Sometimes it helps to gently tie vines or stems in the desired direction or to brace or weight them as necessary to encourage the stems to grow out past the bottom of the container before branching upward. Otherwise, some try to grow up into the bottom of the planter.

1. Install a hanging hook for each bucket before you plant, making sure that it will bear the weight of the pot plus soil (don't forget that the soil will be wet!).

2. Cut or drill a hole in the bottom of the bucket for each plant that will go in it. For large plants such as tomatoes, one hole per container, dead center, 1 to 2 inches in diameter, works well. For smaller plants, such as pole beans and peas, use six to eight holes maximum, and for peppers, eggplant, and strawberries, three or four is sufficient. The holes need to be large enough that you can fit the transplants through them, either head (foliage) first or feet (roots) first, as well as large enough to accommodate the stem of the plant once it matures.

3. Hang the bucket and thread each plant through a hole either by carefully pushing the rootball from the outside of the planter in or by very gently pulling the leaves through from the inside.

4. Once a seedling is in place, add moistened planting soil, a little at a time, gently pressing it as you go, until the transplant is stable. If you're putting in more than one plant, add some potting medium around each one to help hold it in place as you put in the others.

5. Continue adding soil to within 2 to 4 inches of the top of the bucket. Water until the excess starts to drain out the bottom.

Beautiful Buckets

Reclaimed buckets don't have to be ugly or plain. They will last many years, so consider decorating them to match their surroundings or to stand out as artwork in their own right. You can paint, decoupage (covered with a waterproofing coat of polyurethane), wrap (try brightly colored yarn, rope, or raffia), cover with fabric or contact paper, create a faux stained-glass masterpiece by gluing on bits of glass in a mosaic pattern, or whatever else your creative mind can concoct.

[Adapted from *Vertical Vegetables & Fruit* by Rhonda Massingham Hart]

DYE YOUR HAIR WITH HERBS

When you use herbal hair colorants, you don't need to put up with burning eyes and scalp until it is time to wash out the color. You don't need to use a timer that dings to alert you when it's time to rush to a sink. In fact, the longer herbal hair colorants are on, the deeper the tone and the more lasting the stain. If coloring your entire head, use about 1¾ ounces of herbal powder for chin-length hair and 3½ to 7 ounces for long hair, depending on length and thickness.

HERBAL COLORANT RECIPES

The color ratios at right are for virgin hair — hair that does not have a line demarcating chemically colored hair from natural, new growth. If you do have chemically colored hair with a line of demarcation, you can still use these ratios, but you will then need to use some ingenuity and instinct to create a second recipe to blend that line of demarcation. The one rule with herbal hair colorants: you can't make dark hair lighter.

cassia

henna

indigo

amla

HAIR COLOR GOAL	EXISTING BASE COLOR	HERBAL COLORANT FORMULA
Carrot hues	Blond, dirty blond, gray, or white	½ pure cassia powder, ½ pure henna powder
Light brown	White, blond, or red	½ pure henna powder, ½ pure indigo powder
Medium brown	Brown or brown with moderate gray	⅓ pure henna powder, ⅓ pure indigo powder, ⅓ pure cassia powder
Warm dark brown	Medium brown, dark brown, or black	⅓ pure henna powder, ⅓ pure amla powder, ⅓ pure indigo powder
Black	Any color	**STEP 1:** 100% pure henna powder for at least 1 hour **STEP 2:** 100% pure indigo powder for at least 1 hour (the longer indigo is on, the darker the black)

[Adapted from *Natural Hair Coloring* by Christine Shahin]

1. Start with pure herbal powder(s), combining powders if needed. (See the colorant formulas on the opposite page.)

2. Add liquid to the powder (use lemon juice or apple cider vinegar for henna and cassia and water for indigo and amla).

3. Mix until the colorant has a pudding consistency, adding more liquid as necessary.

4. Let the mud sit for at least 2 hours if you're using henna or cassia.

5. Apply the mud to your hair with gloved hands, being sure to include the hairline around your face.

6. Wrap your head in plastic.

7. Wrap a scarf around the plastic (or use a thermal cap). Let the mud sit for 1 to 4 hours, depending on the strength of the stain desired.

8. Rinse out the mud. Shampoo, condition, dry, and style as usual.

Add enough liquid to herbal powder to make a thick pudding.

MAKE TOOTHPASTE AND HAIR CONDITIONER

An easy way to save a lot of money (over the years, anyway) is to make your own toothpaste and hair conditioner. Plus, you know exactly what is going into your mouth and onto your hair! Keep the toothpaste in a jar by the sink.

Toothpaste

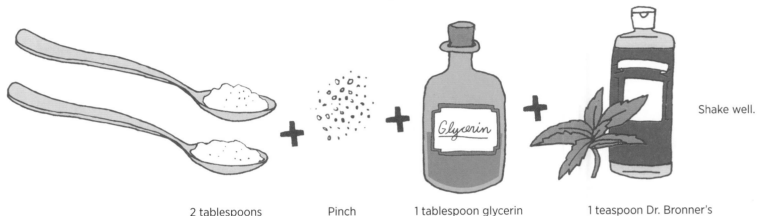

2 tablespoons baking soda

Pinch of salt

1 tablespoon glycerin (optional)

1 teaspoon Dr. Bronner's peppermint Castile liquid soap

Shake well.

Hair Conditioner

Boil water equal to half your container's volume.

Steep yucca — or any saponin-containing local plant — with ¼ cup rosemary and 2 tablespoons hibiscus.

Strain and pour into your container. Fill the rest of the container with white vinegar.

[Adapted from *The Good Life Lab* by Wendy Jehanara Tremayne]

Field biologists and naturalists often keep notebooks to sketch what they observe. Drawing nature is a way of internalizing what you learn and observe. For example, when you draw a plant with flowers, try following this sequence of tips and questions.

LEARN ABOUT NATURE BY DRAWING IT

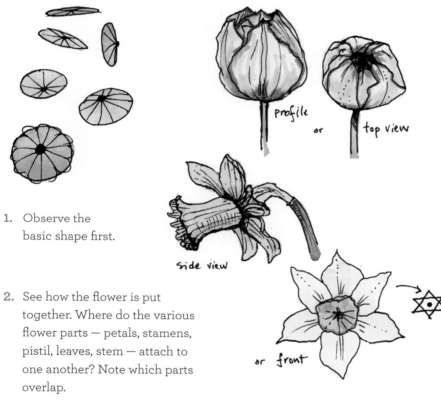

profile or top view

side view

or front

1. Observe the basic shape first.

2. See how the flower is put together. Where do the various flower parts — petals, stamens, pistil, leaves, stem — attach to one another? Note which parts overlap.

Repeated parts, don't draw all details → only a few flowers

3. Keep the drawing simple. If you're doing a complex flower head, like goldenrod or ragweed, do only part of the whole.

4. The flowers may be placed quite differently on different kinds of plants. Where is the flower on your plant placed?

5. Record where this flower grows; whether it is the flower of a tree, plant, or grass; and whether it is wild or cultivated. Record the habitat in which you found it.

6. Keep a record of when various flowers bloom over the course of a year. You can learn a lot about weather, habitat, and soil type by tracking where and when particular flowers bloom.

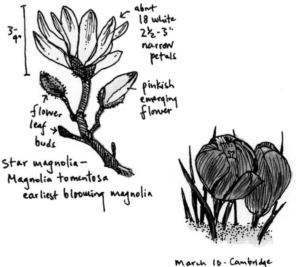

3¾" abnt 18 white 2½-3" narrow petals

pinkish emerging flower

flower leaf buds

star magnolia — Magnolia tomentosa earliest blooming magnolia

March 10 · Cambridge neighbor's orange crocuses in 1" of snow

[Adapted from *Keeping a Nature Journal* by Clare Walker Leslie]

MAKE PRINTS FROM NATURE

You can make beautiful stationery, cards, wrapping paper, and other artwork by printing with leaves and other found objects from nature. Water-soluble printing inks work well, but almost any ink or paint can be used for nature printing, so try whatever product you like working with. Begin with flat leaves, such as sage, maple, hydrangea, and dandelion. Leaves with interesting shapes and protruding veins give satisfying results. Try printing on as many papers as possible to find your favorites, but begin with newsprint, kozo, copier paper, and other inexpensive, smooth-textured papers for practice.

TOOLS AND MATERIALS

- Water-soluble inks
- Glass or freezer-paper palette
- Vehicle or extender (mixing medium for the ink)
- Pigment mixers
- Dabbers (pads) and/or brayers (rollers)
- Leaves and other natural objects to print
- Tweezers
- Newsprint for test prints
- Newsprint or paper towel cover sheets
- Papers for printing

1. **PREPARE THE INK AND PALETTE.** Put a small amount of ink onto your palette. If desired, add a few drops of mixing medium or water and mix together. Use the mixer to drag some of the ink along the palette, making a thin smear a few inches long.

2. **PREPARE THE DABBER.** Pick up a dabber by the narrow end and dab the wide end, up and down, in the ink smear. You don't want globs of ink on your dabber, just a nice even film. Test this by pressing the dabber, using medium pressure, on a piece of newsprint. Ideally, a little square of evenly distributed ink will appear. Use a clean dabber for each color.

3. **INK THE LEAF.** Place a leaf, underside up, on the palette or on a piece of scrap paper. Hold the stem end of the leaf with your finger and dab ink over the entire surface. Don't saturate the leaf with ink or the veining pattern won't print clearly.

4. **PRINT THE LEAF.** Pick up the leaf by the stem end with tweezers and place it inked side down on newsprint or other test paper. Place a cover sheet over it and press the entire leaf with your fingers or the heel of one hand. For large leaves use both hands; anchor the center of the leaf with the thumb of one hand while using the other hand to successively press all around, radiating from the center to the edge of the leaf. Remove the cover sheet, then lift the leaf straight up and off the paper with clean tweezers.

5. **CHECK THE RESULTS.** If the leaf print looks heavy, with little detail, use less ink or less pressure. If the leaf looks pale, with spotty detail, use more ink or more pressure when printing. Always make test prints. With the exception of delicate flowers, the first print is rarely the best one.

6. **MAKE MORE PRINTS!** Depending on the sturdiness of the leaf, one leaf might make 5, 10, or sometimes 40 impressions. One inking can make two or more prints, each one lighter than the last. Once you're satisfied with your test prints, move on to using good-quality papers. Print a variety of leaves, flowers, and other objects; use more colors, and print on fabrics and other surfaces.

[Adapted from *Hand Printing from Nature* by Laura Bethmann]

Step 1

Step 2

Step 3

Step 4a

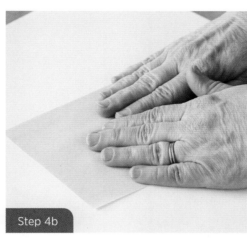

Step 4b

Step 4c

This basic basket is fun to make and can be quite useful. Make one for your desk to organize things like index cards, sticky notes, or small notebooks. Or make one for your craft table to hold odds and ends. It's a wonderful catch-all that reuses a paper bag and takes only a little time to put together. You can also experiment with other types of paper, such as old maps. The finished bag measures 4½ inches wide, 4½ inches long, and 3 inches deep.

WEAVE A PAPER BASKET

TOOLS AND MATERIALS

- Scissors
- 1 brown paper grocery bag
- Ruler
- Bone folder, letter opener, butter knife, or any tool that will help crease a fold

PREPARING THE PAPER

1. Cut down the seam on one side of the bag.

2. Cut along the fold around all sides of the bottom to make one long, flat rectangular piece of paper. Discard the bag bottom.

3. From the long rectangle, cut 16 strips that are 1 inch wide and 14 inches long and 5 strips that are 1 inch wide and 21 inches long.

4. Fold all the strips in half lengthwise so they are ½ inch wide and double thickness.

5. Press the fold line with the bone folder to achieve a crisp edge. If you don't have a bone folder, something like the side of a letter opener or the edge of a butter knife will work.

WEAVING THE BASKET

6. Lay out eight of the 14-inch strips next to each other vertically, with the ends even.

7. In the center of the vertical strips, insert a 14-inch strip horizontally so it goes over one strip and under the next all the way across.

8. Insert a second 14-inch strip horizontally into the vertical strips, but this time go over the vertical strips that you went under in the previous row and under the strips that you went over.

9. Repeat steps 7 and 8, moving outward from the center and working your way first above and then below that horizontal center strip.

10. When you have used all of the 14-inch strips, the woven area should form a square in the center of the vertical and horizontal strips. This will be the bottom of the basket.

Continued on next page

As you weave in the strips, snug them together so they touch the previous row.

Step 3

Step 7

Step 9

[Adapted from *The Weaving Explorer* by Deborah Jarchow and Gwen W. Steege]

11. Fold the side strips up from the bottom, being careful to keep the bottom grid tight. Pinch and fold the strips as they turn the corner from the bottom to help hold the shape of the bottom square.

12. Insert one of the 21-inch strips horizontally, alternating over and under, to begin forming the sides of the basket. Use paper clips to help stabilize the strips you're weaving, then reposition the clips as you move along.

13. Repeat step 12, but weave over the strips you went under in the previous row and under the strips you went over. Continue in this manner, working up the sides and tightening the individual strips as you go along so you pull up any slack. Overlap the beginning and end of each strip as you weave each round.

14. Weave as high as you want the basket to be. This example is five horizontal strips high.

15. Go back and tighten up all the strips again, working any slack to the top edge of the basket.

FINISHING

16. Trim both ends of the 16 strips, fold them over, and tuck them into the previous row.

Step 11

Step 12

Step 16

This is the simplest and cheapest way to start crafting your own paper at home. The paper you make will be round, unless you experiment with containers in other shapes to put on top of your screen. For the pulp, you can use any kind of recycled paper, from the Sunday funnies, magazines, and bags to wrapping paper, envelopes, and labels from cans and jars.

MAKE PAPER IN A TIN CAN

TOOLS AND MATERIALS

- Large container such as a coffee can, juice container, or milk jug, with one end cut out to catch water runoff
- Drain pan
- At least one 6" square of rigid screen, such as hardware cloth or plastic needle-work canvas, to serve as support screen
- At least two 6" squares of nonmetal fine-mesh window screen, to serve as paper-making screen
- Container of equal or smaller size as the one above, with both ends cut out (whatever the size and shape, that's what your paper will be)

- Recycled paper, to make the pulp
- Blender
- Measuring cup
- Two tall cups for pouring pulp
- Sponge
- Paper towels
- Flat piece of wood or other flat item for pressing
- Clothes iron and a surface appropriate for using it

1. Set the large container with one end cut out in the drain pan, with the open end facing up. Place a support screen over the open end, followed by a papermaking window screen.

2. Place the container with both ends cut out over the papermaking screen. If the containers are of the same size, match their rims.

Steps 1 and 2

Continued on next page

[Adapted from *Trash-to-Treasure Papermaking* by Arnold E. Grummer]

3. Tear up an appropriate amount of recycled paper into small pieces and put them in the blender. As an example, for a container that is 4 to 5 inches in diameter, you'd want about 7 square inches of paper. Add about 1½ cups water to the blender. Put on the lid and run the blender for 20 to 30 seconds.

4. Pour half of the blender's contents into each of the two tall cups and add ½ cup water to each cup.

5. With a cup of pulp in each hand, dump the contents of both cups at the same time into the top container. Pour from opposite sides so that the streams from both containers hit each other. Let all the water drain into the bottom can.

6. Raise the top container straight up off the screen. Lift both screens (with your new sheet of paper on them) and remove the base container. Place the screens back into the drain pan or onto a flat surface that is not harmed by water. Place another 6-inch square piece of window screen over the new sheet.

7. Press a dry sponge down on top of the window screen and new sheet, then remove it and squeeze the water from the sponge. Continue pressing and squeezing until the entire sheet has been covered and the sponge removes little, or no more, water.

8. Carefully, starting at any corner, peel off the top window screen. Lay down three folded paper towels on top of each other. When folded, the towels must be bigger than the new sheet. If they're not, get bigger towels, or don't fold them. Pick up the screen with the new sheet on it and turn it over onto the towels so the new sheet is on the top towel.

9. Apply the sponge as in step 7, this time pushing down with as much force as possible. Apply pressure over the entire new sheet. This is so the new sheet will stay with the towels when the screen is peeled off. Starting slowly at a corner, peel off the window screen, leaving the new sheet on the towels. If the sheet rises with the screen, apply the sponge again with all the force you can. If the sheet still rises with the screen, carefully peel a corner of the new sheet from the screen and separate them with care. At the end of this step, the new sheet should be on top of the paper towels.

10. Fold three more paper towels. Place them on top of the new sheet. Take a flat piece of wood, or other flat item, and press down hard on top of the dry towels.

11. Remove the top wet towels and replace them with dry ones. Repeat pressing, replacing wet towels with dry ones, until little water is removed with the dry towels. When the new sheet has become strong enough, lift it off the wet towels beneath it. Replace the wet towels with dry ones. The idea is to get as much water out of the new sheet as possible. *Note:* Do not throw wet towels away. Lay them out to dry and reuse them in future papermaking.

12. Put the new sheet on an ironing board or other dry, clean surface that will not be harmed by heat. Turn a clothes iron to its top heat setting and iron the new sheet dry. Move the iron slowly but steadily, so all parts of the sheet dry at about the same rate. *Note:* Placing a thin cloth over the sheet for ironing is wise. It protects the iron's surface from possible heat-sticky additives that might have been in the recycled paper.

Step 3

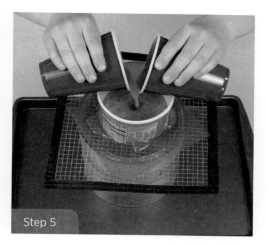

Step 4

Step 5

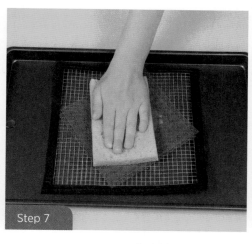

Step 6

Step 7

Step 8a

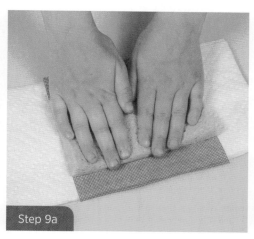

Step 8b

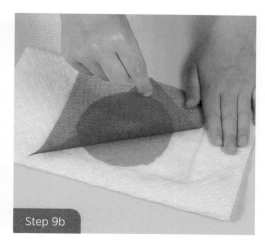

Step 9a

Step 9b

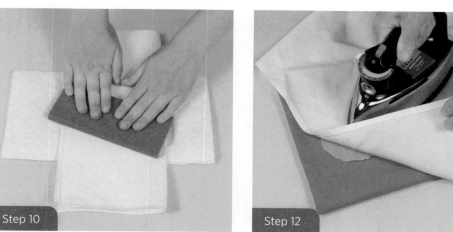

Step 10

Step 12

MAKE A POP-UP
PAPER LANTERN

Candles are a natural centerpiece for a tabletop. Why not add another dimension by covering your candle with this beautiful shade? A piece of translucent vellum paper softens the candlelight and keeps it from glaring through the holes in the pop-ups.

TOOLS AND MATERIALS

- One 20¼" × 6" piece of lightweight card stock (grain should be in the 6-inch direction)
- Ruler
- Pencil
- One 1¼" × 6" piece of card stock
- Craft knife or scissors
- Cutting mat
- Bone folder
- White glue or ¼" double-sided tape
- One 8⅝" × 5¾" piece of heavy vellum
- Glass votive candleholder
- Tea light or votive candle

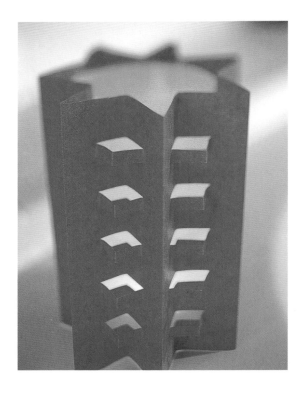

FOLDING THE ACCORDION

1. Lay the larger piece of card stock on your work surface and use the ruler to place a mark ¼ inch in from one of the short ends. Fold the card stock up at that mark. This ¼-inch edge will become the seam.

2. Accordion-fold the paper into pleats 1¾ inches wide, starting at one end and making the first fold so that it meets the fold of the ¼-inch seam.

MAKING A CUTTING TEMPLATE

3. Create a cutting template with the smaller piece of card stock using the diagram at right as a guide. Use a craft knife or scissors to remove the tabs.

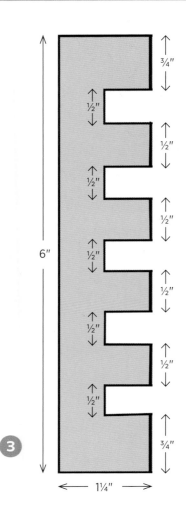

3

6"

¾"
½"
½"
½"
½"
½"
½"
½"
½"
½"
½"
½"
¾"

1¼"

[Adapted from *Paper Illuminated* by Helen Hiebert]

CUTTING THE POP-UPS

4. Unfold the first pleat on the accordion-folded paper, starting at the side opposite the ¼-inch fold, and lay it on the cutting mat. Place the template on that first panel with the edge of cut notches at the fold. Carefully draw and then cut the slits. Make only the vertical slits — do not make any horizontal slits, as you did when making the template.

5. Place a ruler or straightedge at the bottom edge of the slits to keep them aligned. Use a bone folder to carefully make score marks between the cuts, which will make the tabs easier to fold.

6. Repeat steps 4 and 5 on all of the folded sections.

FOLDING THE POP-UPS

7. Starting with the first pleat, take one scored section and fold it over, creasing along the scored line. Fold it in one direction and then bend it backward and crease it in the other direction.

8. Continue creasing the other sections in the pleat.

9. Open the entire pleat and push the creased sections through the fold so that they pop up.

10. Repeat steps 7 through 9 on every pleat.

FINAL ASSEMBLY

11. With the pop-ups showing as mountain folds (popping out like peaks), apply white glue or a piece of double-sided tape to the ¼-inch seam and attach it to the edge of the pleat on the opposite side.

12. Apply a piece of double-sided tape to one of the shorter edges of the vellum. Attach that edge to the opposite side to create a cylinder.

13. Place the cylinder inside the paper lantern and place them both over the glass votive candleholder. Place the tea light or the votive candle inside the votive holder.

MAKE A FLOWERPOT SMOKER

If the thought of smoking meat and fish conjures up images of heaps of hardwood, a large smokehouse, and a big investment of time and cash, think again. You can smoke food on a much smaller scale: in a clay pot smoker.

MATERIALS

- One 1,000-watt (or greater) hot plate
- One 12"- to 16"-diameter ceramic pot
- Round grill grate (sized to fit inside the ceramic pot)
- One additional ceramic pot or tray (for a smoker lid)
- One eyebolt with two washers and nuts
- One 6"-long wood dowel
- Two to four scrap pieces of 2"-thick brick or patio block
- Pie pan for holding wood chips
- Silicone caulk (if needed)
- Three scrap wood blocks

Cutaway View

Nut
Washer
Eyebolt
Bolt
Wooden handle

grate

brisket

Silicone grate support

wood chips

pie pan

hot plate

Brick pieces

To GFCI-protected outlet

1. Purchase your materials. Since you'll acquire them from a variety of sources, measure as you go and purchase the parts in this order:

   ✳ **HOT PLATE.** The smaller the better, but it should be at least 1,000 watts. Anything smaller may not maintain the needed temperature.

   ✳ **FLOWERPOT.** Make certain the bottom is large enough to accommodate the hot plate and its control knob, plus a little elbow room.

   ✳ **GRATE.** It should nestle about three-quarters of the way up the tapered sides of the pot. Grates can be found at hardware stores and online.

   ✳ **COVER.** This can be another pot or a pot tray. It can fit over, inside of, or directly on the lip of the pot; just make sure it seals fairly well and doesn't slide off.

   ✳ **HANDLE HARDWARE.** Here we construct a handle with an eyebolt and dowel, but you can use whatever hardware works with your cover. Be creative; there are lots of ways to make the handle.

2. Use a masonry or glass-and-tile drill bit to create a hole (or enlarge an existing hole) in the bottom of the flowerpot for the plug of the hot plate to pass through. To minimize the chance of damage, place the pot on a bag of sand to support the area as you drill.

3. Assemble a handle for the lid using an eyebolt, two washers, two nuts, and a 6-inch length of wood or wood dowel.

4. Test-fit your parts. Place a few 2-inch-thick brick or patio block scraps inside the pot to prop up the hot plate for air circulation. Place the wood chip pan on the hot plate, insert the grate, and then position the top. If your grate wobbles, create three support lips for it to rest on using dabs of silicone caulk.

5. When everything fits, you're ready to start smokin'. Position the smoker outside on a noncombustible surface in an area sheltered from the elements. Prop the pot on three scrap wood blocks or bricks. Make sure the hot plate is protected from moisture, and always plug it into a GFCI-protected outlet. Don't leave the smoker unattended. Keep curious pets, kids, and neighbors away from the designated "smoking area."

[Adapted from *The Backyard Homestead Book of Building Projects* by Spike Carlsen]

BAKE BREAD
IN A
FLOWERPOT

Yes, you can bake bread in a terra-cotta flowerpot! It's only fitting that loaves baked in flowerpots be a showcase for good stuff from the soil, like carrots, onions, and herbs. The vegetables are finely chopped or grated and then dried in the oven to concentrate their flavors. Buy two new terra-cotta pots (5½ to 6 inches in diameter and about 5 inches tall) just for this purpose; you'll "season" the pots, like you would a cast-iron skillet, before their initial use.

MAKES 2 SMALL LOAVES

INGREDIENTS

1–2 teaspoons cooking oil, for oiling the baking sheet and bowl

1½ cups grated carrots

1 celery stalk, finely chopped

½ medium onion, finely chopped

2 cups lukewarm water (105°F–110°F/41°C–43°C)

1 tablespoon sugar

1 packet (¼ ounce) active dry yeast

¼ cup fine yellow cornmeal

4¼–4½ cups unbleached all-purpose flour

2 tablespoons unsalted butter, softened, plus more for greasing the flowerpots

2 teaspoons salt

2 tablespoons chopped fresh sage or 2 teaspoons dried

2 teaspoons fresh thyme or ¾ teaspoon dried

1 cup grated sharp cheddar cheese

1 tablespoon unsalted butter, melted, for brushing the flowerpots and loaves

Safflower or light olive oil, for seasoning the flowerpots

Sunflower seeds, for coating the loaves

[Adapted from *The Harvest Baker* by Ken Haedrich]

1. Preheat the oven to 300°F/150°C.

2. Oil a large rimmed baking sheet very lightly. Spread the carrots, celery, and onion evenly in a single layer on the sheet. Place in the oven and roast for 45 minutes to 1 hour, until shrunken and shriveled but not brittle dry. Transfer the sheet to a cooling rack and allow the vegetables to cool.

3. Pour the water into a large bowl. Stir in the sugar and sprinkle on the yeast. Stir once or twice with a fork and set aside for 5 minutes.

4. Add the cornmeal and 3 cups of the flour to the water. Using a wooden spoon, stir well for 100 strokes. Set aside for 10 minutes.

5. Add the 2 tablespoons softened butter, salt, sage, and thyme to the dough. Stir well. Stir in the veggies and cheese. Add enough of the remaining flour, about ¼ cup at a time, to make a firm dough that pulls away from the sides of the bowl. Using your wooden spoon, work the dough vigorously against the sides of the bowl for 1 minute or so.

6. Flour your work surface and turn the dough out. Using floured hands, knead the dough for about 8 minutes, dusting with flour as necessary to keep the dough from sticking. Oil a large ceramic or glass bowl with a teaspoon or two of cooking oil. Add the dough, rotating it to coat the entire surface with oil. Cover the bowl with plastic wrap and set aside in a warm, draft-free spot for 1 to 1½ hours, until the dough has doubled in bulk.

7. While the dough rises, season your flowerpots: Preheat the oven to 450°F/230°C. Wash and dry the pots well. Rub the insides thoroughly with safflower or light olive oil. Place the pots on a baking sheet and place in the oven. Bake for 1 hour. Don't be surprised if a strong odor develops as the pots heat. Remove the pots and cool thoroughly.

8. Butter the pots well with softened butter and line with strips of parchment paper brushed with melted butter. Cover the bottom hole with a little circle of buttered aluminum foil and sprinkle the inside of the pots with sunflower seeds.

Step 8a

Step 8b

9. When the dough has doubled, punch it down and turn it out onto a floured surface. Knead the dough for 1 minute, then divide it in half. Shape each half into a ball and place them in the pots. Cover the pots with plastic wrap and put them aside in a warm, draft-free spot until the loaves have almost doubled in bulk, about 40 minutes to 1 hour.

10. Move one of your oven racks to the lowest position and move the second rack up high or take it out of the oven. Preheat the oven to 400°F/200°C.

11. As soon as the loaves appear to have doubled, brush the top of each one with a little melted butter. Use a sharp serrated knife to make a shallow slash right across the middle of each loaf.

12. Bake the loaves for 30 minutes, then reduce the heat to 375°F/190°C and bake for an additional 15 to 20 minutes, until the tops of the loaves are a rich golden brown. Transfer the pots to a cooling rack. Cool for about 5 minutes, then slide the loaves out of the pots and let cool on their sides. When completely cool, store in plastic bags in the refrigerator.

TELL THE DIFFERENCE BETWEEN A SHEEP AND A GOAT

Many people have trouble telling sheep from goats. Some hair sheep breeds are very goatlike, and Angora goats resemble woolly sheep. Their voices differ, however: sheep generally stick to some variation of "baa," while goat calls vary by breed from sedate "mehs" to ear-splitting screams. Here are some other similarities and differences between them.

GOATS

SHEEP

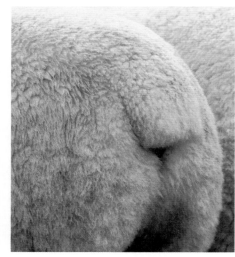

Lips
The sheep's upper lip is divided by a distinct groove, while the goat's lip has only a superficial groove.

Horns
Most goats are born with horns but may be disbudded. Goat horns are usually narrower than sheep horns and tend to sweep up or back.

Some sheep breeds are horned in both sexes; some are polled (naturally hornless); and in some breeds, most rams have horns but ewes usually do not. Rams' massive horns grow down into spirals by their faces; ewes' horns are more slender and upright. Sheep do not respond well to disbudding.

Beards
Many goats have beards. Sheep never have beards, though some hair sheep rams have manes.

Tails
Goat tails are naturally short and fringed, and they usually stick up unless the animal is frightened or ill.

Sheep tails take many forms but always hang down and often are docked (shortened).

[Adapted from *The Backyard Sheep* by Sue Weaver]

Goats must be milked once or twice a day at the same time of day, every day, with no respite. So why milk a goat? To make goat cheese (page 58), of course! Besides being very creamy and delicious, goat's milk cheese can also be a profitable niche for people who want to make some money from their goats. Plus, goat's milk is more easily digested than cow's milk, and it has more calcium, protein, riboflavin, and vitamins but less lactose and saturated fat. Direct the first stream into a strip cup, not the pails.

MILK A GOAT

1. Close off the top of the teat with your thumb and forefinger so the milk will flow out of the teat, not back into the udder.

2. Close your second finger, and the milk should start to squirt out.

3. Close your third finger. Use a steady pressure.

4. Close your little finger and squeeze with your whole hand. Strive for a smooth, flowing motion. Don't pull on the teat; just squeeze gently.

5. Release the teat and let it fill up with milk. Repeat the process with your other hand on the other teat.

6. When the milk flow has ceased, "bump" the udder, as kids often do while nursing, and you'll get a few more squirts. You never get all the milk, but it won't go away. It will be there the next time you milk.

7. Coat the teats with a teat dip to prevent bacteria from entering the orifice.

[Adapted from *Storey's Guide to Raising Dairy Goats* by Jerry Belanger and Sara Thomson Bredesen]

MAKE GREEK YOGURT

Greek yogurt is just yogurt that has been drained of much of its whey, so it is thicker and creamier than regular yogurt. Fermented, probiotic dairy products like yogurt are among the best "functional foods" — that is, foods that promote health beyond providing basic nutrition. This is thanks to the probiotic microbes they contain, which produce a wide range of by-products and benefits that transform already nutritious milk into something approaching a superfood. Happily, yogurt is very easy to make at home. You will need an incubator (such as a warm oven, well-insulated ice chest with a warm water bottle, or an electric yogurt maker) to keep the yogurt warm.

MAKES ½ GALLON

INGREDIENTS

½ gallon milk

⅛ teaspoon powdered yogurt culture

1. **CLEAN TOOLS AND EQUIPMENT.** Scrub all fermentation tools well, then rinse with hot water and air-dry.

2. **HEAT-TREAT THE MILK.** Place the milk in a saucepan and heat on the stove top over medium heat until it reaches 180°F/82°C. Hold it there for 10 minutes.

3. **BRING THE MILK TO INCUBATION TEMPERATURE.** Fill the sink with cold tap water, then place the pan of milk in the sink and let it cool to 115°F/46°C. Pour the milk into your incubation vessel.

4. **ADD THE CULTURE.** Sprinkle the powdered yogurt culture on top of the milk and let sit for 1 minute, then whisk it in.

5. **INCUBATE.** Place the cultured milk in an incubator and incubate at 110°F/43°C for 8 to 12 hours.

6. **DRAIN.** Line a colander with cheesecloth and place in a large bowl. Place your yogurt in the cheesecloth. Cover the top of the colander with a towel to protect it from pets or dust. It should be at a cool room temperature (between 65°F and 72°F/18°C and 22°C). Let drain for 3 to 4 hours, depending on your desired thickness, stirring every 30 minutes or so. Pour the yogurt into an airtight container.

7. **CHILL.** Fill the sink with cold tap water and place the yogurt container in the water until the ferment is cool. Move the ferment to the freezer for 1 or 2 hours, then place it in the refrigerator.

Step 2

Step 3

Step 4

[Adapted from *Homemade Yogurt & Kefir* by Gianaclis Caldwell]

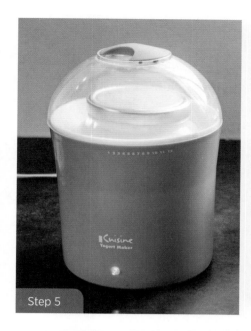

Step 5

Step 6

Step 7

Fresh Yogurt Begets Fresh Yogurt

You can also incubate your yogurt with ⅛ cup of your favorite fresh yogurt instead of powdered yogurt culture. To do so, in step 4, combine the yogurt with ¼ cup of the warm milk in a small bowl and whisk until smooth, then add the mixture to the rest of the milk.

MAKE FARMHOUSE CHEDDAR

Making hard cheese transforms milk protein and butterfat into a delicious culinary delight that is both nourishing and long-lasting — that is, if you can control yourself until your prize is properly matured. This recipe is a tasty and satisfying foray into hard-cheese making and can be made with either cow's or goat's milk. Unlike traditional cheddar, this cheese does not require the process of cheddaring (cutting the drained curds into strips and allowing them to set at 100°F/38°C for 2 hours), thus saving a lot of time.

MAKES 2 POUNDS

INGREDIENTS

- 2 gallons milk
- ½ teaspoon calcium chloride diluted in ¼ cup cool, unchlorinated water
- 1 packet direct-set mesophilic starter culture
- ½ teaspoon liquid rennet (or ½ rennet tablet) diluted in ¼ cup cool, unchlorinated water
- 2 tablespoons cheese salt

1. Warm the milk to 90°F/32°C (or 85°F/29°C for goat's milk).

2. Add the calcium chloride solution and stir well to combine. Sprinkle the starter over the surface of the milk, wait 2 minutes for the powder to rehydrate, then stir well. Cover and allow the milk to ripen for 45 minutes.

3. Add the diluted rennet and stir gently with an up-and-down motion for 30 seconds.

4. Cover and let set at 90°F/32°C (or 85°F/29°C for goat's milk) for 45 minutes, or until the curd gives a clean break (when the tip of a knife inserted slightly at a 45-degree angle separates the curd firmly and cleanly).

5. Cut the curds into ½-inch cubes.

6. Place the curds in a sink full of hot water and slowly heat the curds to 100°F/38°C (or 98°F/37°C for goat's milk), increasing the temperature by 2°F/0.5°C every 5 minutes for 30 minutes. Stir gently every 3 minutes to keep the curds from matting. As the heat increases, you will see more and more whey, and the curds will shrink noticeably.

7. Cover the container and let the curds set for 5 minutes. Transfer the curds to a cheesecloth-lined colander. Tie the corners of the cheesecloth into a knot and hang the bag in a convenient spot to drain for 1 hour at 72°F/22°C or higher.

8. Place the drained curds in a bowl and break them up gently with your fingers into walnut-size pieces.

9. Mix in the salt.

Continued on page 60

[Adapted from *Home Cheese Making* by Ricki Carroll]

Step 1

Step 2

Step 3

Step 4

Step 5

Step 6

Step 7

Step 8

Step 9

10. Firmly pack the curds into a 2-pound mold lined with cheesecloth, then neatly fold the cheesecloth over the top.

11. Press the cheese at 10 pounds of pressure for 10 minutes. Remove the cheese from the mold and gently peel away the cheesecloth. Turn over the cheese, re-dress it, and press at 20 pounds of pressure for 10 minutes. Unwrap, flip, rewrap, and press at 50 pounds of pressure for 12 hours.

12. Remove the cheese from the mold and carefully peel away the cheese-cloth. Air-dry the cheese at room temperature on a wooden board until a nice rind has developed and the surface is dry. This may take 2 to 4 days, depending on the weather. Turn the cheese several times a day so moisture will not col-lect on the bottom, and rub off any mold growth.

13. Bandage, wax, or oil the cheese if desired. To bandage the cheese, cut a piece of butter muslin as wide as the depth of the cheese and 1½ times its circumference in length. Cut four circular pieces to act as caps for the top and bottom, making them larger than the cheese so they will fold over the sides. Rub a thin coat of lard or solid vegetable short-ening on the cheese and place two caps at each end. Wrap the bandage around the cheese, sticking it down as you go.

14. Age the cheese at 52°F to 56°F/11°C to 13°C and 80% to 85% relative humidity for at least 1 month, turn-ing twice a week and rubbing off any unwanted mold growth.

Step 10

Step 11

Step 12

Step 13, bandaging

Step 13, waxing

If you have a woodland orchard or just a couple of trees you'd like to restore, begin by clearing the area around your trees. Since the trees have likely been under shade for many years, it's best to slowly introduce them to increasing levels of sunlight. Once a tree has been given a growing season to adjust to increased light conditions, you can take the following steps to restore it.

RESTORE A FORGOTTEN FRUIT TREE

1. **STUDY THE SHAPE OF THE TREE.** Before you pull out your loppers and saw, take some time to study the shape of the tree or, more specifically, the shape that the tree *could be*, given the benefit of time and judicious pruning. Strive for creating a central leader and a shape that resembles a pyramid.

2. **REMOVE WATER SPROUTS.** Begin by removing any vertical branches or water sprouts. Water sprouts are vigorous vertical shoots that redirect nutrients from the rest of the tree, thereby discouraging fruit formation. Water sprouts can be pruned in summer to encourage the tree to focus its energy on fruit buds. Old vertical wood should also be removed to encourage a single central leader.

3. **REMOVE BRANCHES THAT CROSS.** Abrasions caused by rubbing are entry points for pests and disease. Additionally, remove any branches that double back into the center of the tree.

4. **REMOVE LATERAL BRANCHES.** If you're intending to graze pigs or sheep in your woodland orchard to glean fallen fruit, consider pruning all lateral branches below 3 feet. This will help discourage climbing, which can break branches and damage the bark.

5. **REPEAT THESE STEPS OVER 2 TO 3 YEARS.** To prevent shock, you must gradually prune trees that have been abandoned and forgotten.

6. **REMOVE DEADWOOD.** After the immediate area around the tree has been cleared, you should remove any deadwood from your fruit tree. Unlike removing live wood, this doesn't need to be done gradually; just make sure your cuts are clean and executed just outside the branch collar (the area of swollen bark where the branch meets its parent branch or the trunk), which will encourage callus tissue to develop, sealing over the wound. If you can, allow the tree a full growing season to adjust to the new light conditions and begin healing the wounds where deadwood was removed.

Note that on this tree the terminal fork was removed to encourage a lower crown, giving greater accessibility during the harvest.

[Adapted from *The Woodland Homestead* by Brett McLeod]

GROW A FRUITING ESPALIER

Fruiting trees and shrubs trained to grow flat against a wall make for eye-catching and productive garden features. Shapes range from fans, palmettes, and candelabras to tiers, fountains, triangles, and diamonds. The key to a successful espalier is having fun and making a design you like. Here's how to create a simple tiered cordon on a masonry wall, a good beginner's project.

1. On the wall, mark with chalk where you want to drill for the eyebolts that will support the espalier wires. Work with a level to keep each tier horizontal. Make your first mark 18 inches from soil level. Sketch in marks at the same height every 2 to 3 feet to the ends of the wall. Add another line of marks 18 inches above the first. Repeat until you reach the top of the wall or the desired height of your espalier.

2. Using a masonry drill, drill holes at every mark, then insert 5- to 7-inch eyebolts with expanded lead anchors into the holes. Thread 14-gauge galvanized wire through the eyebolt at one end of a row, winding the tail around the longer side five or six times to fix it in place. Stretch the long wire horizontally to the next eyebolt, threading it through the second hole, drawing it taut, and securing it as before. Continue threading and securing until you reach the end of the row. There should be 4 to 6 inches between the wire and the wall to allow for good air circulation. Repeat for the other rows.

3. For one tree or shrub, pound a vertical 4-foot stake in the ground at the planting site, which should be about 6 inches in front of the wall and at the center of the wires. Then plant a bare-root whip (a young, typically unbranched shoot) next to it. If the tree is grafted onto rootstock, set the bulge or bud union about 2 inches above ground level to keep the graft from growing roots. Keep the trunk straight by loosely tying it to the upright stake with a piece of twine looped around it in a figure eight. (You will slacken the twine as the trunk grows and remove the stake when the pattern of growth is established.)

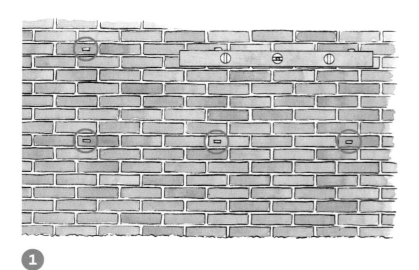

1

2

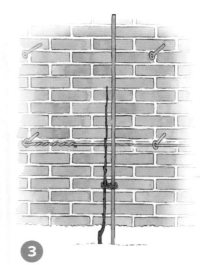

3

[Adapted from *The Homeowner's Complete Tree and Shrub Handbook* by Penelope O'Sullivan]

4. With sharp pruners, snip off the top of the whip right below the bottom wire. Be sure to make your cut at a spot about where two buds show on either side of the stem.

5. When new shoots develop, select one to train upright (the main stem) and two to train to either side. Attach the side shoots to the wire with twine. Avoid making the ties so tight that the trunk and branches don't have room to grow. Never use wire to attach branches to the horizontal wires. Rub all other developing shoots off the trunk until the main stem reaches the second wire, and shorten shoots on the limbs by pinching.

6. When the main stem reaches the second wire, trim it just below the wire as in step 4, and then train the main stem and two side shoots as in step 5. Repeat this process for each level.

7. When growth reaches the top wire, cut off the top of the trunk but keep two branches on the sides. Take out the stake and secure the trunk to the horizontal wires. Check each year to see if ties need replacing. If you see dead, diseased, or damaged branches during the growing season, remove them. Also, take off wayward shoots that spoil the lines of the espalier.

This pear tree is being trained in a horizontal espalier.

Popular Trees and Shrubs for Espalier

* Camellia (*Camellia* species)
* Flowering quince (*Chaenomeles speciosa*)
* Lemon, lime, orange (*Citrus* species)
* Cotoneaster (*Cotoneaster* species)
* Dwarf apple, crabapple (*Malus* species)
* Mock orange (*Philadelphus coronarius*)
* Firethorn (*Pyracantha coccinea*)
* Yew (*Taxus* species)
* Viburnum (*Viburnum* species)

CARVE A WOODEN SPOON

Wooden spoons are easy to make, even for a novice, and it's a great activity to do while sitting around a campfire. Make a variety of sizes for your kitchen, or give them away as gifts.

1. Create a blank about 1 foot by 2 inches by 1 inch.

2. Carve a notch into both sides of the blank, about a third of the way from one end.

3. Draw a spoon shape on one of the blank's flat surface. If you're in the field, you can sketch using charcoal from your firepit.

4. Using the notches from step 2 as stop cuts, baton down both sides of the blank.

5. Carefully place an ember on the blank where the depression of the spoon will be. Hold the ember in place using a green sapling, and gently blow on the ember.

6. Scrape out the charred area of the spoon with a stone until you reach a fresh layer of wood.

Step 2

Step 4

Step 5

Make sure not to blow so hard that you create a flame.

[Adapted from *Wilderness Adventure Camp* by Frank Grindrod]

Step 7

7. Repeat steps 5 and 6 until the depression in your spoon is as deep as you want it to be.

8. Finish carving the handle of the spoon until it is comfortable to hold in your hand and smooth.

Step 8

Batoning

Batoning is a technique used to split a piece of wood by striking the spine of your knife with a baton-size stick. Practice using a round of birch, maple, or hop hornbeam wood that is 1 to 1½ feet long and 5 to 6 inches in diameter as your baton. For safety, be sure to use a sheath knife with at least a three-quarter tang, not a lock blade.

1. Hold your knife in a forward grip. Stand your piece of wood on a flat, sturdy surface. Place the blade sharp side down into the end of the wood.

2. Using the baton, strike the middle of the knife spine. This will set your blade.

3. Gently tap the baton on the knife spine to set the blade deeper into the wood.

4. Maintain pressure on the knife handle, keeping it straight up and down. Do not twist the knife. Continue striking the spine of the knife blade, changing the exact spot that you hit to avoid damaging your knife blade.

Step 2

Step 1

Step 3

BRAID A RUG

The craft of rug braiding, like so many other good things, is rooted in necessity. People of an earlier day found that they could use what they had — in this case, "rags" of worn clothing — to create the rugs they needed for warmth on the drafty floors of their inefficiently heated homes. Less of a practical necessity now, a beautifully braided rug can be the focal point of a room.

MATERIALS

- Strips of wool fabric in three different color schemes, cut on the bias, 3" wide
- Sharp sewing scissors
- Thread (heavy-duty for piecing strips and carpet for lacing braids together; do not use nylon thread)
- Safety pin
- Bodkin (a flat, blunt "poker" used to lace the braids together)
- Crochet hook
- Tape measure or yardstick

SEWING THE STRIPS

1. Sew a strip of color A to a strip of color B in a bias seam.

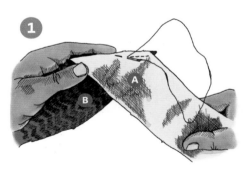

2. Fold color C into a four-ply tube-strip with the raw edges inside.

3. Fold the raw edges of strip AB in to meet at the center of the strip.

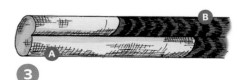

4. Insert the raw edge of folded strip C at the seam joining colors A and B and sew firmly in place.

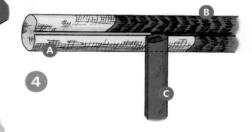

5. Fold the top half of strip AB down to cover the raw edges of strip C. You can now have a "T" with color C sandwiched between layer 1 and 2 and layer 3 and 4 of strip AB.

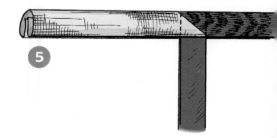

[Adapted from *Braiding Rugs* by Nancy Bubel]

BRAIDING

6. Put C over A toward the left.

7. Put B over C toward the right.

8. Put A over B.

9. Repeat the braiding steps until you reach your desired length, and mark the end of the starting braid with a safety pin. The projected length of the rug minus its projected width equals the length of the starting braid, plus a few inches to make up for shrinkage. To make a 7' × 9' rug, your starting braid should be 2' 3".

10. Double the braid back on itself so that you have two rows of braids side by side. Force both sections of the braid to lie flat as you form this rounded corner.

LACING THE RUG

11. Thread your bodkin (a blunt needle) with a double strand of heavy button-and-carpet thread about a yard long.

12. Knot the end of the thread and, starting at the pin-marked corner, poke the bodkin *between* the braid folds.

13. Take several stitches to secure the thread and then begin to lace by inserting the bodkin through every other braid fold, alternating from left to right. Pull firmly with your right hand as you hold the braids flat with your left.

14. For the first six to ten rounds — *at the corners only* — the stitches on the body of the rug must be closer together than those on the braid

you're attaching. So after lacing through a loop on the outer braid, and then through the next loop on the body of the rug, you then *skip* a loop on the outer braid and lace the following loop to the *very next* loop on the body of the rug.

15. Complete the rug by tapering the last 6 to 8 inches of the braid. To do this, trim each strip so that it tapers

to about half its original width at the cut end. Braid these narrow ends, carefully rolling in the edges, and lace the tapered butt firmly to the rug, retracing the last few lacing stitches for extra firmness. Leave a 2 to 3-inch length of the lacing thread and weave it back between the braids, using a crochet hook, to form a secure, invisible ending.

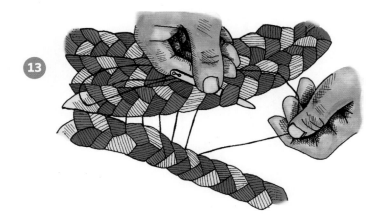

KNOW YOUR HONEY BEES

Honey bees are fascinating creatures. They show a level of social organization so extreme that individuality is meaningless. No one bee in a social group competes against another for food or mating opportunities in the way that mammals, birds, and even most other insects do. A honey bee's total devotion to its colony's well-being results in breathtaking acts of heroic self-sacrifice and brutal acts of premeditated murder.

In this insect opera there are three principal players: the queen, the drones, and the workers. Every colony of bees has one queen. She is the only female capable of laying productive eggs. Workers are fully formed females, but their ovaries are undeveloped. Drones are the males of the colony and mate with the queen.

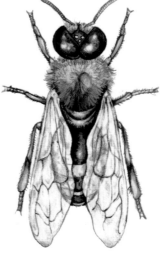

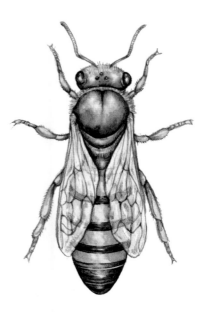

WORKER

* Smallest in size
* Functional barbed stinger

DRONE

* Looks fatter than the queen, with a thick waist and rounded abdomen
* Large eyes meet in the center

QUEEN

* Longest bee in the colony
* Smooth, hairless thorax
* Wider hips than a worker
* Abdomen tapers gradually

[Adapted from *Storey's Guide to Keeping Honey Bees* by Malcolm T. Sanford and Richard E. Bonney and *Homegrown Honey Bees* by Alethea Morrison]

Bees are sticklers. They want exactly ¼- to ⅜-inch passageways — called bee space — in their hive. Any smaller space they'll seal up with propolis (resin collected from trees). Any larger space they'll fill with comb. The movable beehive invented in 1852 by L. L. Langstroth consists of vertically hung combs placed just the right distance apart to maintain bee space. It is still the most commonly used beehive today.

PUT TOGETHER A BEEHIVE

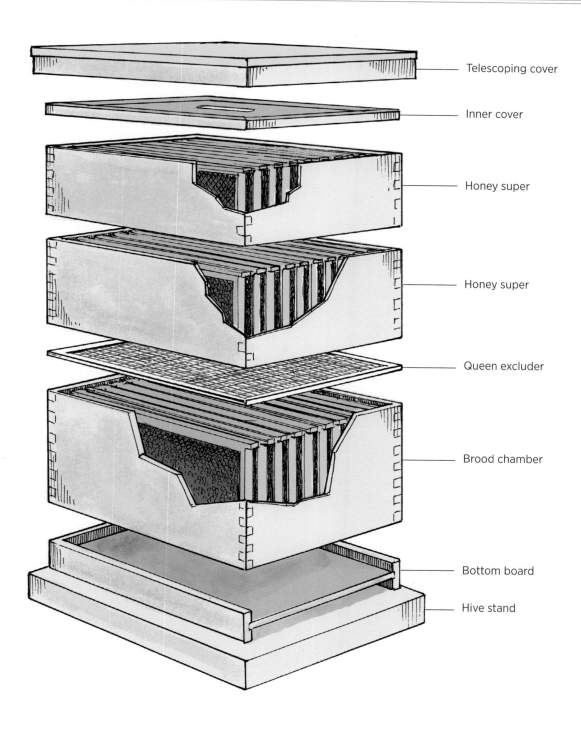

Telescoping cover

Inner cover

Honey super

Honey super

Queen excluder

Brood chamber

Bottom board

Hive stand

[Adapted from *Homegrown Honey Bees* by Alethea Morrison]

EXTRACT HONEY

Honey bees build a wax comb to hold their honey. A low-tech way to extract honey from the comb is the "squish and drain" method. To go slightly higher tech, install a honey gate — a spout with an on/off lever — in a plastic bucket (it will require drilling a hole); you can dispense the filtered honey from this bucket into canning jars for storage, which will make the process much easier and neater. Each frame should yield 2½ to 3 pounds of honey.

1. **CUT THE COMB.** Cut the comb from the frames and let the comb fall into a shallow plastic bin. Set the now-empty frame in another bucket.

2. **BREAK IT UP.** Break up the comb with your hands, a potato masher, or some other tool. This will result in a pulpy, sticky mess.

3. **STRAIN.** Set a fine-mesh strainer over a food-safe plastic bucket. Pour the sticky mess into the strainer and let drain. It will take about 16 hours for the honey to slowly drip into the bucket. To speed up the process, use a salad spinner to spin batches of the comb, separating the wax and honey.

4. **STRAIN AGAIN.** The strained honey will still contain bits of wax and other debris. Line a strainer with dampened butter muslin and strain again to get clear honey.

5. **LET SIT IN THE BUCKET.** Let the honey sit in the bucket for a day or so to reduce the amount of air bubbles in it.

6. **STORE.** Fill clean jars with the honey. Cap, cover, and store at room temperature. (This process is much easier if you've installed a honey gate on your collection bucket.) The honey will keep indefinitely, but like all natural products, fresh honey tastes best.

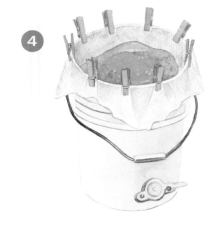

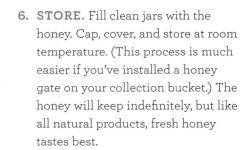

Be Sure to Clean Up!

Be forewarned: Honey attracts ants, flies, and other insects, so try to keep everything very, very clean.

[Adapted from *The Backyard Homestead Book of Kitchen Know-How* by Andrea Chesman]

Electuaries, or medicinal herb-infused honeys, are a sweet way to make the medicine go down. Crafting them is a simple process, but at the same time, there is a distinct art in ensuring that the herbs you choose work well both with each other and with the honey.

MAKE A MEDICINAL HONEY

1. Decide which powdered herbs you are going to use. You might include only one herb, or you might want to create a more complex formula (see the sidebar on page 72 for some suggestions).

2. Pour 1 cup of honey into a bowl.

3. Measure out the necessary amount of your powdered formula for 1 cup of honey. Generally, you really only need between 5 and 8 teaspoons of powder for your electuary to be effective. This ratio of powder to honey will result in an electuary that is sticky but still easily spreadable. Feel free to use your intuition here. If you want to add more powder, do it. If you wind up adding too much powder and the honey stiffens up, then you can either roll it into pills or add more honey to loosen it up again.

Note: In some people who are particularly sensitive, a lot of herbs, when amplified through the honey, can cause very quick, startling results. It's not always a good idea for your formula to work too well! Tonic herbs should, in most cases, be allowed to work in a slow and steady fashion. You should not experience sudden dramatic results, as they can often be uncomfortable. If you find yourself in this situation, either add more honey to your blend to make it less concentrated or take ½ teaspoon at a time instead of 1 teaspoon.

Continued on next page

Step 1

Step 2

Step 3

[Adapted from *Sweet Remedies* by Dawn Combs]

4. Sift your dried ingredients into the bowl of honey. Sifting is not required, but it will make blending the honey and herbs together much easier. Many powdered herbs tend to clump while in storage. If you don't break them up before adding them to the honey, it can take longer for them to soak into the mixture.

5. Stir everything together with a spoon until the blend is completely mixed. Then stir in any extra ingredients you desire, such as fresh herbs or fruits, oils, or other goodies.

6. Cover your bowl with a lid and set aside for at least 24 hours (in the refrigerator if you added anything fresh). You can use your electuary immediately if you must, but it will taste best and have the best mouthfeel if you allow time for the herbs and honey to marry. Before you use your electuary, you will want to stir it again. The herbs will tend to push to the top at first until they are completely saturated.

7. Store your finished electuary in a container with a lid to prevent contamination or evaporation of your honey. If you have added any liquid or anything fresh to your electuary, then it will need to be stored in the refrigerator and should be used within 2 to 3 months. If you have added only dried powder, then your electuary is shelf stable and will be good indefinitely.

TO USE: Your electuary can be "dosed" in 1-teaspoon servings or added to other foods to enjoy.

Step 4

Step 5

Step 6

Step 7

Medicinal Honey Formulas to Try

Sleep Well Honey

For those who have trouble falling asleep, this remedy is effective when taken as a 1-teaspoon serving within 30 minutes before bed. For those who wake in the middle of the night, try smaller, more frequent servings of ½ to 1 teaspoon every 10 to 15 minutes until you're back asleep.

POWDERED HERB FORMULA

1 part hops powder
1 part passionflower powder
1 part skullcap powder

MEDICINAL HONEY

6 teaspoons powdered herb formula
1 cup raw honey

Happy Honey Spread

Try this spread for anxiety and depression. Each herb is equally important, but feel free to play with the amount to match your own taste preference. Enjoy 1 to 3 teaspoons daily. *Note:* Less is more with lavender. Too much will make your formula bitter.

POWDERED HERB FORMULA

1 part chamomile powder
1 part eleuthero root powder
1 part lavender powder
1 part rose petal powder
1 part St. John's wort powder

MEDICINAL HONEY

6 teaspoons powdered herb formula
¼ teaspoon raw pollen
1 cup raw honey

MAKE A WATER FILTER FROM A 2-LITER BOTTLE

You can use a plastic 2-liter bottle (such as a soda bottle) to make a water filter with just a few additional materials. This filter will remove sediment and other debris from the water but will not purify it of bacteria and other pathogens. The safest way to purify water is to boil it.

1. Cut the bottom off a 2-liter bottle.

2. Remove the cap and cover the small opening with a coffee filter, held on with a rubber band.

3. Stuff the neck of the bottle with cotton balls.

4. Layer with 3 inches each of activated charcoal, fine sand, and gravel, in that order, with a coffee filter between each layer. You can purchase all of the components online or, in small quantities, from places that sell aquarium supplies. (A word of caution about the charcoal: It is messy. Wear clothes you don't care about and latex gloves. A dust mask is a very good idea. Plan to work outside.)

5. To use, position the filter like a funnel over a clean container and pour water in slowly. Add more water as needed to fill the container.

6. When you see that the cotton balls are beginning to discolor, it is time to take apart your filter. You can reuse the sand and gravel, but replace the charcoal, coffee filter, and cotton balls.

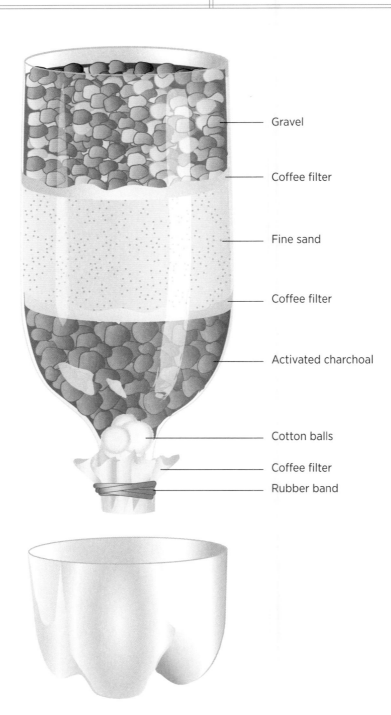

Gravel

Coffee filter

Fine sand

Coffee filter

Activated charchoal

Cotton balls

Coffee filter

Rubber band

[Adapted from *Prepping 101* by Kathy Harrison]

A water still uses the heat of the sun to evaporate water, which is then cooled and collected. It is easy to make, and the water does not need to be treated. Try to position the still where the sun will be hot and the soil moist by selecting areas with green vegetation. Adding nonpoisonous plants to the pit will increase the amount of water collected. Move the still to another area every few days.

MAKE A STILL
FOR COLLECTING WATER

1. Dig a hole 3 feet deep and 4 feet wide.

2. Place a container in the bottom of the hole. Lay out a length of plastic tubing so that it reaches from the container to the the top of the hole. Anchor the tubing to the top edge of the hole.

3. Cover the hole with a plastic sheet that is weighted down in the middle, forming a cone a few inches above the collecting receptacle.

4. The sun's heat will warm the soil and cause the evaporation of moisture, which will collect on the underside of the plastic and trickle down to the point of the cone, where it will fall into the container. You can suck water through the tube to avoid disturbing the still.

A water still is a traditional, time-tested method for gathering water.

[Adapted from *The Natural First Aid Handbook* by Brigitte Mars]

GROW A GARDEN TO HELP YOU SLEEP

Chronic insomnia is multifactorial and sometimes tricky to solve, but valerian, skullcap, passionflower, and California poppy help point your body in the right direction — toward your bed! All of these work best as tinctures (see page 78 for basic instructions). Dilute 1 to 4 mL of tincture in a little water and take shortly before you hit the hay. Tinker around a bit — most people find one perfect plant that suits them better than any other, but blends work well, too.

CALIFORNIA POPPY

(*Eschscholzia californica*)

Native Americans relied on poppy to induce sleep and mediate pain. Its safe, nonaddictive constituents produce a mild, tranquilizing effect. Think of it for people who wake in the middle of the night and can't go back to sleep, as well as those who struggle with spinning thoughts or pain that interferes with slumber. This Southwest native thrives in full sun and dryish soil. In cooler climates, seed it along a south-facing fence, wall, or hill. All parts can be used, but the roots are strongest.

More Ways to Use Sleep-Inducing Herbs

* Chamomile tea, plain or with spearmint
* Lemon balm and holy basil tea, lightly sweetened with honey
* Ashwagandha honey milk
* Linden tea, for gentle calm
* Magnolia bark tincture, for those who wake early with a racing mind
* Passionflower and skullcap tincture blend

[Adapted from *Grow Your Own Herbal Remedies* by Maria Noël Groves]

PASSIONFLOWER

(*Passiflora incarnata*)

Simply gazing into the otherworldly, mandala-like passionflower flower could lull you to sleep. In addition to its amazing beauty, intricacy, and sweet, calming aroma, passionflower may well be our most effective safe sedative and sleep aid. It works for almost anyone, quelling mind chatter to lull you into deep sleep. Although not as well studied as valerian, its effects in studies have been more profound, both as a simple herb (that is, on its own) and when combined with other sleep herbs. It's useful fresh or dried and also as tea.

SKULLCAP

(*Scutellaria lateriflora*)

Think of skullcap when you can't get to sleep because *everything* gets on your nerves — from the stress of the day, a light outside the window, or a worry about tomorrow to a mosquito flying around the room or your bed partner's obnoxious breathing. Skullcap "caps your skull," nourishes your nerves, and brings your reactions down a notch so you can get some shut-eye. This creek-side wildflower can be hit or miss in the garden, with alternating years of abundant and then puny growth. It prefers rich soil and good moisture. Some years it comes back; some years it doesn't. It's best when fresh or freshly dried. Stock up your apothecary in good years. It can also be enjoyed as a tea.

VALERIAN

(*Valeriana officinalis*)

Even though valerian is the most studied and most famous herb for sleep, it's actually the least reliable for a broad group of people. Valerian suits anxious, thin-framed people who tend to be cold with taut muscles. For "valerian people," it loosens those muscles and improves sleep latency for a deeper, more restorative night's sleep. For others, it may not work at all, or it may make them groggy or agitated, or overstimulate them. In the garden, valerian produces beautiful tall, pleasantly aromatic flowers that self-seed aggressively in good soil. Pull up the stinky roots in spring or fall for medicine.

MAKE A TINCTURE
TO EASE ACHES AND PAINS

This multipurpose mix can be used topically and internally for joint, bone, tendon, and ligament pain, for both acute and chronic issues. You can make separate tinctures to combine as needed or make one combination blend in spring from scratch. Tinker with the herb proportions based on how much you can harvest. You can use this basic process for making other tinctures with fresh plants.

INGREDIENTS

- 1 ounce fresh Solomon's seal root
- 1 ounce fresh horsetail
- ⅔ ounce fresh mullein root
- 5⅓ ounces high-proof alcohol, such as Everclear 151

1. Weigh then coarsely chop your plant material with clippers or scissors.

2. Shove the material into an 8-ounce jar — squeeze in as much as is humanly possible to get in there.

3. Add enough alcohol to entirely fill the jar. You may need to hold the plant material down as you fill the jar. Use a knife or chopstick to poke around and remove air bubbles. Put on the lid. No need to shake. Open the jar a few days later to top off the contents with a little more alcohol, as needed (it's important to keep the plant material covered).

4. After at least 1 month, strain the mixture through a cloth. Squeeze out as much extract as you can with your hands. A potato ricer, wheatgrass juicer, or hydraulic tincture press will also work here.

5. Pour the tincture into a dark glass bottle and store in a cool, dark, dry spot. It will keep for 3 to 10 years.

Step 1

Step 2

Step 3

Step 4

How to Use the Tincture

Take 0.5 to 1 ml (15 to 30 drops, diluted in water) as needed, one to four times daily. You can also rub a bit directly on the affected area. Topically, you can use the tincture straight, shake it vigorously with oil (comfrey-infused oil would work well), or stir it into premade cream.

[Adapted from *Grow Your Own Herbal Remedies* by Maria Noël Groves]

Herbs with invigorating scents and stimulating properties work amazingly well at energizing your body both mentally and physically, without jitters and the ensuing letdown. The essential oils in this recipe can reduce adrenal, mental, and physical fatigue, while providing a feeling of balanced energy. These drops are safe for use by folks 12 years of age and older. This is an aromatherapeutically concentrated formula, so use only as directed. You'll need a 4-ounce plastic squeeze bottle or dark glass bottle with a pump, dropper top, or screw top.

MAKE ANTIFATIGUE ESSENTIAL OIL DROPS

INGREDIENTS

- 30 drops balsam fir essential oil
- 30 drops Scotch pine essential oil
- 20 drops cedarwood essential oil
- ½ cup jojoba, almond, extra-virgin olive, or sunflower oil

1. Combine the balsam fir, pine, and cedarwood essential oils in the bottle, then add your base oil of choice. Screw the top on the bottle and shake vigorously for 2 minutes to blend.

2. Label the bottle and set it in a cool, dark location for 24 hours so that the oils can synergize.

3. Store at room temperature, away from heat and light; use within 1 year (or 2 years if you used jojoba oil).

TO USE: Shake well before using. Massage a few drops into the sole of each foot or onto your chest every morning after showering, or anytime during the day when you need a shot of balanced energy. Alternatively, once or twice per day, you can have someone massage a few drops onto your lower back, directly over your kidneys and adrenal glands, to help reduce adrenal stress. Let the oil soak in for 5 to 10 minutes before getting dressed.

Bonus Uses

If you're suffering from a cold or the flu, massage a few drops into your feet and chest to help combat the chills, soothe body aches, and open respiratory passages, encouraging deep, oxygenating breaths. This formula also makes a pain-easing rub for arthritic hands, wrists, elbows, shoulders, and feet.

[Adapted from *Stephanie Tourles's Essential Oils* by Stephanie Tourles]

READ YOUR WEEDS
FOR PASTURE MANAGEMENT

Certain weeds in your pasture can tell you about soil deficiencies and which fertilizer amendments may be needed to correct them. Familiarize yourself with these weeds to get a sense of the advantages of using them as soil fertility indicators. And have fun exploring the fascinating world of weeds. They open an intriguing window into the soil and are a wonderful source of information to guide your pasture management strategy.

Redroot pigweed

REDROOT WEEDS

Redroot weeds (plants in the Amaranthaceae family) such as redroot pigweed (*Amaranthus retroflexus*) are a sign that the iron-manganese ratio is out of balance: there's either far too much iron or far too little manganese. Redroot weeds also indicate a soil that is excessively high in potassium and magnesium and low in phosphorus and calcium.

QUACK GRASS

Quack grass (*Elytrigia repens*) is also a sign of an improper iron-manganese ratio. It makes an excellent pasture grass, and grazing and manure recycling will help correct this fertilizer imbalance over time.

KNAPWEED

Knapweed (*Centaurea maculosa*) grows in soils that are low in calcium, low in humus, and very low in phosphorus.

BURDOCK

Burdock (*Arctium lappa*) indicates low-calcium, high-potassium soils.

OXEYE DAISY

Oxeye daisy (*Leucanthemum vulgare*) grows in low-phosphorus, high-potassium, high-magnesium soils.

[Adapted from *Grass-Fed Cattle* by Julius Ruechel]

YARROW

Yarrow (*Achillea millefolium*) likes low-calcium, low-phosphorus, low-humus soils.

BROADLEAF PLANTAIN

Broadleaf plantain (*Plantago major*) grows in compacted, poorly aerated soils.

CURLED DOCK

Curled or sour dock (*Rumex crispus*) is another plant that loves compacted soils and is characteristic of soils that are low in calcium and extremely high in magnesium, phosphorus, and potassium.

LAMB'S-QUARTER

Lamb's-quarter (*Chenopodium album*) grows in low-phosphorus, high-potassium soils. Because cattle manure is quite high in potassium, these plants are often found in areas where manure concentrations have accumulated.

FOXTAIL BARLEY

Foxtail barley (*Hordeum jubatum*) is characteristic of low-calcium, high-magnesium, compacted, poorly drained soils.

ST. JOHN'S WORT

St. John's wort (*Hypericum perforatum*) favors soils that are dry, calcium deficient, phosphorus deficient, magnesium rich, potassium rich, and salty. Also be aware that the plant can cause extreme photosensitivity in cattle, leading to irritability; severe sunburn to the nose, skin, and udder; and even death.

Signs of Calcium Deficiency

A whole host of plants indicate a calcium deficiency in the soil. They include bitterweed (*Helenium tenuifolium*), stinging nettle (*Urtica dioica*), broom sedge (*Andropogon virginicus*), trumpet vine (*Campsis radicans*), horsetail (*Equisetum arvense*), and wild buckwheat (*Polygonum convolvulus*). Because many of these weeds concentrate calcium, they are excellent sources of calcium for cattle if they choose to eat them. Wild buckwheat also indicates low phosphorus and an excess of potassium.

USE WEEDS TO TREAT BITES AND RASHES

Being able to treat a bite, sting, or rash right on the spot can save you a good bit of pain and discomfort. Two of the best plants for skin irritation are what we think of as common weeds: plaintain and jewelweed.

JEWELWEED. Often grows near poison ivy and is an excellent treatment for it. Crush and rub the fresh aerial parts of this plant on the affected area, preferably as soon as you're exposed, then rinse it off. You can also simmer the whole fresh plant, cool, strain, and freeze the liquid in ice cube trays to apply as needed.

PLAINTAIN likes to grow where people walk — along pathways, in lawns, through concrete sidewalks. A fresh leaf poultice quickly and effectively draws out venom, splinters, and irritation when applied quickly to bug bites, bee stings, and poison ivy. Here's what to do:

1. Chew fresh plantain leaves into a paste or mash them with a mortar and pestle. If you're working with dried plantain powder, moisten it with clean water, vinegar, honey, or an appropriate liniment/tincture to make a paste.

2. Apply the mashed herb or paste to the affected area. If needed, cover and wrap with vet wrap, bandage, gauze, or other cloth to hold it in place. Replace every half hour to 2 hours, as needed. Gently irrigate the area with saline solution or a diluted liniment between dressings.

Step 1

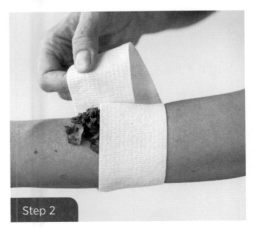
Step 2

[Adapted from *Grow Your Own Herbal Remedies* by Maria Noël Groves]

Nix the plastic wrap and sew a couple of these covers instead — they can be whipped up in the time it takes your lasagna to bake. You'll feel better about not producing more trash, and you'll be able to walk into your next potluck party knowing that your casserole or salad bowl is outfitted well.

MAKE A REUSABLE DISH COVER

MATERIALS

- ½ to ¾ yard of oilcloth (any width will do as long as it fits your container)
- 1 spool of contrasting thread
- Tissue or tracing paper
- Fold-over elastic

1. With the wrong side of the fabric facing up, position your dish, pan, or bowl upside down in the center and trace around it. Measure and mark a line 1½ inches bigger all around than the traced line (a compass is the best tool if you're drawing a circle). Cut along the larger marked line.

2. Draw your lettering and any other design elements on a lightweight piece of paper (tissue paper works well). Position the paper with the sketched design over the right side of the fabric. (The paper keeps the presser foot of the sewing machine from sticking to the oilcloth.) Topstitch over your design, through both the paper and the fabric. Tear away the paper.

3. Fold the elastic over the edge of the fabric. Using a zigzag stitch, sew it all around the edge of the circle, pulling the elastic as taut as possible.

[Adapted from *Improv Sewing* by Nicole Blum and Debra Immergut]

MAKE BEESWAX CANDLES

These little candles are easy and fun to make, and they smell great. If you choose not to scent them with essential oils, they will give off a slight honey scent. Also, beeswax candles are naturally dripless and smokeless and don't create soot like paraffin candles do.

TOOLS AND MATERIALS

- Small jelly jars
- Beeswax
- Shallow pan
- Essential oil of choice, for fragrance (optional)
- Toothpick (optional)
- Wicks (available at most craft stores)
- Pencil
- Scissors

1. Fill the jars halfway with beeswax. If your beeswax came in a large chunk, you'll want to chop it into small pieces before filling the jars.

Step 1

[Adapted from *Girls' Home Spa Lab* by Maya Pagán]

Step 2

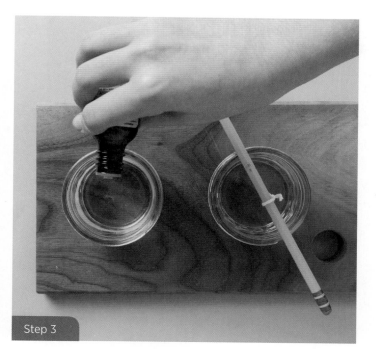

Step 3

2. Carefully place the jars in a shallow pan of water on the stove. Heat slowly until the wax has completely melted.

3. Remove each jar from the heat. Add a few drops of essential oil to the melted wax, if desired. Stir briefly with a toothpick.

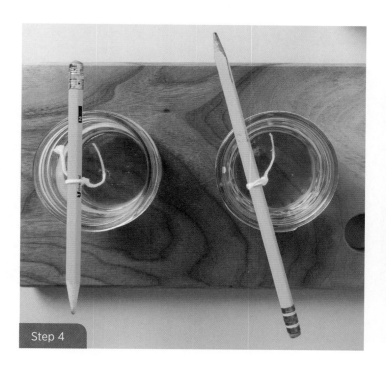

Step 4

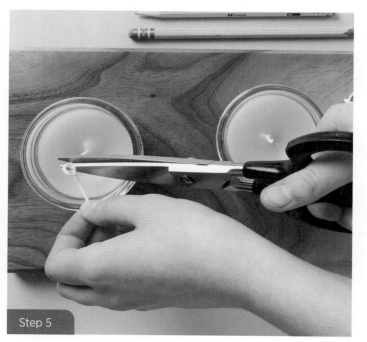

Step 5

4. Dangle one end of the wick down into the wax. The bottom of the wick should touch the bottom of the jar. Tie the other end of the wick to the middle of a pencil, and lay the pencil over the jar rim so the wick is centered in the jar. Trim the extra wick above the knot on the pencil so it doesn't dangle back down into the jar.

5. Let cool overnight. Then remove the pencil and cut the wick about ½ inch above the cooled wax.

STORE POTATOES
SEVEN WAYS

If you've spent your time and attention growing potatoes, you want to make sure they don't rot before you eat them. First cure or dry the potatoes for 7 to 10 days (if you have clay soil, you may want to lightly rinse off excess soil, then pat the spuds dry). To cure, lay them out in a dim room and cover them with a cloth or towels to block out sunlight. During this time, the skins will dry, small wounds will heal over, and new layers of skin will form where the outer layer peeled or rubbed off. After 3 or 4 days, turn the potatoes over so all sides can dry.

1 Place cured potatoes in a burlap bag, tuck the bag into a plastic storage bin left open a wee bit, and keep in an unheated basement, where temperatures are between 45°F and 55°F/7°C and 13°C.

2 Line plastic laundry baskets with newspapers, with potatoes arranged in layers between more newspapers (as shown at left). Place the packed, covered baskets in an unheated garage, preferably with temperatures between 45°F and 55°F/7°C and 13°C.

3 In the basement, make short towers of potatoes by stacking them between layers of open egg cartons. Cover the towers with cloth to protect the potatoes from light.

4 Line small cloth shopping bags with plastic bags, fill them with potatoes, and store in a cold space under the stairs. A similar method: Sort potatoes into paper bags, then place the bags in milk crates to prevent bruising.

5 Use an old dresser in a cool room or basement for storing potatoes in winter. Leave the drawers partially open for ventilation.

6 In a shady spot outdoors, place a tarp over the ground and cover it with an inch of loose straw. Pile on potatoes and cover with more straw, a second tarp, and a 10-inch blanket of leaves or straw.

7 Bury a garbage can so that its bottom half is at least 12 inches deep in the soil. Place potatoes in the can with shredded paper or clean straw. Secure the lid with a bungee cord, and cover with an old blanket if needed to shade out sun.

[Adapted from *Homegrown Pantry* by Barbara Pleasant]

When winter comes, the taste of fresh vegetables can feel like a distant memory. Thankfully, if you take time to store them correctly, they don't have to be. For vegetables that like to be cold and dry, store them in a place that is unheated or underheated during the winter — provided that it is fairly dry. For crops that like to be cold and damp, an unheated basement or root cellar is a good choice.

STORE WINTER VEGETABLES

WARM AND DRY, WITH THE POSSIBILITY OF SUN. Potted herbs can be overwintered on a warm, sunny windowsill. A spot like this is also good for ripening tomatoes from yellow-green to red. Dried herbs and beans cure best where it's warm but not too sunny.

COOL AND DRY. Onions, garlic, green tomatoes, pumpkins, and other winter squash store well in a dry spot that stays around 50°F/10°C, like this closet.

COLD AND MOIST. If you've got a cold (just a couple of degrees above freezing), damp cellar, you've got the perfect spot to store Brussels sprouts (in a bucket of moist sand), carrots (buried in moist sand), potatoes, and celery (potted up), among other vegetables — not to mention canned foods.

COOL AND MODERATELY MOIST. Apples last the longest in a cool spot (just a couple of degrees above freezing is best) that's somewhat moist. They hasten the ripening of other produce, so they need to be stored separately; an insulated garage works very well.

[Adapted from *The Vegetable Gardener's Bible* by Edward C. Smith]

GIVE A
FULL BODY
MASSAGE

Massage is a good way to help relieve physical stress and pain. It is also a great way to connect with a partner and help him or her relax. Below is a simple technique you can use. Wash your hands thoroughly before the massage, and trim your fingernails if necessary.

1. Pour 4 ounces of oil (see the sidebar on page 89) into a bowl for easy access.

2. Oil your hands and rub them together to warm the oil.

3. Start with the person lying faceup with his or her body covered by a sheet (and blanket, if needed). Apply the oil to the throat using gentle side-to-side strokes.

4. Gently swipe across the chin, above the lips, and then across the forehead.

5. Using your fingertips, gently massage in upward strokes, starting at the jaw outside the mouth, coming up along the side of the nose, then across the bridge of the nose.

6. Make several spiraling, circular motions spanning the entire forehead, ending up above and outside the eyes.

7. Press the cheekbones using slight pressure from the outside to the inside.

8. Use a spiral, circular stroke on the cheeks.

9. Press along the sides of the neck, working outward to the shoulders.

10. Massage the crown of the head using the fingertips. Press gently, working down and around to the back of the skull.

11. Uncover one arm, leaving the rest of the body draped. Gently holding the wrist, shake the arm from side to side. With both hands around the arm, gently squeeze, working back and forth starting at the shoulder and working down to the hand.

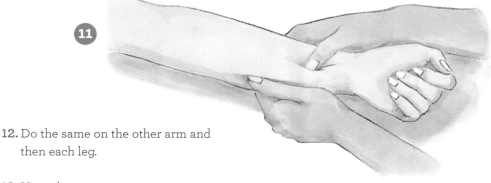

12. Do the same on the other arm and then each leg.

13. Have the person turn over, so you can work on the back. Starting at the base of the spine, gently push on the spine, working up to the top of the shoulders. Rub the shoulders and top of the back all over.

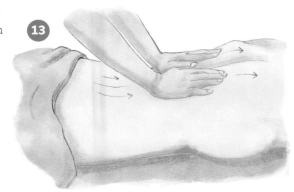

[Adapted from *The Herbal Home Spa* by Greta Breedlove]

An aromatherapy foot massage is the perfect antidote to frayed nerves, low energy, and tired feet. Put a little oil or cream on your hands and rub them together vigorously to warm them before beginning the massage. Complete all the steps on one foot before moving on to the other.

GIVE A FOOT MASSAGE

1. **STROKE THE TOP OF THE FOOT.** Stroking stimulates circulation and warms the foot. Holding your partner's foot in your hands, use your thumbs to begin a long, slow, firm stroking motion on the top of the foot, starting at the tips of the toes and sliding back away from you, all the way to the ankle. Retrace your steps back to the toes with a lighter stroke. Repeat this step three to five times.

2. **STROKE THE BOTTOM OF THE FOOT.** Starting at the base of the toes, use your thumbs to stroke from the ball of the foot and over the arch to the heel, and then back again. Use long, firm strokes, slightly pressing the sole with your thumbs as you stroke. Repeat this step three to five times.

3. **ROTATE THE ANKLE.** Ankle rotations loosen joints and relax feet. Cup one hand under the heel, behind the ankle, to brace the foot and leg. Grasp the ball of the foot with your other hand and turn the foot slowly at the ankle three to five times in each direction. With repeated foot massages, any stiffness will begin to recede. This is a particularly good exercise for anyone suffering from arthritis.

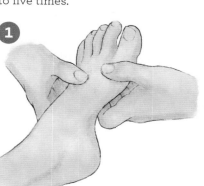

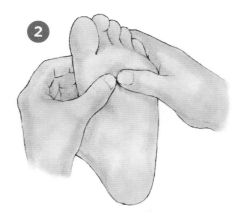

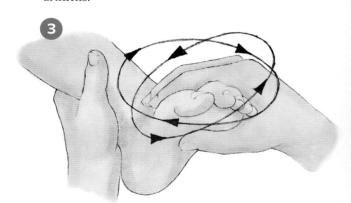

Simple Lavender Massage Oil

Massage is often done with straight vegetable oil. The next step up is aromatherapy oil, which is easy to make and offers the healing elements of both the herbs and their aroma.

✳ ⅔ cup grapeseed oil
✳ ⅓ cup wheat germ oil
✳ 10 drops vitamin E oil
✳ 6 drops lavender essential oil

Combine all the ingredients in a dark bottle that has a spout. Shake well before use.

Continued on next page

[Adapted from *Natural Foot Care* by Stephanie Tourles]

4. **DO TOE PULLS AND SQUEEZES.** Toes, like fingers, are quite sensitive to the touch. This massage step is very calming. Grasp the foot beneath the arch. With your other hand, beginning with the big toe, hold the toe with your thumb on top and index finger beneath. Starting at the base of the toe, slowly and firmly pull the toe, sliding your fingers to the top and back to the base. Now repeat, but gently squeeze and roll the toe between your thumb and index finger, working your way to the tip and back to the base. Repeat these two movements on the remaining toes.

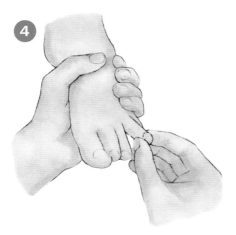

5. **DO TOE SLIDES.** Grasp the foot behind the ankle, cupping under the heel. With the index finger of your other hand, insert your finger between the toes, sliding it back and forth three to five times.

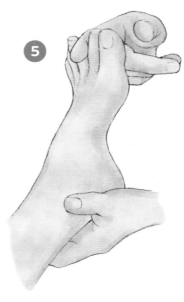

6. **PRESS THE ARCH.** This releases tension in the inner and outer longitudinal arches. Hold the foot as you did in step 5. Using the heel of your other hand, push hard as you slide along the arch from the ball of the foot toward the heel and back again. Repeat five times. This part of the foot can stand a little extra exertion on your part, but don't apply too much pressure.

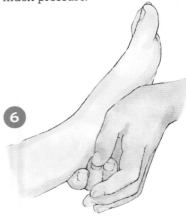

7. **STROKE AGAIN.** Repeat steps 1 and 2. This is a good way to begin and end a foot massage.

Benefits of Foot Massage

FOR THE GIVER: Giving a friend or loved one a foot massage is very soothing and calming for you, and it can actually cause your blood pressure to decrease. It's a very caring, nurturing, and bonding experience to share with another person.

FOR THE RECEIVER: Obviously, this is really the best position to be in. Foot massage will help reduce your stress, boost circulation, and relieve blood stagnation from wearing ill-fitting shoes. In addition, it will dramatically relax your body; soothe foot muscles; undo knots and tension in your toes, the balls of your feet, your arches, and your ankles; and soften your feet if a massage cream or oil is applied.

Specially designed soft, slow, gentle stretching exercises can bring relief to those with carpal tunnel or other repetitive strain injuries. You will notice a slight resistance to the movement at the beginning of the stretch, which will fade as the tissue releases. This loosening is the beginning of change and healing. For each of these exercises, start with 1 set of 10 repetitions and build up to 3 sets of 10 each time.

RELIEVE CARPAL TUNNEL SYNDROME

GENTLE WRIST FLEX

1. Extend one arm in front of you with your palm and fingers facing up.

2. Place your other hand sideways across the outstretched palm, as if you were reaching for a handshake.

3. Press gently against your outstretched palm and fingers for a mild extension. Repeat on the opposite side. This is an easy and important stretch to do when you are spending a lot of time in front of a computer.

4. For this slightly more vigorous stretch, hang your hand, palm side down, over a shelf, table, or armchair. Use your other hand to bend it down as far as is comfortable. Repeat with the opposite hand.

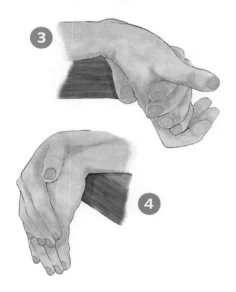

WISHING POSE PRESS

1. Bring your hands together, with your palms touching and fingers interlaced.

2. Pressing your palms together, push your right hand backward with the force of the left.

3. Reverse, pushing your left hand backward with the strength of the right. The pressure should emanate from the palms, not the fingers. Bend just until the stretch begins to feel uncomfortable.

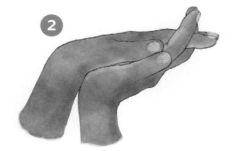

WINGS WRIST STRETCH

1. Bring your palms together in front of your chest, fingers pointed up.

2. Keeping your palms together, slowly raise your elbows up as far as possible without discomfort. Release. Repeat slowly.

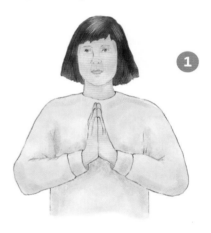

[Adapted from *Natural Hand Care* by Norma Pasekoff Weinberg]

SHEAR A SHEEP IN 1O STEPS

Shearing is a major job that has to be done every year on most breeds of sheep. It's a skill that takes practice to perfect and requires good endurance. Many shepherds hire a professional shearer, who can shear a sheep in a few minutes. State universities offer courses in shearing, which can be done with good old hand shears or with electric clippers. Here's an overview of the process.

1. Slip your left thumb into the sheep's mouth, in back of the incisor teeth, and place your other hand on the sheep's right hip. Bend the sheep's head sharply over her right shoulder and swing the sheep toward you.

2. Lower the sheep to the ground as you step back. Start by shearing the brisket, and then shear up into the left shoulder area. Place one knee behind the sheep's back and your other foot in front. Then trim the top of her head, her cheek, and side of her neck as far as the shoulder.

3. Place the sheep on her rump, resting against your legs. Shear down the shoulder and then down the left side.

4. Hold her left front leg up toward her neck, and from this position shear her side and belly.

[Adapted from *Storey's Guide to Raising Sheep* by Paula Simmons and Carol Ekarius]

5. With only a minor shift in the position of the sheep, you are now ready to shear the back flank. Pressing down on the back flank will straighten out the leg, making it easier to shear. Then shear along her backbone and a few inches beyond, if possible. Then shear the left side of the crotch.

6. The job is half done. Keep your feet so close to the sheep's belly that she cannot get up.

7. Holding one ear, start down the right side of the neck. Hold the ear firmly but not tightly — you don't want to hurt her. Then hold the sheep with your left hand under her chin and around her neck and shear the right shoulder.

8. Pull the sheep up against you to expose her right side, so that you can shear down that side. Then shift position and shear farther down the side and the rump.

9. Shifting position again, finish the right flank and shear the sheep's rear end and right side of the crotch.

10. The job is done, and within a minute the sheep is back on her feet and eating grass.

MAKE 4 LITTLE PROJECTS FROM SCRAPS OF FELTED WOOL

Save those scraps! Small pieces of felted wool hold unlimited potential. Here are just a few of the possibilities. (See page 96 for how to felt wool sweaters.)

EYEGLASS CASE

This useful scrap project can be made to fit whatever you need to hold, whether it's eyeglasses, your phone, or some other gadget requiring a case. Simply fold a piece of scrap cloth over your glasses, or the object you want to hold, to get a general sense of the required size. Allowing enough material for a ½-inch seam allowance, cut the scrap into a tidy rectangle. Leaving the short end open, use a running stitch to sew the other sides together. There is a densely felted strip attached to the back, cut long enough to fold over the open top of the case and button to the front.

Make the tab fit neatly to hold in contents.

Cut a short snip for a buttonhole so the button fits snugly.

FINGER PUPPETS

These little puppets are fun, quick, and easy to make from the smallest scraps around. Make them fit the fingers they will sit on. If the right buttons are not available, use tiny bits of cloth with a small stitch in the middle for eyes. Add wings and feet or stay simple. Make a handful!

[Adapted from *The Sweater Chop Shop* by Crispina ffrench]

BUSINESS CARD CASE

To make your one-of-a-kind card holder, start with a stack of business cards, which are traditionally 2 by 3½ inches. Cut a rectangle ¾ inch wider than the cards and almost three times their height. Fold the cloth around the cards and stitch up the sides with a running stitch. Decoratively edge the flap of the case with blanket stitch. If the cloth is heavily felted, you can make tiny slits for buttonholes. If the cloth is looser knit, it's best to use Velcro or snap tape, and add decorative buttons just for flair.

BABY BOOTIES

Here's a project for larger scraps of extra felty cloth. They're pretty slippery on the floor, making them best for kids too small to walk. Adjust the pattern shapes shown to fit the foot you wish to cover. Sew the back heel seams first, then sew around the circumference of the sole to the shoe top with a running stitch. Make tiny slits for buttonholes in the top ankle bands, and sew buttons to the bottom ankle bands. The buttonholes should be tight going over the button. Be sure to sew the buttons on securely. If you are worried about buttons being a choking hazard, use a small strip of Velcro instead.

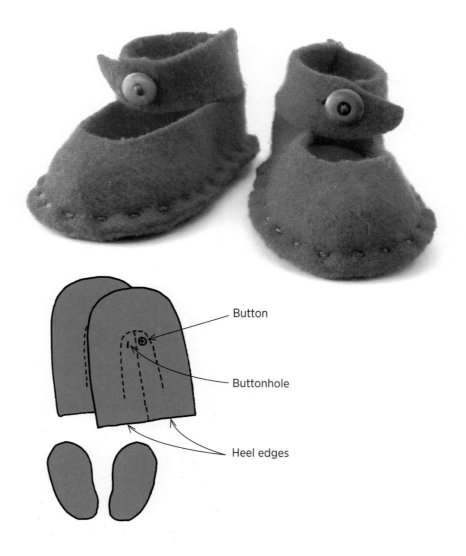

Button

Buttonhole

Heel edges

MAKE POT HOLDERS FROM RECYCLED SWEATERS

Making pot holders from old sweaters is quick and simple, and they are a great gift any time of year. Plus, because they are constructed with wool, they are fire-retardant and insulating, making them super-functional yet cute. The simplest design is to use a single 7- by 7-inch square top. Once you've learned the basic technique, try patching pieces together to make colorful tops.

TOOLS

- Sharp fabric scissors
- Rotary cutter, pad, and extra blades *or* a 7" × 7" pattern made from cardboard
- Permanent felt-tip marker
- Extra long straight pins
- A size 16 yarn darner needle

MATERIALS

- Felted wool sweater
- One 7" square of woven cotton cloth for backing
- One 1" × 6" strip of nonraveling cotton jersey (such as T-shirt material)
- Persian wool or embroidery floss

Felting Wool Sweaters

To prepare sweaters for making pot holders or for other sewing projects, they must first be felted. This requires heat, moisture, and friction, which can be provided by your home washing machine and dryer. Here are a few tips:

✳ Use a hot-water wash, a cold-water rinse, and the usual amount of whatever laundry soap you have on hand.

✳ Make sure the sweaters can move freely in the washer, but don't use too much water or they will float and not get enough friction. If you desire a thicker, more shrunken finish, wash the sweaters in a load with your regular laundry.

✳ Dry the sweaters on high heat.

✳ If, after one cycle, you still haven't achieved the desired felted texture, repeat the process once or twice more. Your sweaters should be felted enough to hold a crisp edge when cut.

[Adapted from *The Sweater Chop Shop* by Crispina ffrench]

PREPARING YOUR MATERIALS

1. For each pot holder, carefully cut a 7- by 7-inch square from both the felted sweater and the woven cotton cloth you have selected. If the felt is thin, cut two or three squares to increase the thickness.

2. Place the felt and cotton squares wrong sides together with the cotton on top. If you are using more than one felt square, stack them together and add the cotton square to the top of the pile, right side up.

3. To make a loop for hanging the pot holder, fold the strip of cotton jersey in half, short ends together. Insert 1½ inches of the two short ends in one corner of the stack, between layers.

4. Pin all four corners in place, being certain that you have "caught" both ends of the hanging loop.

Once you've mastered the single-square pot holder (facing page), you can create a playful look by patching together a variety of fabrics.

SEWING

5. Thread your needle with a 2-yard length of Persian wool or embroidery floss. Beginning at the corner with the hanging loop, insert your needle under the cotton top layer and push down through the loop and the wool bottom layer(s) of fabric. Pull the yarn through to the bottom of the pot holder, concealing the knot under the top cotton layer.

6. Make a reinforced X stitch through the hanging loop and all layers in that corner. Stitches should be neat and strong and can show on both sides of the pot holder. This stitch will anchor the hanging loop and keep the layers in place; it also allows pin removal in this corner, making it easier to hold.

7. Finish your X stitch with thread coming out of the fabric about ½ inch in from the cut edges of the layers, and begin to blanket stitch around the edges of the pot holder. Be sure you are catching all the layers. Keep your corners neat and square by double stitching the first and last stitches of each side seam.

8. When you get back to where you started, tie an overhand knot close to the surface of the material. Run the needle and yarn about 1 inch between the layers to conceal it. Snip the yarn off at the surface of the pot holder.

9. Iron the finished pot holder with lots of steam to make a nice flat finish.

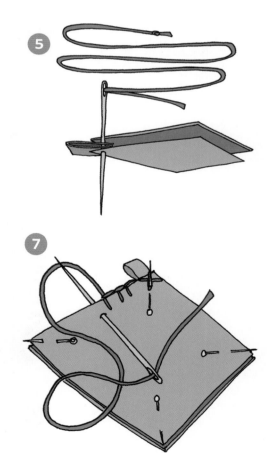

REWIRE A TABLE LAMP

If a lamp doesn't work, the problem can only be in one of three places: the plug, the cord, or the socket. Unless the lamp is rather new, you might as well replace all three. You don't have to buy an entire socket — shell, insulator, and cap. You can buy just the interior electrical part; it's cheaper.

Before you start, however, study the illustration below to familiarize yourself with lamp terminology.

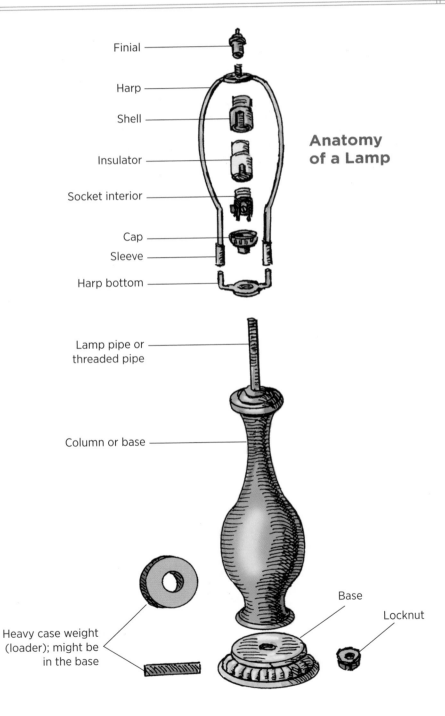

Anatomy of a Lamp

- Finial
- Harp
- Shell
- Insulator
- Socket interior
- Cap
- Sleeve
- Harp bottom
- Lamp pipe or threaded pipe
- Column or base
- Heavy case weight (loader); might be in the base
- Base
- Locknut

TOOLS AND MATERIALS

- Screwdriver
- Electrical cord
- Sharp knife or single-edge razor blade
- Wire stripper
- Socket interior
- Automatic plug
- Replacement felt
- Craft glue
- Scissors

1. **REMOVE THE HARP.** It's easier to take the shell off the socket if the harp is out of the way first. With the lamp unplugged, lift the two little sleeves where the top attaches to the bottom of the harp. Squeeze the sides of the harp near this attachment and remove the top part.

2. **TAKE THE SOCKET APART.** Look at the socket where the shell meets the cap. You'll see the word *press* near the switch opening. Push in on this with your thumb and tilt the shell toward the opposite side. The shell will come off, exposing the socket. If you're unable to loosen the shell, insert a small screwdriver at the *press* point. This will usually dislodge it.

[Adapted from *Antiques on the Cheap* by James W. McKenzie]

3. **DISCONNECT THE OLD CORD.** When you remove the shell, the cardboard insulator usually remains in it. If it's still covering the socket, pull it off. Loosen the two screws holding the lamp cord to the socket, and pull the cord from the bottom of the lamp. You might have to take the felt off the base of the lamp to access the cord.

4. **INSERT THE NEW CORD.** Feed the new cord, which should be 6 to 8 feet long, through the base and through the lamp pipe and socket cap. Allow yourself plenty of slack at the top and tie a loose, ordinary knot in the cord several inches from the end. With a sharp knife or razor blade, slit the insulation between the two wires, just enough to start the separation. Pull the two wires apart a couple of inches, and strip about ½ inch of insulation off each wire. Roll each wire between your thumb and index finger to twist all those little fine wires together.

5. **CONNECT THE NEW WIRES.** If you're using a polarized cord and plug (one prong wider than the other), you'll note that one wire is copper colored and the other is silver. Just match the wire colors to the colors of the screws on the socket. What this does is place the grounded side of the circuit on the threaded outer portion of the socket — the part you could most easily touch by accident. If the cord doesn't have two different-colored wires or if the plug isn't polarized, you can place the wire under either screw.

6. **PUT THE SOCKET TOGETHER.** Making sure there are no stray strands of wire, tighten the screws securely. Work the loose knot up as close to the bottom of the interior as possible, pull the slack out of the cord from the bottom, and replace the shell and insulator. You'll feel it snap into place as you push the shell into the cap.

Wiring socket with knot

7. **REPLACE THE PLUG.** There is no reason to use old-fashioned screw-type plugs when rewiring lamps. Instead, use an automatic plug. To attach one to the wire, squeeze the prongs together and pull the insiders out. Insert the end of the cord through the hole in the cover and, holding the prongs spread outward, force the cord as far as possible into the opening between the prongs. Squeeze the prongs together and push the mechanism back into the cover, seating it firmly. If the plug has one prong wider than the other and the cord has a silver and copper-colored wire, the silver side goes to the wide prong.

8. **REPLACE THE FELT.** Normally, you'll destroy the felt on the bottom of a lamp when you rewire it. You can buy replacement felt from parts suppliers (even self-stick) or, for a lot less money, in small sheets at craft stores. Use a thick craft glue. Spread a coat on the base and set the lamp on top of the felt. After the glue has dried, trim the excess close to the base with sharp scissors.

There are several varieties of "automatic" plugs that attach without the use of tools.

RE-COVER A LAMPSHADE

Here's an easy way to add style to an old lamp. Not every old shade will re-cover well. You want either of the following: (1) a straight-sided hexagonal (or other sectional) shade; or (2) a shade that has no ribs, only a top and bottom ring, or a shade with straight, not bowed-in, ribs connecting the top and bottom rings. Repair procedures for these two types of shade differ somewhat. We'll begin with a hexagonal shade and then move on to one with circular rings.

HEXAGONAL SHADE

1. To remove the covering from a hexagonal shade, cut and rip it off in any manner, but don't bend the frame.

2. To mark the new cover, place the frame on a sheet of poster board or other stiff paper, and use a pencil to trace around the outside of one of the sections.

3. Cut out the section, staying outside the marks to allow a little room for adjustment later on. Use the cutout section as a pattern to make the other sections.

4. To attach the first section of the new cover, run a bead of glue along the outside of one section of the frame. (Use a thick craft glue that will stick to metal and paper.) Attach the paper to the frame with spring-type clothespins around all four edges. Let the glue dry, or accelerate the drying with a hair dryer. Trim any overlap of the paper with a sharp razor blade.

5. Attach other sections in the same manner, using clothespins to secure three edges. Hold the fourth edge of the section against the frame by weighting it with a bag or two of beans. For the final section, clip it at the top and bottom and weight it on each side.

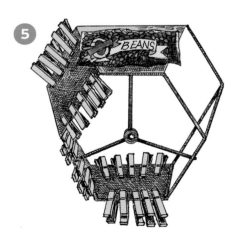

Tracing a frame

Covering attached and weighted

Decorating the Shade

After you've re-covered your shade, you can decorate it or glue fabric onto it using spray adhesive or diluted glue. If you want to cover the top and bottom edges of the shade around the rings, use a ribbon that is at least 50 percent cotton; otherwise, the glue won't adhere to it. The type of ribbon most commonly used is a variety called grosgrain ("grow grain"). After measuring and cutting the ribbon, apply glue to a section and wrap the glue-covered portion over the wire, pressing it against the paper on the inside and outside of the shade. Use a clothespin to hold the ribbon in place temporarily as you work on the next section. When you reach the end, just overlap it, glue, and clamp it into place.

[Adapted from *Antiques on the Cheap* by James W. McKenzie]

SHADE WITH CIRCULAR RINGS

1. To remove an old fabric covering, cut and rip it off in any manner possible without bending the frame. If the frame is covered with paper, parchment, or plastic, a gentler approach is necessary in order to preserve the old cover for use as a pattern. Use a razor blade to cut the trim that covers the rings. Next, carefully insert the blade under the edge of the seam that joins the end of the covering and work this glued seam loose. You might have to work from both the inside and the outside. At this point, the entire covering should come off the frame, and you will be holding an arc-shaped piece of material. Use the scissors to tidy the ragged edges.

2. If you're able to use the old cover as a template for the new one, mark the new cover by laying the old one on a sheet of poster board or other stiff paper and tracing around it. If you don't have a pattern to work from and the frame is one piece (not two unattached rings), rub a little crayon or colored chalk on the outer edges of the rings and roll the frame on the paper. This will mark a pattern.

3. Cut the marked paper, staying slightly outside the marks to allow for adjustment later on.

4. Starting with the top ring, attach the paper with a spring-type clothespin. Continue all the way around the ring, placing the clothespins side by side. Repeat for the bottom ring. You might have to loosen pins here and there to adjust the fit as you go. The cover should fit snugly to the frame.

5. Once it is attached, glue the covering to the frame. To do this, remove every other clothespin from the top ring. Then, with the bottle of glue or a glue applicator, reach inside the shade and apply a bead of glue along the paper where it touches the frame. This will "tack" the paper to the frame.

6. Repeat this process for the bottom ring and for any inside ribs. When the glue dries, remove all the clothespins and apply glue to the spaces that were covered by the pins.

7. There should be about ½ inch of overlap where the two ends of the arc come together. Using your finger or a piece of stiff paper, coat the underside of the overlapping edge with a little glue (too much glue will squeeze out from under the paper onto the outside). Lay the shade on its side, seam down on a clean surface, and place a bag or two of beans inside the shade. The weight will press the surfaces together. Leave the beans in place until the adhesive sets and the seam is sealed.

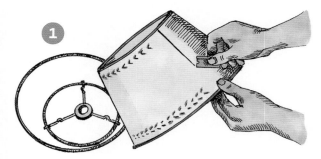

Use a single-edge razor blade to cut the old paper cover away from the frame.

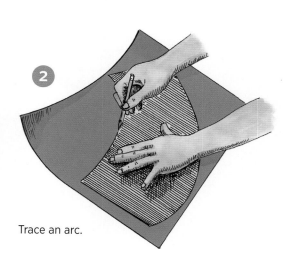

Trace an arc.

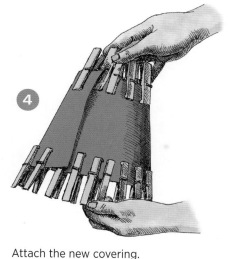

Attach the new covering.

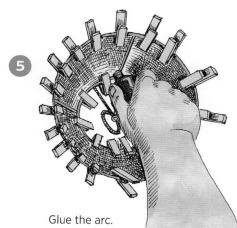

Glue the arc.

MAKE BEER THE EASY WAY

Malt extract brewing is the simplest way to make beer, and most people start out this way. Malting is the trickiest stage of brewing, and using malt extract means that you don't have to mash grain. This recipe is for a bitter — the standard English pub beer. This beer has a lot of character, despite its simplicity. It's popular with homebrewers because it's fast and easy to brew. It is not a long-keeping beer, so you can brew it, drink it up, and make some more. Refer to a handy guide like *Brewing Made Easy* by Joe and Dennis Fisher for instructions on priming and bottling your beer.

MAKES ABOUT 5 GALLONS

INGREDIENTS

- 3.3 pounds amber hopped malt extract syrup
- 2 pounds plain light dry malt extract
- 1 ounce East Kent Goldings flavoring hops
- ½ ounce East Kent Goldings aroma hops
- 1 packet Fermentis Safale S-33 ale yeast

EQUIPMENT

Star San sanitizer

5-gallon food-grade plastic bucket

6.7-gallon plastic fermenting bucket with lid

Thermometer

16-quart stainless steel pot

Long-handled metal or plastic stirring spoon

Medium-sized stainless steel strainer

Fermentation lock

1. Mix up a gallon of sanitizing solution (¼ ounce Star San in 1 gallon water) in the food-grade plastic bucket. Pour ½ gallon into the fermenting bucket, seal with the lid, and slosh it around until the sides of the bucket and the bottom of the lid are coated in foam. Return any unused solution to the mixing bucket and place the rest of your equipment in it. A few minutes of immersion should sanitize the equipment throughout.

2. Add 1½ gallons cold water to the fermenting bucket. Seal with the lid and set aside.

3. Immerse the unopened can of hopped malt extract syrup in hot water for about 10 minutes to make it easier to work with. Trim off the top of the plastic bag of dry malt extract. This prevents steam from hydrating the extract and causing a sticky mess.

4. Heat 1½ gallons cold water in the brew pot to a high enough temperature to melt the malt extracts (100°F to 120°F/38°C to 49°C).

5. Remove the brew pot from the heat. Pour the hopped malt extract syrup into the brew pot and scrape any remaining syrup away from the sides of the can. Add the dry malt extract and stir well to dissolve. Return the brew pot to the heat and boil for 30 minutes.

6. Add the flavoring hops. These will contribute flavor and aroma to the finished beer.

7. Remove the brew pot from the heat when the wort (unfermented solution) has boiled for 45 minutes. Add the aroma hops, cover the pot, and steep for 5 minutes. Remove the cover and allow the brew pot to cool until it can be safely handled.

[Adapted from *Brewing Made Easy* by Joe Fisher and Dennis Fisher]

8. Carefully pour the boiled wort through a strainer and into the fermenter with the cold water.

9. With the spent hops over the fermenter, rinse the hops with ½ gallon 180°F/82°C water.

10. Add enough cold water to the fermenter to make 5 gallons. (On a standard primary fermenter bucket, the 5-gallon mark is indicated by the thick plastic collar. It is also useful to mark gallon increments on the outside of the bucket with a permanent marker.) Stir thoroughly with the sanitized spoon to mix the water with the wort.

11. Measure the temperature of the wort. It needs to cool down to around 70°F/21°C before you can add the yeast. Be sure to rinse the thermometer and shake it down; otherwise, it will give you a false reading. Temperatures of 90°F/32°C and up are fatal to yeast; temperatures between 60°F/16°C and 70°F/21°C are ideal for ales (a few degrees above or below that range is fine).

12. Add the yeast and stir in gently with the sanitized spoon.

13. Attach the fermenter lid and the fermentation lock. The fermentation lock must be filled with water. (The gasket in the lid is usually a pretty tight fit for the stem of the airlock. It helps to push against the gasket from the underside of the lid while twisting the airlock.)

14. Allow to ferment for 7 to 10 days in a quiet spot, out of direct light, at temperatures between 60°F/16°C and 70°F/21°C.

15. Prime, bottle, and cap the beer once the fermentation is complete. Priming (adding corn sugar) is a necessary step for carbonation. This chore goes a lot faster if you have two people: one to fill the bottles and one to cap. From setup to cleanup, priming and bottling usually takes only an hour or so.

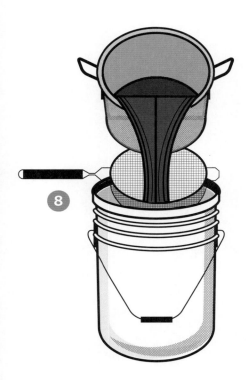

What Is Malt Extract?

Malt extract is the product of grain mashing, in which malt grains (barley that has been partially germinated, dried, and roasted to produce different brewing characteristics) are steeped at controlled temperatures to extract the brewing sugars. Then the resulting liquid is reduced until it is a syrup that contains only about 20 percent water.

POUR A BEER
FOR GREAT FOAM

To get the best head on a beer, pour boldly down the center of an absolutely clean glass. It will foam up, but this is good. Really. Allow it to settle, and then repeat until you have a full glass. By delaying gratification and allowing a large amount of foam to build up and then shrink, you have created a dense, creamy foam, filled with tiny, long-lasting bubbles. As a side benefit, you have knocked some of the excess gas out of the beer, and the result will be more like the smooth creaminess of draft beer.

1. Pour straight down and let it foam up.

2. Let the foam settle.

3. Pour, wait, and repeat until the glass is filled to the appropriate level. Enjoy!

[Adapted from *Tasting Beer* by Randy Mosher]

BUILD A RAISED GARDEN BED

Raised beds have several advantages over their ground-level counterparts. They avoid soil compaction, are at a more manageable height for tending, and tend to be less weedy. Designs abound for wood-framed raised beds, and frames made from 2×6, 2×8, or 2×12 boards or 4×4 timbers are very popular. The basic setup for a frame is the same for all of these materials, but 6"-long galvanized spikes or timber screws are needed to connect 4×4s. The following instructions are for a bed that is approximately 4 feet wide and 6 feet long with sides made from 2×6s.

1. Find or cut two 6-foot lengths for the long sides and two 45-inch lengths for the short sides.

2. Set the boards into position and screw or nail them together at one corner. If you're using screws, predrill pilot holes in the wood. Alternatively, you can cut a length of 2×2 scrap lumber to serve as a corner brace and drive nails or screws through the frame pieces directly into the brace.

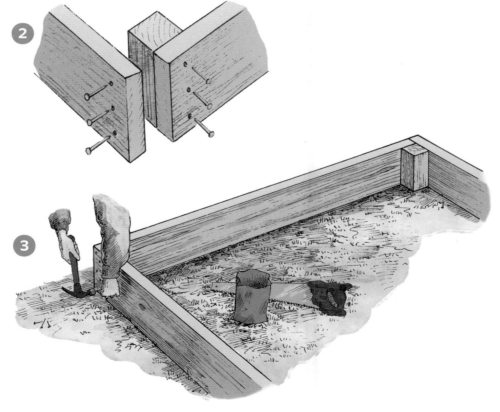

3. Fasten together the other two frame boards at the opposite corner. Now check to see whether the frame is squarely aligned. One way to do this is to measure the distance diagonally across the frame, and then measure across the other diagonal. If the two distances are equal, then the corners are square. When you're sure the frame is squared up, add fasteners at the two remaining corner joints.

[Adapted from *Building Raised Beds* by Fern Marshall Bradley]

4. Use a level to check that the frame is level, or simply get down on the ground and eyeball it. If there are high or low spots, add more soil or dig out soil as needed until the frame is level all around.

5. For beds that are longer than 6 feet, add a center brace to reinforce the frame and prevent the weight of the soil from distorting the shape of the frame over time. Or you can drive sturdy metal garden stakes into the soil along the outside face of the long sides of the frame and use screws to fasten the stakes to the framing.

6. For taller frames that use a second set of boards or timbers, stagger the end joints. This makes for sturdier joints that are less likely to shift out of place over time. Fasten the two tiers together by driving spikes or screws down through the second course into the timbers below (you may need to drill pilot holes first).

BUILD A GARDEN DOLLY
FROM A GOLF CART

Here's the perfect use for that old pushcart. (Even if you don't have a cart sitting around, you can often buy one at a garage sale or flea market for a few bucks.) The bottom golf bag rest gives you the perfect place for perching a homemade plywood tray, the big wheels allow you to navigate rough or muddy terrain, and the overall design makes the dolly easy to steer and push. You can customize yours to haul garden tools, pots, hoses, mulches, chicken feed, or anything else you want.

Tip: Every golf cart is a little different, so before you pick up your tools, scratch your head a little. Figure out how much space you have between the wheels and how you're going to attach the tray to the cart. Once you have the basics figured out, go for it.

MATERIALS

- Scrap ½" or ¾" plywood
- One 4- to 6-foot 2×2
- 1⅝" or 2" screws
- L-brackets (optional)
- U-bolts (with washers and nuts; optional)
- Pipe straps (optional)
- Hooks and other hardware, as desired

Exploded View of Open-Front Box

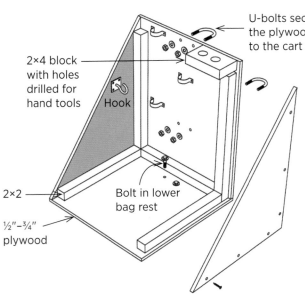

2×4 block with holes drilled for hand tools

Hook

U-bolts secure the plywood box to the cart

2×2

Bolt in lower bag rest

½"–¾" plywood

1. Build the open-front box or tray out of ½- or ¾-inch plywood. Reinforce the box by gluing and screwing 2×2s into the corners or using metal L-brackets.

2. Secure the plywood box to the cart in at least three places for stability. Use U-bolts, pipe straps, or screws.

3. Accessorize your dolly. Add pairs of pipe clamps to hold long-handled tools and hooks for hauling hoses, ropes, and wire. Drill holes through 2×4 scraps and secure them to the box to create hand tool holders. Remove the upper curved bag rest, or leave it in place to help support tall objects you might be hauling.

[Adapted from *The Backyard Homestead Book of Building Projects* by Spike Carlsen]

Your meat-loving dog will sit up and beg for this easy-to-make recipe. Hey, where is it written that cookies must be sweet to taste good?

BAKE
GRAVY COOKIES
FOR YOUR DOG

MAKES 4 DOZEN SMALL COOKIES

INGREDIENTS

Cooking spray, for the baking sheet

2½ cups whole-wheat flour, plus more for dusting

2 small jars beef-based baby food

6 tablespoons low-sodium beef gravy

½ cup nonfat dry milk

½ cup water

1 egg

1 tablespoon packed brown sugar

1. Preheat the oven to 350°F/180°C. Lightly coat a baking sheet with cooking spray.

2. Combine all the ingredients in a large bowl and mix well.

3. Dust your hands with flour and shape the dough into a big ball. Dust a rolling pin with flour and use it to flatten the ball into a disk.

4. Cut the dough into fun shapes with a cookie cutter. Transfer the cutout shapes to the baking sheet.

5. Bake for 25 minutes, or until lightly browned. Allow the cookies to cool before serving. Store in the refrigerator in an airtight container for up to 2 weeks.

Serve one cookie a day for a dog of up to 30 pounds, or two cookies for a dog over 30 pounds. Break cookies into small pieces to use for training treats.

[Adapted from *A Kid's Guide to Dogs* by Arden Moore]

TEACH YOUR DOG TO WEAVE THROUGH YOUR LEGS

If your dog acts like your shadow and always seems to want to be close by your side, she may be a good candidate to learn the art of weaving in and out of your legs. Your goal is to have your dog perform a figure eight through your legs. As with all training, it starts with one step at a time.

1. Cue your dog to sit, facing you and up close. Stand tall with your legs wide apart.

2. Holding a treat in your left hand, tuck that hand behind your left leg, so your dog can see the treat. Say "Weave" as you encourage her to reach through your legs for the treat.

3. When she pokes her head through your legs, say "Good weave!" Then reward her with the treat. Continue to work on having your dog follow the treat through your legs. Always make it playful and fun.

[Adapted from *A Kid's Guide to Dogs* by Arden Moore]

4. Once your dog knows to follow your hand, position her so she is sitting on your right side and looking up at you. Hold a treat in your left hand.

5. Take a big step forward with your left leg and lower your left hand under your outstretched leg to entice your dog to put her head through your legs. If she doesn't understand what you want at first, hold the treat closer and move it slowly away from her.

6. Lure her by moving your hand forward so that she follows it with her whole body. As soon as she's through your legs, say "Good weave" and give her the treat.

7. Moving slowly, repeat the action with your right leg, holding a treat in your right hand. Always hold the treat in the same hand as the leg you step forward on and reward her at every step. As she learns what you want, you can treat her every few steps.

8. Once your dog can move back and forth between your legs, it's time to pick up the pace and make the movement nice and smooth. You may feel like an orchestra conductor with the treat in your moving hand, but it's worth the payoff — this is a really fun trick!

SET UP A DOG AGILITY COURSE

Agility courses consist of 10 different obstacles that the dog navigates with his owner running beside him. The goal is to run the course in the shortest length of time with the least number of faults. The course layout changes for every competition; some agility courses combine jumps and weaves but leave out the other obstacles. A standard course has all three — jumps, weaves, and obstacles — but can be arranged to be more or less difficult.

▼JUMPS (HURDLES)

The jump setup involves two upright supports that are a minimum of 32 inches high with one 4- to 5-foot adjustable horizontal bar set between 4 and 30 inches off the ground. The crossbar must be lightweight so it moves if the dog hits it; it can be made of PVC, wood, or plastic; it may have side wings on the supports. Jumps can be set up as a single obstacle or in a series.

▶TIRE JUMP

This circle is made of PVC pipe or foam with a diameter of 20 to 22 inches. The form for the dog to jump through hangs in a frame and is adjusted to between 4 and 30 inches from the ground. The tire is fastened at the top and sides of the frame but swings free at the bottom.

▶LONG JUMP

The long jump is a set of 6- or 8-inch-wide steps that ascend upward and outward, creating a horizontal jump that is set from 16 to 52 inches, depending on the height of the dog.

[Adapted from *Canine Sports & Games* by Kristin Mehus-Roe]

START

100

90

3. Tunnel

1. Weave poles

80

2. A-frame

70

4. Teeter

60

5. Tire

 **7. Jump**

50

FINISH

40

T **6. Table**

10. Jumps

30

8. Chute

20

10

9: Dogwalk

10   20   30   40   50   60   70   80   90   100

A typical agility course: the obstacles are numbered in the order of approach.

▼TUNNEL

This flexible tube is made of heavy nylon with an inside diameter of 24 inches. It can be 10 to 20 feet long. It may be set up as a straight tunnel or in a curve. The tunnel is kept in place with 20-pound bags of sand or 3-gallon bags of water.

►WEAVE POLES

A succession of upright plastic or PVC poles form one of the more challenging obstacles. The poles are between 36 and 48 inches in height and between 20 and 21 inches in distance from one another (measuring from the middle of one pole to the middle of the next pole). Depending on the level of competition, there will be 6 to 12 weave poles in a set. The object is for the dog to run through the poles (entering between the first and second pole going from the right to the left), alternating from one side to the other without missing any.

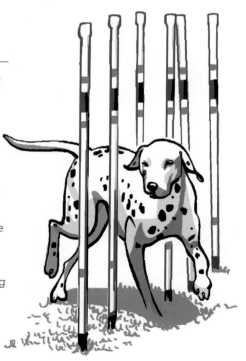

▲CHUTE

This two-part tunnel has a rigid opening section that is a maximum of 30 inches in length with a 22½-inch minimum inside diameter. The attached tube is made of lightweight fabric and is a maximum of 8 feet long. The circumference flares to 96 inches at the chute opening. The dog enters at the opening and must push through the fabric sleeve, or tube, to exit.

Continued on next page

▲PAUSE TABLE (BOX)

Depending on the organization, this will be either a raised table or an outlined box on the ground. The dog must stay in either a sit or a down for a specified length of time before the handler releases him to finish the course.

▲A-FRAME

This obstacle consists of two ramps joined at the top to make an A shape. The ramps are 8 or 9 feet in length and 3 to 4 feet wide. The total height ranges from 5 feet to 5 feet 11 inches, depending on the venue. The dog must climb up one side of the A-frame and down the other.

Contact Zone

The A-frame, the teeter, and the dog walk are contact obstacles — that is, each has a 42-inch yellow contact zone at the beginning and end of the apparatus. The dog must touch the yellow part with at least one paw as he enters and leaves the obstacle or he will be penalized.

▶TEETER

Similar to a child's teeter-totter, the teeter is 12 feet long, 12 inches wide, and 24 inches high at its tipping point. The dog must walk up one side of the teeter, tip it, and then walk down the other.

◀DOG WALK

Requiring careful maneuvering, the dog walk consists of two sloped ramps with a 6- to 12-foot-long board in between. The center board is 46 to 50 inches high. The ramps and center board are usually 12 inches wide. The dog must ascend one ramp, cross the center board, and descend the other ramp.

No one likes finding a hole in one of their favorite socks. If the damaged area is small, you can mend it with thread, but if it is a large hole or tear, you should secure a fabric or interfacing patch on the wrong side and darn over the patch for greater durability and to make the mending job quicker.

DARN SOCKS

1. Secure your thread by working several stitches in an undamaged part of the cloth.

2. Work a running stitch around the damaged area a couple of times.

3. Work several straight stitches across the opening, starting and ending the stitches close to the running stitches.

4. Work a series of stitches perpendicular to the parallel rows, weaving the threads over and under the parallel threads in the desired pattern.

5. To fasten off, don't knot the thread; instead weave the ends into the stitches.

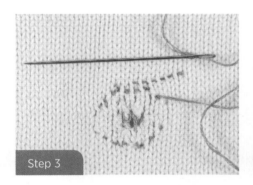

Step 3

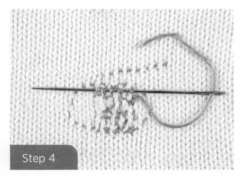

Step 4

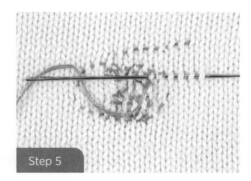

Step 5

Darning Eggs

Darning eggs are useful tools for holding a sock or sleeve as you are working on it, but they can be difficult to find these days. You might pick one up at a thrift shop or estate sale, but another option is to make your own. Find a shaker peg and a wooden egg or sphere in the wood craft section of your local craft supply store. Drill a hole in the wooden sphere, fill it with wood glue, and insert the shaker peg. Paint or decorate it any way you wish!

[Adapted from *Mend It Better* by Kristin M. Roach]   **115**

PATCH CLOTHING

Instead of throwing out that torn or stained piece of clothing, patch it! A cloth patch opens up many options for decoration as well as concealment. When placing the patch on the outside, use fabric that contrasts the garment. Make it a decoration instead of just trying to hide a hole.

1. Set the iron to the heat temperature specified by the garment's care instructions, and press the area where you will be applying the patch so it's nice and flat.

2. Trim any stray threads around the hole to be patched.

3. Cut the patch fabric ½ inch larger on all sides than the hole to be patched. If you are using lightweight fabric or fabric that frays a lot, add 1 inch all around so you can turn the edges to the wrong side for a more finished look.

4. **IF YOU ARE USING A SEWING MACHINE,** sew a zigzag stitch around the edge of the damaged area to help prevent further fraying. Pin the patch over the hole and zigzag stitch around the edge. If you are using a lightweight fabric, turn the edges of the patch under before applying it for a finished look.

IF YOU ARE SEWING BY HAND, work a whipstitch around the damaged area. This serves the same purpose as the zigzag stitch in machine stitching. Pin the patch in place and use a blanket stitch to secure it to the garment and give the patch a finished edge.

Make a Woven Patch

This woven patch is a cross between weaving and embroidery. You can weave a patch to decorate or repair; use it to add something special to your favorite jacket or to cover a hole in your favorite jeans. Try to keep the patch small — 1 to 2 inches at most — or it can bunch up the fabric.

1. First, sew a series of long, close-together warp threads over the hole and tie off the last stitch.

2. Then use a different color thread to weave over and under the warp threads.

3. Use a fork or your fingers to push the weft threads close together as you go. Tie off the thread on the back of the fabric.

[Adapted from *Mend It Better* by Kristin M. Roach]

UNCLOG A DRAIN WITHOUT CHEMICALS

Sinks are commonly clogged by hair, grease, and soap that prevent water from draining properly. But don't despair, you can solve the problem without resorting to dangerous chemicals or calling a plumber. In fact, you have a few options.

Before taking anything apart, try plunging the drain with a plunger (first run a little water into the sink). You can also try flushing the drain by inserting a garden hose, stuffing a towel around and inside the drain hole to seal it, and turning on the hose.

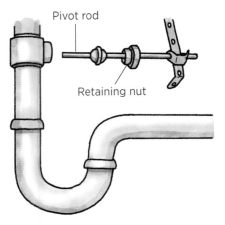

Pivot rod

Retaining nut

CLEANING THE WATER STOPPER

Most bathroom sinks have a water stopper built into the fixture, except for older sinks that have a removable rubber drain plug. Underneath the sink and behind the drainpipe, there is a pivot arm that regulates the up-and-down motion of the water stopper. The arm is held in place by a retaining nut.

1. Unscrew the nut and push the arm toward the back of the sink. This lifts the stopper up from the drain hole.

2. Clean the stopper and the drain with a disassembled coat hanger or some other instrument that will reach into the drain.

3. Reassemble the arm, tighten the retaining nut, and check the drain.

[Adapted from *The Woman's Hands-On Home Repair Guide* by Lyn Herrick]

CLEANING THE DRAIN TAP

You may need to clean the drain trap — the U-shaped pipe under the sink. The drain trap is filled with water at all times to prevent contaminants from entering your house through the pipe. Unfortunately, it sometimes becomes clogged.

1. Place a small bucket or pan under the trap to catch any water that remains in the sink drain.

2. Some traps have a plug at the bottom that can easily be removed for cleaning. Unfasten the plug using an adjustable wrench. If your pipe does not have a cleanout plug, remove the entire trap, using a plumber's wrench to unfasten the two nuts that connect the trap to the drainpipe.

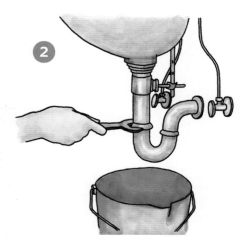

3. Once the plug or trap is removed, clean out the trap with your fingers or with a disassembled wire coat hanger.

4. Replace the plug or reattach the trap to the drainpipe, fastening the nuts tightly so the trap does not leak but not so tightly as to damage the threads.

5. Turn on the water to test the drain and check for leaks.

USING A SINK AUGER

Sometimes the clog is farther down the pipe. In this case, you will need a sink auger. To assemble the auger, insert the end of the snakelike coil into the auger handle.

1. Place a bucket under the trap to catch any water remaining in the drain.

2. Remove the drain trap with a plumber's wrench by unfastening the two nuts that connect the trap to the drainpipe.

3. Insert the blade of the snake into the pipe that enters the wall. Allow the snake to run freely into the pipe. When the coil stops running into the pipe, you have reached the blockage or a bend in the pipe.

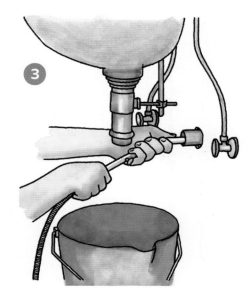

4. Tighten the screw handle and rotate the auger handle in a clockwise direction. This moves the snake coil around the bend in the pipe or enables it to cut through the blockage.

5. Pull the snake from the drain pipe. Reattach the drain trap, turn on the water, and test the drain.

THAW FROZEN PIPES

If a pipe freezes, don't panic. First check the weather forecast, and if the temperature is set to rise above 32°F/0°C, the pipes may thaw on their own, with no damage. Usually pipes freeze just at the points where they are exposed to the cold. This is common near sills, exterior walls, and uninsulated spaces. Here's how to help the thawing process. When you heat the pipe, turn on all affected faucets so that the frozen water can expand and the vapors from the melting ice can escape.

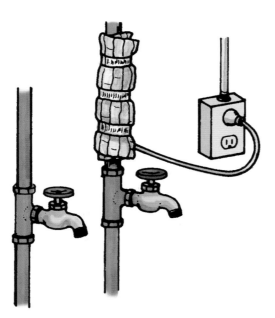

Try wrapping an electric heating pad around the frozen pipe.

Wrap rags around the freeze-up and soak them with hot water.

Use a hair dryer to heat the spot, if you have an outlet nearby.

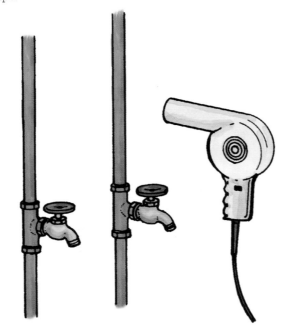

Pinpointing the Culprit

To locate the freeze-up, turn on the water faucets. Follow the frozen pipe back to a juncture. Then test water taps off this second pipe to determine whether the pipe has frozen farther downstream. Once you have located the culprit section of pipe, you probably can pinpoint the location of the freeze-up by looking for a bulge or feeling for where the pipe is coldest.

[Adapted from *What to Do When the Power Fails* by Mary Twitchell]

There is nothing worse in the deep of winter than finding a leak from a burst pipe. If a pipe does burst, you can buy a pipe cutter and pipe repair kit at your local hardware store. You could also buy a length of snug-fitting heater tubing at your local car parts store, along with two clamps. Before starting on a plumbing project, always remember to turn off the main water supply. These are quick-fix solutions. Consult a plumber for long-term strategies.

FIX A BURST PIPE

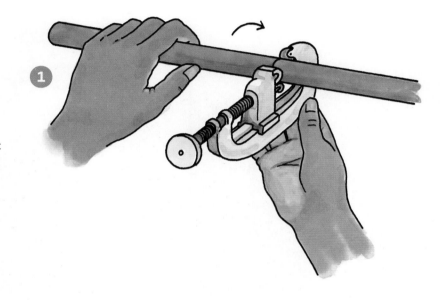

1. Use a pipe cutter to cut away the broken section of pipe. Be careful not to bend or dent the pipe by tightening the cutter too quickly. If you are using a repair kit, do not cut away more than the repair length specified on the package.

2. If you are using a repair kit, follow the instructions on the package. Make sure the cut ends of the pipe are square and clean. Slip one end of the repair piece onto one of the pipes. Using the tool provided, push the repair piece onto the other pipe.

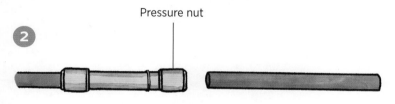

Pressure nut

If you are using heater tubing, cut a piece to fit with 2 extra inches on each end. Slip the clamps onto the tubing and the overlapping ends onto the pipe. Tighten the clamps.

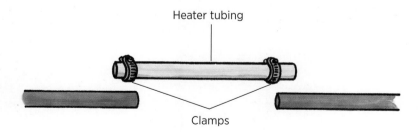

Heater tubing

Clamps

[Adapted from *The Woman's Hands-On Home Repair Guide* by Lyn Herrick]

A bountiful, healthy vegetable garden needs compost. Compost is both partially decomposed organic matter — mostly plants and the manures of plant-eating animals — and the soil-dwelling microbes that do the decomposing. When you make compost, you're doing what nature does all the time, only a little faster. Composting is nature's method of recycling. The instructions below are for a hot compost pile.

MAKE COMPOST
IN FOUR EASY STEPS

1. Begin making your compost pile by adding successive layers of straw, green material (grass clippings, kitchen scraps, and nonpoisonous weeds that haven't gone to seed), and soil, lasagna-fashion, until the pile is about 4 feet high. As you spread on the layers, fluff them to allow spaces for air to circulate through the pile.

2. Compost needs moisture just as it needs air. Your goal should be to get a mixture that feels something like a squeezed-out sponge — damp to the touch, but definitely not soggy. Add water to the brown layer (the straw), which is the driest, as you build the pile.

3. When you've finished making the pile, cover it. This reduces evaporation from the top of the pile and also prevents accidental overwatering from rain. You can cover it with a nylon-reinforced tarp or with black plastic, which absorbs sunlight and adds warmth to the pile. Don't use white plastic; it reflects sunlight and can keep the compost pile too cool.

4. You'll get better results with a hot compost pile if you check it and tend it regularly. Using a compost thermometer, preferably one with a long probe, take the temperature of the pile daily. If everything is going as it should, the pile should reach 140°F to 160°F/60°C to 71°C within a few days. Whenever the temperature starts a steady drop, turn the pile. With each turning, moisten the pile if necessary, fluff it for aeration, and move the material from the outside into the center. Your compost is ready when it looks like dirt and you can no longer identify what it was made of.

What Can You Compost?

Just about anything organic can be made into compost, but some things are better for composting than others. You'll end up with more balanced compost, and have it sooner, if you're a little choosy about what goes into it. If you're really particular, you may want to be sure that your compost ingredients are organically grown. Chop up any large pieces.

The following materials make great compost:

* Bean shells and stalks
* Broccoli stalks (but not the roots)
* Cabbage stalks and leaves (but not the roots)
* Citrus rinds
* Clover
* Coffee grounds
* Corncobs (chopped)
* Cucumber vines
* Eggshells (crushed)
* Farm animal manures
* Flowers
* Fruit peels
* Grass clippings (in thin layers)
* Hay
* Hedge clippings
* Leaf mold and leaves
* Lettuce and other greens
* Melon vines, leaves, and rinds
* Potato skins and vines (unless diseased)
* Rhubarb leaves
* Shells (clam, crab, lobster, mussel, or oyster, ground up and well buried in the pile)
* Tea leaves
* Vegetable peels, stalks, and foliage
* Weeds

[Adapted from *The Vegetable Gardener's Bible* by Edward C. Smith]

BUILD A
MOVABLE
COMPOST BIN

This type of compost bin has been a popular choice for many years. It is easy to assemble and use — particularly when the compost is ready to turn. You simply take the sides apart, reassemble them beside the compost pile, and fork the pile back into the bin.

MATERIALS

- Two dozen 36"-long 2×2 cedar balusters
- Four pieces of 36" × 38½" hardware cloth (with ½" squares)
- Sixty 2½" pan-head exterior screws
- Two pounds ¾" galvanized poultry staples
- Eight 2½"-long hook-and-eye latches

TOOLS

- Carpenter's square
- Combination square
- Hand saw
- Power drill
- ⁵⁄₃₂" and ⅛" twist drill bits
- Driver bit to match the screws
- Staple gun
- Pliers
- Awl
- Hammer
- Two clamps and wood blocks
- Tin snips

1. Cut eight of the balusters into corner braces (C) with 45-degree angled ends; you will have sixteen braces measuring 18 inches from tip to tip.

2. Assemble each of the four panels, as shown in figure 1, first attaching the upright balusters (B) to the ends of the top and bottom balusters (A). It's easier if you predrill the screw holes. Then fasten the four corner braces (C) in place. Working on a flat surface, attach a piece of hardware cloth to each panel, stapling every 3½ inches or so along the perimeter and the braces. Use pliers to pull the cloth taut as you work.

FIGURE 1

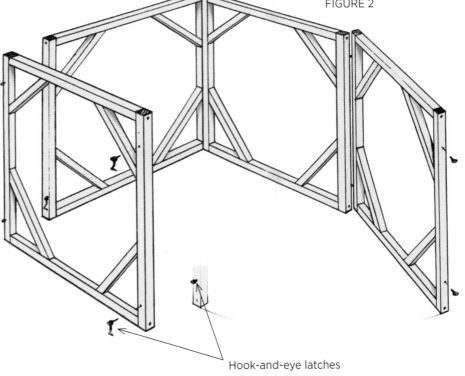

FIGURE 2

Hook-and-eye latches

[Adapted from *The Vegetable Gardener's Book of Building Projects* by the Editors of Storey Publishing]

3. Attach the panels to one another with hook-and-eye latches positioned 6 inches from the tops and the bottoms, as shown in figure 2. You can make a handy template for predrilling holes for the latches by marking spots 2¼ inches apart on the back of a business card and then holding the card against the wood and using an awl to poke through the card into the wood. Drill the holes with a ⅛-inch bit, angling them slightly toward the center of the wood (see figure 3).

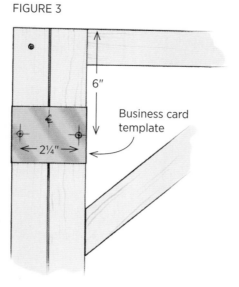

FIGURE 3

6"

2¼"

Business card template

MAKE COMPOST WITH WORMS

Earthworms' natural home is the great outdoors, but they can easily be raised in bins that are kept indoors — and that's a great way to continue composting through the winter in ruggedly cold climates. Any place where the temperatures range between 55°F and 75°F/13°C and 24°C is a good place for an indoor worm bin. When bins receive proper care, they are not smelly or messy, and the worms inside multiply like mad. You can easily harvest 5 gallons of excellent vermicompost from a 15-gallon plastic storage bin every 4 to 5 months.

MATERIALS AND SUPPLIES

- 1 (12-gallon or larger) plastic storage bin with lid
- Drill and ¼" bit, or hammer and sharp nail
- Dry newspapers, including color inserts (enough to make a stack 6" high)
- Bucket or sink filled with water
- 4 cups peat moss or weed-free compost
- 2 cups gritty garden soil
- 2 cups plain cornmeal
- Rubber gloves
- Spray bottle filled with water
- Earthworms (at least 200; 500 is even better)
- 2 cups chopped vegetable and/or fruit scraps
- Long spoon, for stirring the worm bin mixture (optional)

1. Remove any labels from the plastic bin, and decorate the top with acrylic paint if you like.

2. Use the drill, or a hammer and a sharp nail, to make numerous holes through all sides of the bin. In the lower half of the bin, make the holes about 6 inches apart. Reduce the spacing between holes to 4 inches apart in the top half of the bin.

3. Working with a few sheets at a time, dunk the newspapers in a bucket or sink of water and then tear the damp paper into pieces no larger than 3 inches long and wide. Some pieces can be in thin strips, while others are ragged patches. Add the torn-up newspaper bits to the bin until it is about half full of lightly moistened pieces.

4. Move the bin to its permanent location and then add the peat moss or compost, soil, and cornmeal to the damp newspaper bits. Put on rubber gloves and toss everything together thoroughly with your hands. Spritz on additional water until the entire mixture is lightly moist.

5. Place the earthworms in the prepared bin. Divide the vegetable and/or fruit scraps into four portions. Spread one portion on top of the soil and cover with 1 inch of bedding. Repeat layers. Put the top on the bin.

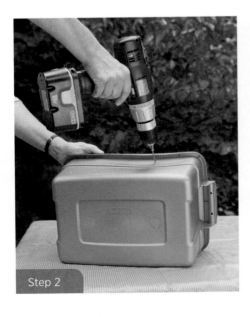

Step 2

Step 3

Step 4

[Adapted from *The Complete Compost Gardening Guide* by Barbara Pleasant and Deborah L. Martin]

Step 5

6. After a few days, stir through the bin with a long spoon or a gloved hand, and spritz water on any parts of the newspaper mixture that seem dry. You can now start feeding your worms kitchen waste, buried in the mixture, up to three times a week.

7. When it's time to harvest, place your vermicompost in a bucket or large bowl and place in good light. The worms will move to the bottom, allowing you to gather the vermicompost from the top of the container after an hour or two. Then return the worms to the bin, or release them outdoors if conditions in the bin seem quite crowded.

Food for Worms

DO INCLUDE:
* ✳ Coffee grounds and tea, including filters
* ✳ Most fruit pulp and peelings
* ✳ Most seed-free vegetable trimmings
* ✳ Eggshells (well rinsed)
* ✳ Bread, pasta, rice, or cereals that are not heavily sweetened
* ✳ Any cooked vegetable (without excessive salt or fat)

DON'T INCLUDE:
* ✳ Seeds from vegetables and fruits
* ✳ Trimmings from cabbage-family crops
* ✳ Garlic, onion, or hot pepper trimmings
* ✳ Citrus rinds
* ✳ Salty foods

IDENTIFY ANIMAL TRACKS

Each critter leaves its own calling card. Whether you're having trouble with a predator in the chicken coop or you just want to learn more about what animals live in your neighborhood, a first step is to look for tracks. If tracks prove hard to find, spread sand on the ground where the animal will likely step, smooth out the sand, and come back later.

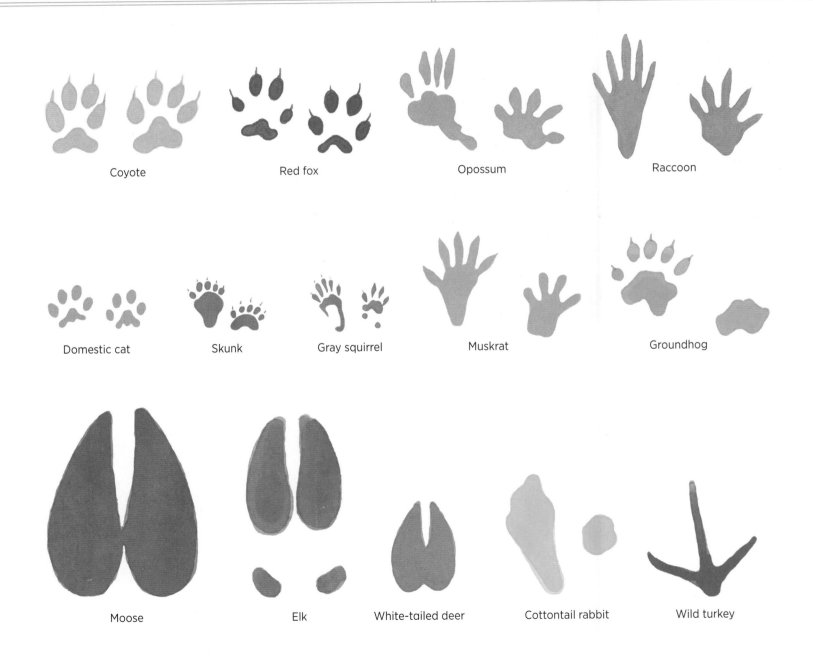

Coyote

Red fox

Opossum

Raccoon

Domestic cat

Skunk

Gray squirrel

Muskrat

Groundhog

Moose

Elk

White-tailed deer

Cottontail rabbit

Wild turkey

[Adapted from *100 Skills You'll Need for the End of the World (as We Know It)* by Ana Maria Spagna]

Signs of wildlife may be easier to spot than the wildlife that made them. Woodpecker holes in stumps and snags, a pile of pinecone scales left by a red squirrel, small circular holes in the dirt where a skunk dug for grubs, deer scat — signs such as these indicate a healthy diversity of wildlife.

SPOT
COMMON SIGNS
OF WILDLIFE

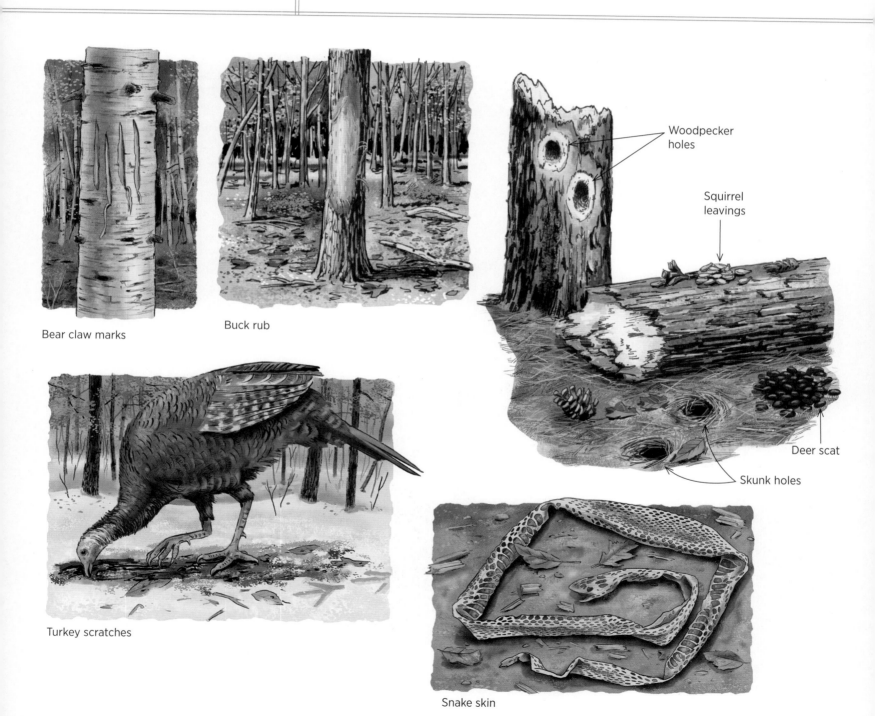

Bear claw marks

Buck rub

Woodpecker holes

Squirrel leavings

Deer scat

Skunk holes

Turkey scratches

Snake skin

[Adapted from *A Landowner's Guide to Managing Your Woods* by Anne Larkin Hansen, Mike Severson, and Dennis L. Waterman]

SPEAK CHICKEN

Chickens use their language to communicate about food, to warn of predators or other threats, and to converse among themselves about what's going on. This "grown-up" language, used by all chickens, starts at about 14 weeks of age.

GREETING

Buh-dup

The *buh-dup* greeting sound is heard among members of the flock as they come and go during the day. They also say it to humans.

WARNING

SCREE-oop-oop-oop

When feeling threatened on her nest, a broody hen makes a sort of a yell that trails into a grumble. It sounds like a tiny dinosaur roaring.

CROWING

Ur, ur, ur, UR-URRR

It is a fallacy that a rooster crows only in the morning. He will crow 24/7 to announce his presence and warn of perceived threats.

ALERT

Grrrrrr, buk, buk, buk, buk, buk, buk, BUKGAW

Chickens make an alert call to signal that danger is near. It starts out as a low, rolling growl and progresses in volume and intensity into a full-out yell. There are two alert calls. The low-pitched alert for a ground predator is accompanied by the chickens running for cover. The higher-pitched alert for a threat from the sky causes the chickens to pause, crouch, and look upward.

DISPUTE

(General squawking and squabbling)

A burst of noisy carrying-on usually means a disagreement is occurring. The flock is not getting along. Typical squabbles may involve a tasty morsel of food, a favorite roosting place, or sorting out a perceived spot in the pecking order.

Buh-dup

[Adapted from *How to Speak Chicken* by Melissa Caughey]

EGG ON THE WAY

Bwah, bwah, bwah, bwah

This call sounds a bit frantic and slightly impatient. It is usually made by a hen while she is pacing outside her favorite nesting box when it is occupied by another hen. Once inside the coveted nesting box, she quiets down and will not "speak" until she lays her egg.

EGG SONG

Buh-gaw-gawk, buh-gaw-gawk, buh-gaw-gawk

The distinctive egg song announces that a hen has laid her egg for the day. It's the only time a hen will be really loud, even louder than the alert call. She starts the call as she leaves the nesting box and continues to celebrate her accomplishment as she returns to the flock. It's not uncommon for other hens to join in. They seem to enjoy celebrating one another's successes.

GOOD NIGHT

Doh-doh-doh

The soft, airy-sounding good-night murmur is like an evening roll call that means "Yes, I'm here and I am okay."

Buh-gaw-gawk, buh-gaw-gawk, buh-gaw-gawk

CATCH A CHICKEN

Chickens need to be caught so that they can undergo routine procedures, including being examined and treated for parasites, being moved for show, and being groomed. Catching one is as simple as bending down and picking it up. If the chickens aren't tame, one of these methods will work.

NIGHT TACTIC

The easiest way to catch a chicken that isn't tame is to pick it off its perch at night. If you have to catch a wily chicken during the day, you'll need to use one of the other approaches.

HELPING HAND

With a helper, slowly herd the bird into the corner of a mesh fence or, better yet, inside a building with the entries closed so the chicken can't get out. Move deliberately, taking great care not to panic the bird. When you and your helper get close enough, clamp down quickly on the bird's two wings or reach beneath it and grasp both legs.

CATCHING CRATE

A catching crate is nothing more than a lightweight but strong wooden or wire box with an opening at one end. Use a pair of panels to guide the chicken into the catching crate's open end.

CATCHING HOOK

To catch a chicken with a hook, slip the hook around one leg and pull toward you. Using a catching hook requires quick thinking and physical agility.

CATCHING NET

When you get close enough to the chicken, toss the net over the bird, then quickly retrieve the bird from inside the net. A really wild chicken might slip out of the net, so clamp the hoop against the ground and hold it tight until you are in a position to get the chicken out.

[Adapted from *Storey's Guide to Raising Chickens* by Gail Damerow]

Certain members of a flock may have a difficult time keeping their fluffy bottoms clean despite their daily dust baths. Soiled bottoms can result from an infection or just loose stools from something in the diet. Most chickens can benefit from a bath once in a while, but chickens who attend poultry shows are always bathed before the show. An egg-bound hen can also benefit from a soak in warm water and Epsom salts.

BATHE A CHICKEN

Setup

Before collecting your chicken, prepare your bathing area:

✳ Find two containers or bins large enough to hold your chicken, along with a small plastic cup for pouring water over the chicken.

✳ Spread out a couple of towels for the containers.

✳ Fill both containers halfway with warm water. Add a few drops of gentle dish detergent to one of them and mix the soap into the water to create some bubbles.

✳ Make a drying station on a table away from the water. Lay out a towel on the table, and plug in a hair dryer where you can reach the table with it.

1. If you think that a chicken will be nervous during her bath, you can cover her entire head with a small towel to help keep her calm. Place the chicken in the bin with the soapy water. Use the cup and your hands to wet the soiled area. Once the feathers are wet, gently rub the dirty feathers with your fingers. Make sure any hardened-on poop is soft before you try to pick it off. Do not be afraid to clean right around the vent.

Step 2

Step 3

Step 4

2. When the chicken is clean, transfer her to the second basin. Use the cup and your hands to rinse the soap off completely.

3. Slide your hands down her body to remove the excess water, then wrap her in a towel to absorb more water. She'll probably be happy to have her head uncovered by now!

4. With the dryer set on warm (not hot) and low, dry the wet feathers. You may need to keep her wings wrapped in a towel to keep her from flapping. Keep the dryer moving continuously until the chicken is completely dry, which should take about 5 minutes.

When you're done, you'll be amazed at how fluffy a clean chicken can be!

Clean chicken!

[Adapted from *A Kid's Guide to Keeping Chickens* by Melissa Caughey]

MAKE BODY BUTTER

This herbal butter made from chamomile and olive oil deeply feeds your skin from the outside and especially benefits inflamed, irritated skin. It also makes a fabulous cleansing cream and facial moisturizer for all skin types. Plus, it's easy to make! Gently heat up some fats and base oils, just like you might melt butter, pour them into a blender, and let cool for a few minutes. Then just drizzle in a mix of water-based ingredients and blend to form an emulsion. The process is similar to making mayonnaise or aioli — and the results are just as rich!

INGREDIENTS

- ¾ cup extra-virgin olive oil or chamomile-infused olive oil
- ¼ cup unrefined coconut oil
- 2 tablespoons beeswax or vegetable emulsifying wax
- 1 tablespoon shea butter (refined or unrefined)
- 1 cup distilled or purified water or chamomile, lavandin, lavender, or rosemary hydrosol
- 1 teaspoon vegetable glycerin
- 10 (200 IU) capsules vitamin E oil
- 30 drops German chamomile essential oil
- 30 drops Roman chamomile essential oil

1. In a small saucepan over low heat or in a double boiler, warm the olive oil, coconut oil, beeswax, and shea butter until the solids are just melted.

2. In another small pan, warm the water or hydrosol and the vegetable glycerin, and stir a few times until the glycerin dissolves in the liquid.

3. Remove both pans from the heat. Pour the oils/wax/shea butter mixture into a blender and allow it to cool until it begins to turn slightly opaque, 5 to 10 minutes. The time will vary depending on the temperature of your kitchen. Do not allow it to cool too much and get too thick or it will not blend properly.

4. Place the lid on the blender and remove the lid's plastic piece. Turn the blender on at medium speed. Slowly drizzle the water and glycerin mixture through the center of the lid into the vortex of swirling fats below. Almost immediately the cream will turn off-white to very pale yellow and will begin to thicken.

5. Blend until all the watery mixture has been added, 10 to 15 seconds, then turn off the blender and check the consistency of the cream. It should have a smooth, glossy texture.

6. If the watery mixture is not properly combining with the fatty mixture, give the cream a few stirs with a spatula, being sure to scrape down any cream residue from the sides of the blender container. Then replace the lid and blend on medium speed for another 5 to 10 seconds. Repeat this process once or twice more, if necessary, until the cream is smooth.

7. Turn off the blender and add the contents of the vitamin E oil capsules by piercing the capsule skin and squeezing the contents into the cream. Add the essential oils. Put the lid back on and blend until the cream is smooth and thick, 5 seconds or so.

Note: If the temperature of your kitchen is above 76°F/24°C, the cream will maintain a softer consistency. (Coconut oil turns from solid to liquid at 76°F/24°C.) If your kitchen is below 76°F/24°C, the cream will be firmer.

8. Pour the finished cream into a storage container or containers. Lightly cover each container with a paper towel and allow the cream to cool for about 30 minutes before capping and labeling. Store in a dark, cool cabinet and use within 60 to 90 days. If your storage area is very warm, use within 4 weeks for maximum potency and freshness.

[Adapted from *Pure Skin Care* by Stephanie L. Tourles]

Step 1

Step 2

Step 3

Step 4

Step 5

Step 6

Step 7

Step 8

Applying Body Butter

Immediately following a bath or shower, slather this butter on your damp skin — really massage it in. Because it's very concentrated, begin with 1 teaspoon at a time. If your skin has an oily residue after 5 minutes, you've used too much. Simply wipe off the excess with a towel and use less the next time around. Use daily.

Use this all-purpose healing salve on scrapes, rashes, cracked skin, hemorrhoids, minor wounds — you name it! It's safe for kids and pets, too. You can either purchase the herbal oils or make your own (see page 138).

MAKE A SUPER
SKIN SALVE

Tip: Wrap the beeswax in a clean, sturdy cloth, then whack it with a hammer on a solid surface to break it into smaller pieces so it melts faster. If you don't have a double boiler, simply use a metal mixing bowl over a pot of boiling water.

INGREDIENTS
- 1 ounce beeswax
- 1 ounce calendula oil
- 1 ounce gotu kola oil
- 1 ounce plantain oil
- 1 ounce St. John's wort oil
- 20 drops lavender essential oil (optional)

1. Melt the beeswax in a double boiler.

2. Add the calendula, gotu kola, plantain, and St. John's wort oils. Stir until the mixture is all liquid and combined. Remove from the heat and stir in the lavender essential oil, if using.

3. Pour the mixture into heatproof jars or tubes. The salve settles and shrinks a bit as it cools. Store in a cool, dark spot, where the salve will keep for approximately a year.

Step 1

Step 3

Step 2

Variations

LIP BALM: The only difference between a lip balm and a salve is your intention. Use the same 1:4 beeswax: oil ratio, using plain or herb-infused oils. My favorite is 1½ ounces coconut oil, 1½ ounces grapeseed oil, and 1 ounce olive oil. Add 2 or 3 drops essential oil per empty lip balm tube for flavor before pouring in the base.

OINTMENT: For a softer consistence than a salve, use approximately ½ ounce beeswax to 4 ounces oil, or to your preference.

[Adapted from *Grow Your Own Herbal Remedies* by Maria Noël Groves]

MAKE HERB-INFUSED OIL

Herbalists often extract herbs in oil to use topically. Rub the infused oil into the skin or use it to make a salve, ointment, cream, or oil-liniment rub. Oil is not a great solvent or preservative. It's apt to go bad easily, especially if you use fresh plant material. But it glides easily over the skin, soothing and moisturizing as it slowly penetrates.

INGREDIENTS

- 7 ounces dried herb
- ½ ounce alcohol (190- to 100-proof)
- 8 ounces olive or other oil

1. Coarsely grind your herb in a blender.

2. Add the alcohol. Stir, blend, or shake to mix thoroughly. The consistency should resemble that of damp potting soil. Cover tightly in the blender or a jar. Let sit for about a day.

3. In the blender, combine the prepared herb with the oil. Cover and blend until the blender gets warm, about 5 minutes.

4. Strain through cheesecloth or muslin, squeezing out as much oil as you can.

5. If the strained oil contains a lot of herb dust, run it through a coffee filter. This slow process may take a few hours and require several filter changes.

6. Store the finished oil in a tight-lidded glass bottle in a cool, dark, dry spot. It should keep for about a year, and possibly longer. Avoid rubber droppers except for short-term use — oil will eventually eat through the rubber.

Step 1

Step 2

Step 3

Step 4

Step 5

Step 6

[Adapted from *Grow Your Own Herbal Remedies* by Maria Noël Groves]

Timber framing is a traditional building system that uses a skeletal framework of both large and small wooden members fastened together with wooden joinery, primarily mortise-and-tenon connections secured with wooden pins. While some connections — especially smaller, nonstructural ones — may be secured with nails, bolts, or other hardware, the majority of connections rely upon wooden joinery.

UNDERSTAND THE ANATOMY OF A TIMBER FRAME

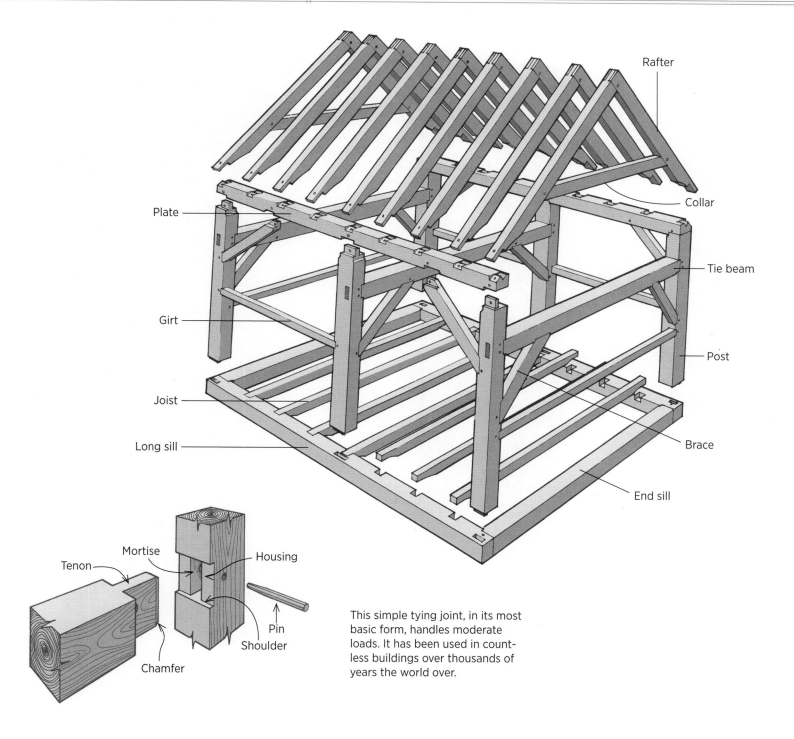

Rafter

Collar

Plate

Tie beam

Girt

Post

Joist

Long sill

Brace

End sill

Tenon

Mortise

Housing

Pin

Shoulder

Chamfer

This simple tying joint, in its most basic form, handles moderate loads. It has been used in countless buildings over thousands of years the world over.

[Adapted from *Hand Hewn* by Jack A. Sobon]

BUILD A HOMESTEAD IN (AND FROM) THE WOODS

Many homesteaders devote themselves to carefully making plans for their garden, hoop house, or chicken coop, but they overlook the homestead woodlot. Just beyond the edge of your lawn is a hidden gem, disguised as thick brambles and gnarled trees. If properly managed, these patches of woodland — whether a quarter acre or a hundred acres — offer you the opportunity to cultivate both additional ground and a more sustainable, self-reliant homestead.

A. Using three-sided logs with lag screws is a fast and economical way to build a log cabin. Insert rubber weather stripping between each course of logs to seal air gaps.

B. When clearing your cabin site, consider leaving several strategically placed tall stumps that can be carved into camp chairs.

C. Slab wood and log-end trimmings make for a functional and attractive bench.

D. Untrimmed boards with a "live edge" make for rustic coffee tables.

E. Cedar shakes for the roof were split with a froe.

F. This woodshed was built using "brainstorm" siding. It adds a rustic appearance and also saves on labor, since only one edge is trimmed.

G. When you're building your woodland homestead, be on the lookout for good stones. Make piles for different types (flat, round, and so on), which can be used for a variety of projects, including a practical stone patio that keeps your feet out of the mud.

[Adapted from *The Woodland Homestead* by Brett McLeod]

This approach is for people who are intent on getting as much food as possible out of their gardens, no matter the size of their plot. There are many reasons why a gardener might do this. It may be that you simply want to feed your household from the garden year-round. Perhaps you'd like to set up a farm stand by the mailbox for supplemental income, or sell a few vegetables at your local farmers' market, or coordinate a community garden. Whatever your reason, this approach will dramatically increase yield while maintaining soil fertility and your sanity.

GROW THE MOST VEGETABLES POSSIBLE

A. Fruit trees (which types and what size — dwarf, semi-dwarf, or full size?)

B. Annual vegetable/herb/flower beds

C. Beehives and mason bee boxes

D. Cistern/water catchment

E. Compost system

F. Fish tank or pond for fish production

G. Greenhouse

H. Habitat plantings, especially for pollinators and other beneficial insects

I. Livestock pens: chickens, ducks, goats, and rabbits

J. Mushroom production area

K. Outdoor dining area with firepit

L. Outdoor wash/pack station

M. Perennial herb beds

N. Pest exclusion fences: deer fence, rabbit fences, and dog fences

O. Produce stand

P. Propagation area

Q. Shrubs: berries

R. Tool and equipment storage

S. Water feature for ducks, frogs, and wild birds

Indoor production area for microgreens and sprouts, kitchen space adequate for food processing, pantry storage, refrigeration/freezing storage, root cellar, and seed storage (freezer, fridge, dresser, cabinet, plastic tubs)

[Adapted from *High-Yield Vegetable Gardening* by Colin McCrate and Brad Halm]   **143**

CAN YOUR BOUNTIFUL HARVEST

If you can boil water, you are capable of canning your own food. The most popular method of canning, known as the boiling-water method, requires very little specialized equipment and can be done in as little as 10 minutes. You will need thick glass canning jars with two-piece lids (like Ball and Kerr jars) and a set of canning tongs (you cannot substitute regular tongs). You can get these things at your local mom-and-pop hardware store, or you can order them online. The canning jars are important — the extrathick glass keeps them from breaking during processing, and the two-piece lid helps form a vacuum seal that keeps your food safe on the shelf.

1. **WASH.** Wash everything with hot, soapy water and arrange it on a clean towel near the stove top, if possible. Separate your lids from your jars, washing them as well, and put the lids in a small heatproof bowl.

2. **LOAD THE CANNER.** Put the rack in the pot, add the glass jars, and fill with enough cold water to cover the jars. Set the loaded canner on your burner, cover it, and bring the water to a boil. You never want to have to wait for your canner to heat up — always have it ready and waiting.

3. **PREPARE YOUR RECIPE.** Now is the time to cook the recipe you will use to pack your jars.

4. **REMOVE THE JARS.** Using canning tongs, remove the jars from the boiling water. Add the boiling water in the first jar to the bowl full of lids to soften their rubber gaskets. Empty the water from the rest of the jars back into the canner and set the jars, right side up, on your work surface for filling.

5. **LADLE THE HOT FOOD INTO THE JARS.** Use a canning funnel or small ladle to keep things neat. Fill the jars as indicated in your recipe, allowing the proper headspace.

Step 2

Step 3

Step 4

Step 5

[Adapted from *Put 'em Up! Fruit* by Sherri Brooks Vinton]

6. **RELEASE TRAPPED AIR.** Swipe your bubble tool (or a chopstick) around the inside of each jar to release any trapped air. Top up, as necessary, to maintain the correct headspace.

7. **CLEAN THE JARS.** Use a dampened paper towel to wipe the rims of the jars. A clean rim will give your lid a better chance of sealing properly.

8. **LID THE JARS.** Lift the lids from the hot water, one at a time, and center them on the jars.

9. **APPLY THE RINGS.** Screw the rings onto the jars until just fingertip-tight, meaning that you use just your fingertips to twist on the rings.

10. **PROCESS THE FILLED JARS.** Submerge the filled jars in the boiling water; they should be covered by at least 2 inches. Put the cover on the pot and process for the time specified in your recipe.

11. **REST THE JARS.** When the processing time is over, turn off the heat, remove the lid of the pot, and let the jars sit in the hot water for 5 minutes.

12. **REMOVE THE JARS.** Using canning tongs, remove the jars from the hot water to a towel-covered surface. Allow the jars to cool for 24 hours.

13. **CHECK THE SEALS.** Check the seals on the jars by removing the rings and gently pushing up on the edge of the lids.

14. **STORE.** Wipe the jars and store, without rings (which can trap moisture), in a cool, dark place.

Step 6

Step 7

Step 8

Step 9

Step 10

Step 13

BLANCH AND FREEZE VEGETABLES

Many kitchen vegetables from asparagus to zucchini can be frozen. Part of the beauty of freezing vegetables is that you can do it in small batches, to use odds and ends from your garden, or in big batches when you are buried in green beans. Use only veggies in excellent condition that have been thoroughly cleaned. Except for peppers, tomatoes, and a few other food crops, veggies should be cooked before they are frozen. Blanching stops enzyme activity that causes vegetables to lose texture and nutrients.

1. Set up a two-piece steamer or pot of water for blanching on the stove. Also set out a large baking dish to use for cooling the blanched vegetables. Bring the water to a slow boil.

2. Thoroughly clean and pare the vegetables into pieces of uniform size.

3. Place about 3 cups of the prepared veggies in the steamer basket or boiling water, put on the lid, and set your timer for a minimum of 3 minutes. Check for a color change,

which indicates that the pieces are almost cooked through. Err on the side of doneness. It is better to go 1 minute too long than to under-blanch the vegetables.

4. Put enough ice cubes in the baking dish to cover the bottom, and transfer the hot, blanched vegetables to the ice bath as soon as you remove them from the steamer or pot. Blanched veggies keep their color best if they are immediately cooled in ice.

5. When the vegetables are cool enough to handle, pack them into freezer-safe containers and freeze immediately. Or arrange the pieces on cookie sheets in the freezer, and place them in freezer-safe containers after they freeze hard.

Veggie Freezing Tips

* When freezing green beans, include a few pods of a purple-podded variety, and use them as blanching indicators. The purple color will change to green when the beans are perfectly blanched.
* Use a silicone muffin pan for freezing pestos or other vegetable or herb purées, or any veggies you often use in small amounts. After the food is frozen hard, transfer to freezer-safe containers.
* Blanch perfect leaves from cabbage or collards and freeze them flat for later use as stuffed cabbage leaves. Blanch and freeze hollowed-out summer squash or sweet peppers for stuffing, too.
* Freeze vegetables and companion herbs together — for example, snap beans with basil or creamed sweet corn with parsley or cilantro. Add the herbs during the last minute of steam blanching, so they barely wilt.
* Add color to your frozen vegetables by including carrots, golden beets, radicchio, or other colorful edibles.

[Adapted from *Homegrown Pantry* by Barbara Pleasant]

Step 1

Step 2

Not cooked

Cooked

Step 3

Step 4

Step 5

DRY HERBS

Drying is an easy way to preserve your fresh herbs. When you are ready to harvest your herbs, choose a dry day and pick after the dew has evaporated. Plants' essential oil content is said to be highest in the morning. Remember, essential oils give a plant its fragrance, flavor, and any health benefits attributed to it.

1. Pat the herbs dry, if necessary, and spread them in a thin layer over drying trays. Dry them in a shady area or in a dehydrator set to 95°F/35°C or lower until the leaves are crisp enough to crumb in your hands. You can also dry them by tying stalks together with a string and hanging them upside down in a shady, well-ventilated area.

2. Remove the dried leaves from their stalks, if necessary, and store in small, tightly sealed containers in a cool, dark place. Dried herbs will keep their flavor for several months but should be discarded after a year.

A GUIDE TO COMMON DRIED HERBS

HERB	PART DRIED	USE
Basil	Leaves	Tomato dishes, soups, stews, meat pies
Bay	Leaves	Soups, stews, spaghetti sauce
Chives	Leaves	Omelets, salads, casseroles
Dill	Flowers, seeds	Stews, cabbage, pickles
Fennel	Leaves, seeds	Soups, casseroles, candies, rolls, cookies
Garlic	Bulb	Italian foods, omelets, chili
Mint	Leaves	Mint jelly, lemonade, roast lamb
Oregano	Flowers	Tomato dishes, spaghetti sauce, pork, wild game
Parsley	Leaves	Soups, sauces, vegetables
Rosemary	Leaves	Salads, lamb dishes, vegetables
Thyme	Leaves	Meat loaf, lamb dishes, onion soup

[Adapted from *The Backyard Homestead* edited by Carleen Madigan]

Vinegar is relatively shelf stable and extracts a decent amount of the healthful constituents of herbs. And vinegar lends its own healing properties, as it is antiseptic, digestion enhancing, and hypoglycemic. In culinary recipes, a splash of vinegar brightens flavor and can be used in salad dressing and marinades. Use apple cider vinegar (preferably raw) for medicinal vinegars, distilled white or apple cider for topical uses, and high-quality clear vinegar (white wine, rice, champagne, organic distilled white) for colorful culinary recipes. Vinegars typically keep for at least a year. Infused vinegars made with fresh herbs may not last as long as those made with dried herbs.

MAKE HERBAL VINEGAR

INGREDIENTS

Fresh or dried plant material

Vinegar of choice

1. If you're using fresh plant material, coarsely chop it. Fill a jar loosely to the top with fresh plant material or approximately halfway with dried plant material.

2. Fill the jar to the top with vinegar. Cover with a plastic lid (vinegar eats through metal, including mason jar lids, though completely lined lids might hold).

3. Shake regularly. Strain when the liquid tastes good, typically after 2 to 4 weeks.

Variation: Oxymel

Oxymels are infused vinegars sweetened and smoothed out with honey. Follow the instructions above using up to 50 percent honey (or to taste). The shelf life varies wildly. Fresh plant oxymels may keep only for 3 to 6 months on the shelf; dried plant oxymels last longer. Store in the fridge or freezer to prolong the shelf life.

Step 1

Step 2

Step 3

[Adapted from *Grow Your Own Herbal Remedies* by Maria Noël Groves]

YOKE AND HITCH

AN OX TEAM

Oxen are normally worked in teams of two, with pairs sometimes hitched together for additional power. Multiple pairs form teams used for logging, heavy transport, and plowing dense soils. Teams are hitched together in tandem, one pair after the other. Before yoking an ox for the first time, be sure the animal is securely tied. When you're ready to hitch, it's usually easiest to approach from the left.

1. Hold the bow in place on the neck of the steer farthest from you (the off steer).

2. Place the bow through the holes in the yoke.

3. Add spacers to maintain the bow depth, and place the bow pin through the hole in the bow.

4. Bring the near (or nigh) steer up and hold the bow in place under his neck.

5. Raise the yoke with one hand while bringing the near steer under the yoke, then lower the yoke onto the near steer's neck.

6. Slide spacers onto the near steer's bow as necessary and fasten the pin. Only one pin per bow is needed.

7. Step the steer furthest from you over the pole, and then step the near steer in, toward the pole, so he is parallel to the pole and the other steer.

8. Push the pole or tongue on the wagon through the yoke ring and then hold it in place with a T-pin.

9. Hitch a chain to the yoke ring with a grab hook on the end of the chain. Then hitch the grab hook back onto the chain.

10. Make sure the chain is neither too long nor too short. Some teamsters will pull the chain back to the steers' flanks. This will provide adequate chain length for the steers' back feet to clear the sled or stoneboat.

What Is an Ox?

An ox is not a separate species or breed but simply a castrated bull used for work. The castration of a bull at an early age changes his growth pattern, so that he develops longer legs and a larger frame. Thus the ox grows taller and heavier than the bull of the same breed when he is castrated before he matures. The ox is also more placid and more easily controlled than the bull.

[Adapted from *Oxen* by Drew Conroy]

Step 1

Step 2

Step 3

Step 4

Step 5

Step 6

Step 7

Step 8

Step 9

Step 10

MOVE A PIG

The most difficult and time-consuming task on a great many farms with hogs is getting them from point A to point B while maintaining a modicum of dignity and your religion. The best way to keep a hog moving is to block the way behind it. As much as possible, allow the hog to move along at its own pace and in the company of other animals to help it remain confident and at ease. It is often far easier to drive two or three hogs back off a trailer than to drive just one hog onto it.

Tip: A plastic trash can on wheels can be used to move two or three shoats (young hogs) quite comfortably for a short distance.

▶ Hogs are wary of shifting light patterns and contrasts in flooring and other footing surfaces when being moved and may balk or turn back from them. Limit changes in light and flooring as best you can.

▲ A rigid board or panel is effective for moving pigs. Pigs respect a solid barrier, and a solid panel must be used to move mature boars.

▲ A "witch's cape" made of plasticized cloth cut to the width of the alley and attached to a stick across the top can be used to move sows and piglets out of a big pen or down a wide alley. In narrow alleys, use half a witch's cape.

▲ A large flag on a short stick works well for moving pigs. The flag is made from a lightweight plasticized cloth and can replace a rigid panel in many cases. Quietly move the flag behind the animals and don't wave vigorously.

152 [Adapted from *Storey's Guide to Raising Pigs* by Kelly Klober and *Temple Grandin's Guide to Working with Farm Animals* by Temple Grandin]

In most cases, it's easier to move a few tame cows or steers by walking ahead of them with a pail of goodies than it is to drive them, but it pays to know how to drive them if you want to. Cattle are easily driven because they have a flight zone. By positioning yourself at certain points in their flight zone, it's easy to direct their movement, be it your friendly dairy cows or a herd of half-wild heifers.

MOVE A COW

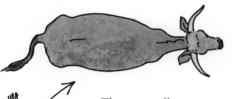

The cow will move forward when you approach her from the rear.

The cow will move back when you approach her from the front side.

The cow will stand still when you stand motionless directly in front of her or when you stand at her side.

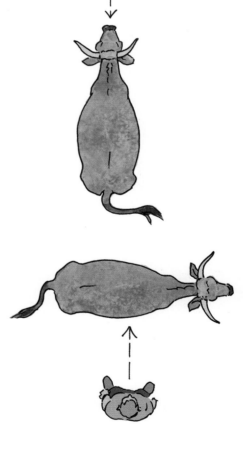

The cow will turn to the right when you enter the space on her left.

The cow will turn to the left when you enter the space on her right.

MAKE A T-SHIRT QUILT

Use old T-shirts to make a quilt of memories, or visit a thrift shop to find T-shirts with fun logos and designs. If you don't have nine T-shirts to cut up for this project, you can use the backs of the shirts, too, and get two squares from each shirt. This quilt is made up of three rows of three squares each to make a quilt about 33 inches square. To make a bed-size quilt, you'll need 36 blocks arranged in six rows of six.

MATERIALS

- 9 T-shirts
- Scissors
- Iron
- 3 yards fusible interfacing
- Chalk
- Clothespins
- Sewing machine and thread
- 1 yard backing fabric
- 1 yard batting
- Straight pins

MAKE THE T-SHIRT BLOCKS

1. Gather your T-shirts and cut off the neck and sleeves at the seams. Next, turn the T-shirt inside out and cut off the side seams so that the fronts and backs of each T-shirt are separated.

2. Iron a square of interfacing to the back of each of the T-shirt pieces you are using in the quilt. This will make the fabric easier to sew and help it keep its shape.

3. Cut out an 11-inch-square piece of cardboard or interfacing to use as a pattern. Flip one T-shirt over so that you can see the design you want on your quilt. Place the pattern piece on top of the image (you'll be able to see the image through the interfacing pattern), and trace around it with chalk.

4. Cut out the quilt block. The back of the block should be covered with the ironed-on interfacing. Repeat steps 3 and 4 for all the T-shirts or until you have nine blocks.

[Adapted from *Sewing School® Quilts* by Amie Petronis Plumley and Andria Lisle]

SEW THE QUILT TOP

1. Lay out the quilt blocks in three rows of three blocks.

2. Stack the rows of blocks and clip them together.

3. Using a zigzag stitch, sew the blocks in each row together. Make sure you do not turn any of the T-shirt blocks upside down.

4. Lay out the rows. Flip each row up one at a time to meet the previous one so that the good sides are facing. Pin the rows together at the block seams.

5. Using a zigzag stitch, stitch the rows together. Repeat until all the rows are sewn together.

6. Trim any extra seam allowance. Iron the seams to one side. The quilt top is ready.

Continued on next page

Step 1

Step 2

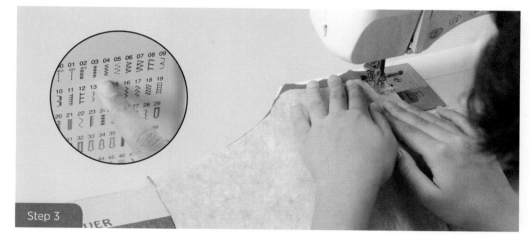

Step 3

Step 4

Step 5

Step 6

Step 1

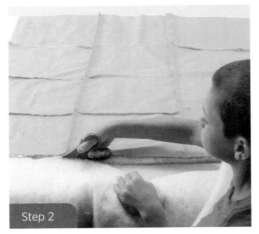
Step 2

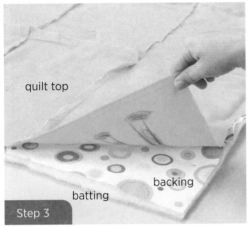
quilt top

backing

batting
Step 3

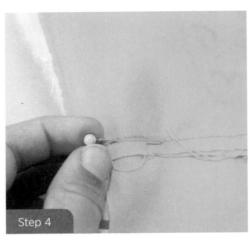
Step 4

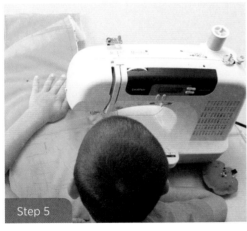
Step 5

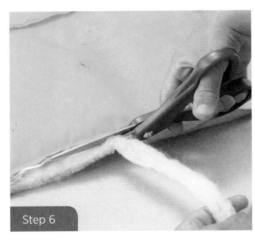
Step 6

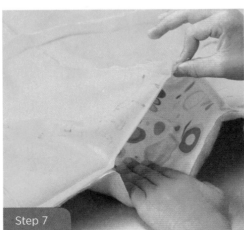
Step 7

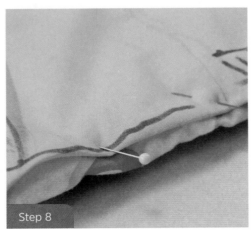
Step 8

BIND THE QUILT

1. Flip the quilt top onto the backing fabric so the good sides are together. Using the quilt top as a guide, carefully cut out the backing.

2. Position the backing fabric and top on the batting, and trim the batting.

3. Stack up the quilt layers in this order: batting on the bottom, then backing fabric, and finally the quilt top. The good sides of the backing fabric and quilt top are facing each other.

4. Pin your quilt together at all the block seams around the edge of the quilt. Add a few pins in the middle, too.

5. Stitch around all four sides of the quilt, leaving an opening about 12 inches long in one side. Take out the pins as you go.

6. Trim any extra batting or fabric that sticks out along the edges.

7. Reach into the opening you left along the edge, grab the opposite side of the quilt, and pull it out through the opening, turning the quilt right side out. Poke out the corners and smooth down the quilt.

8. Tuck in the edges of the opening and pin it together. Then use a sewing machine to edgestitch all the way around the quilt.

QUILT

1. Tie quilting is an easy way to hold together the three layers of your quilt. Thread a needle with craft thread but don't tie a knot in the end.

2. At the corners where the quilt blocks meet, poke your needle all the way down through the three layers of the quilt and then back up to the top.

3. Tie a knot. Cut the threads, leaving a small tie.

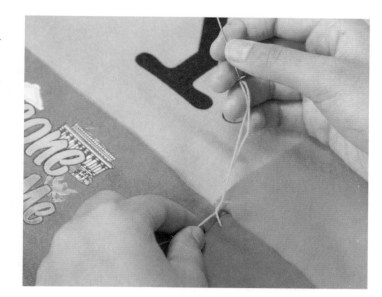

MAKE A CARDIGAN FROM A T-SHIRT

As a layer to toss on over a dress or T-shirt, this piece is as easy to wear as it is to make. Use a short- or long-sleeve tee that you've never really loved, or even one that has become a tiny bit too small. Either way, you'll find that it deserves renewed respect once it's dressed up with a sophisticated stitched edge.

MATERIALS

- Lightweight or regular-weight long-sleeve T-shirt
- 1 spool of contrasting thread
- 30" length of silky ribbon or tape (such as rayon seam tape)

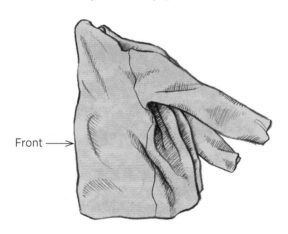

Front →

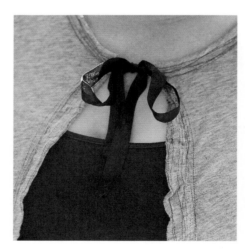

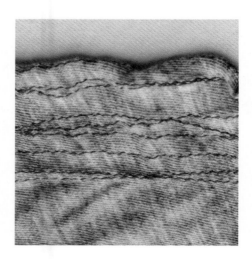

1. **CUT THE SHIRT.** Fold the T-shirt in half at the center of the front panel with the back panel pulled out of the way and the neck and side seams aligned, as shown. Use sharp scissors to cut along the fold, right through the center front.

2. **ATTACH THE RIBBON TIES.** Cut the ribbon into two 15-inch lengths. Knot one end of each piece of ribbon and fold the opposite ends ½ inch to the wrong side. Pin the folded ribbon ends to the T-shirt at the inside top corners of the opening so the ribbons extend toward each other. Trim any excess ribbon beneath the knots.

3. **STITCH THE LINES.** Using a straight stitch, topstitch a meandering line from a bottom corner of the front opening, up the front, over the ribbon's folded end, around the back neckline, over the second ribbon, and back down the opposite side to the bottom. Repeat, to sew five or six closely spaced lines.

[Adapted from *Improv Sewing* by Nicole Blum and Debra Immergut]

MAKE QUICK STRAWBERRY JAM

Home-preserved jam is much better than anything you could find on a store shelf anywhere, ever. This is a quick and easy way to keep strawberry jam on hand. Pomona's Universal Pectin gives the jam just enough gel. Be sure your strawberries look good, with no rot or mold — jam isn't the place to use seconds.

MAKES ABOUT 4 CUPS

INGREDIENTS

- 1 cup sugar
- 1 teaspoon Pomona's Universal Pectin
- 4 cups strawberries, hulled
- 1 teaspoon calcium water (included in the Pomona box)
- ¼ cup bottled lemon juice

1. Combine the sugar and pectin powder in a small bowl and set aside.

2. Place the strawberries in a medium saucepan and crush with a potato masher to release the juice and break up the fruit.

3. Slowly bring to a boil, stirring frequently to avoid scorching.

4. Stir in the calcium water and lemon juice.

5. Slowly pour in the sugar-pectin mixture and stir to dissolve.

6. Return to a boil, stirring to ensure that the mixture is heated thoroughly. Then remove from the heat and let rest for 5 minutes, stirring occasionally to release air bubbles from the jam.

[Adapted from *Put 'em Up!* by Sherri Brooks Vinton]

7. Skim off any foam.

8. If refrigerating, ladle into bowls or jars. Cool, cover, and refrigerate for up to 3 weeks. If canning, use the boiling-water method (page 144), leaving ¼ inch of headspace when you fill the jars and processing for 10 minutes, then remove the canner lid and let the jars rest in the water for 5 minutes.

9. Remove the jars and set aside for 24 hours. Check seals, then store in a cool, dark place for up to 1 year.

DRY FRUIT

The next best thing to having fresh fruit to eat is having dried fruit that you grew yourself. Apples, pears, plums, and other tree fruits are prime candidates for drying, and you can dry seedless grapes into raisins. When properly dried and stored, dried fruits can last for up to 2 years, which matches the bearing cycles of many backyard trees. You'll need a 1,500 mg tablet of vitamin C for this process.

1. Dissolve one 1,500 mg tablet of vitamin C in 1 quart of water. To prevent discoloration, dip all fruits in this acidic solution before they are arranged on trays.

2. Place the prepared pieces in the dehydrator and dry at 135°F/57°C for 3 to 12 hours, depending on the fruit, or until the fruit no longer feels wet to the touch. Allow to rest for a few hours to equalize moisture.

3. Finish drying until the pieces are leathery.

Step 1

Step 2

Step 3

Make Your Own Fruit Leather

Any type of concentrated fruit "butter," such as apple, plum (shown here), or even pumpkin butter, can be dried in sheets that can be rolled up like leather. Check the owner's manual of your dehydrator for directions on drying fruit leathers in your dehydrator, which usually involves spreading the fruit purée over non-sticky silicone sheets and drying it. You can also use small plates. If the leather sticks to the plate after it has dried, an hour in the freezer will make it pop free. Because fruit leathers retain some moisture, it is best to store them in the freezer.

[Adapted from *Homegrown Pantry* by Barbara Pleasant]

If you have chickens, you may occasionally find an egg and not know how long ago it was laid. There are two easy ways to determine its age: by holding a flashlight up to it (called "candling") or by placing it in water. Although a floating egg is quite old, it's not necessarily unsafe to eat. But if an egg has a mottled yolk or otherwise doesn't look right to you, or if it has an off-odor, discard it.

TEST THE
FRESHNESS
OF AN EGG

CANDLING. Using a small, bright flashlight, examine the interior of the egg. If the yolk looks vague and fuzzy, the thick white albumen surrounding it is holding it properly centered within the shell and the egg is fresh. As the egg ages and the white grows thinner, the yolk moves more freely. If you can clearly see the yolk, the albumen has thinned and the egg has aged.

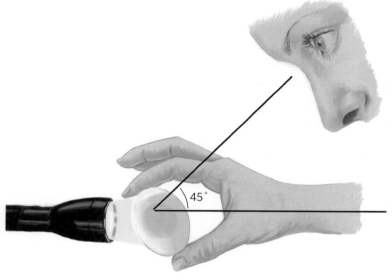

45°

FLOAT TEST. Place the egg in water. Older eggs develop pockets of air under the shell as the inner shell membrane pulls away from the outer shell membrane. If the egg floats, it's old.

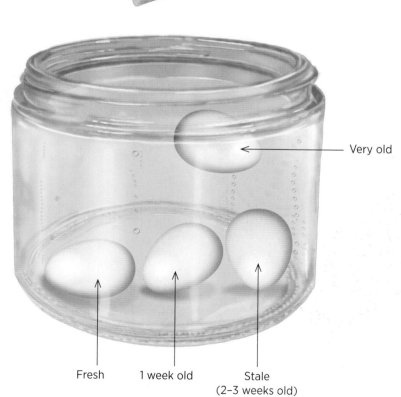

Very old

Fresh   1 week old   Stale
(2–3 weeks old)

[Adapted from *Storey's Guide to Raising Chickens* by Gail Damerow]

IDENTIFY
10 POPULAR
CHICKEN BREEDS

There are hundreds of breeds of chickens around the world, but these 10 breeds are popular in backyards across the United States. They are all good at laying eggs, and some make good meat birds, too.

AMERAUCANAS, known as "Easter Egg" chickens, produce blue eggs in various shades. Ameraucana hens will often lay nearly year-round without supplemental light. The birds are quite hardy, with active but friendly personalities.

ANCONAS are closely related to Leghorns. The birds have an active (some would say flighty, though easy to tame) disposition, and they are excellent foragers. Hens lay longer into the winter without supplemental light than most breeds. They lay white eggs.

BARNEVELDERS were developed in the Barneveld region of the Netherlands as birds that would lay well into the long, damp winter months of northern Europe. They are docile yet active. Hens lay eggs with a unique, dark coppery tinge.

HAMBURG chickens are stylish and graceful. They are small yet active, and they are particularly good fliers. Thanks to their excellent foraging ability, they do very well in backyard and barnyard settings. Hens mature early and are prolific layers of relatively small white eggs.

Feather Patterns

Over 30 genes affect the feather colors and patterns of chickens, yielding the amazing visual array fanciers have come to enjoy. Feather patterns include lacing, barring, penciling, spangling, stippling, and striping.

[Adapted from *Storey's Illustrated Guide to Poultry Breeds* by Carol Ekarius]

LEGHORNS are one of the most popular breeds in the world, thanks to the birds' exceptional laying ability, adaptability, and hardiness. Hens lay lots of large white eggs, with one of the best feed-to-egg conversion ratios of any pure breed.

MARAN chickens are well known for their large eggs, which are the darkest brown of any chicken egg, bordering on a dark chocolate to coppery color. The color results from a recessive gene, so if you cross a Maran with another breed, the dark eggs will become lighter.

ORPINGTONS produce a heavy carcass and plenty of brown eggs. They are quite docile and even somewhat affectionate toward handlers. They are very cold-hardy and mature quickly, and the hens are good brooders and mothers.

PLYMOUTH ROCKS are another dual-purpose breed. This was the most common bird in America at the end of the nineteenth and beginning of the twentieth centuries. It is cold-hardy, friendly, and adaptable to either confinement or free range. Hens lay brown eggs.

RHODE ISLAND REDS are one of the best dual-purpose chicken breeds (meaning they lay a lot of eggs but also have a meaty frame) and are hardy birds. Hens lay brown eggs.

SUSSEX chickens are graceful birds, with a long and broad back giving way to a tail that sits at a 45-degree angle from the body. They are adaptable, calm, and curious. Hens lay a fair number of medium-sized brown eggs.

FIELD DRESS
A DEER

If you are a hunter, field dressing a deer is an essential skill you need to know to preserve your meat for later use. The deer should be bled completely and its entrails removed, and it should be chilled immediately following the kill. Handle the deer with rubber gloves while field dressing to be certain that any bacteria are not transmitted to you. Carry some disinfectant to scrub your hands, if necessary. If there is any doubt whatsoever that your game is not healthy and sound, have it inspected by a veterinarian before it is eaten or processed.

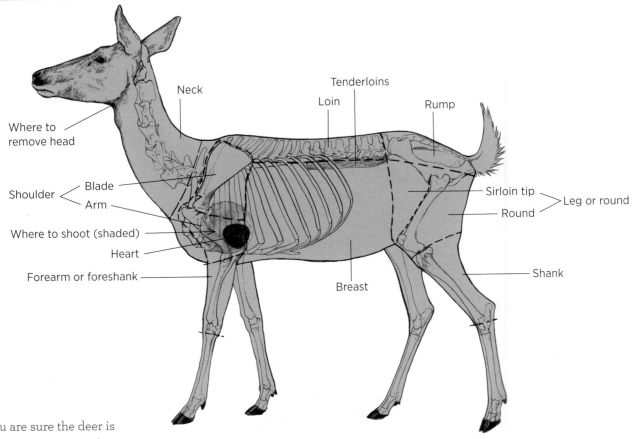

Neck
Tenderloins
Loin
Rump

Where to remove head

Shoulder
Blade
Arm
Sirloin tip
Leg or round
Round

Where to shoot (shaded)

Heart
Shank

Forearm or foreshank

Breast

1. As soon as you are sure the deer is dead, and with it lying on its side, cut deeply around the bung (the anus, or the anus and vulva in the doe) with your hunting knife. Pull it out and tie it off with a string.

2. Roll the deer onto its back, and make a small cut just behind the rear end of the breastbone. Insert the knife at a 45-degree angle with the blade facing up, and cut forward under the breastbone. Be careful not to puncture the stomach.

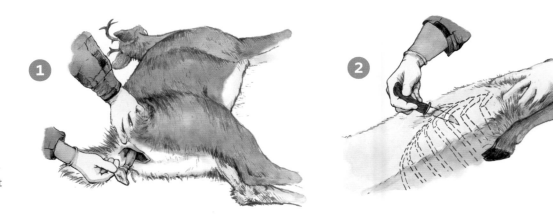

[Adapted from *Basic Butchering of Livestock & Game* by John J. Mettler Jr., DVM]

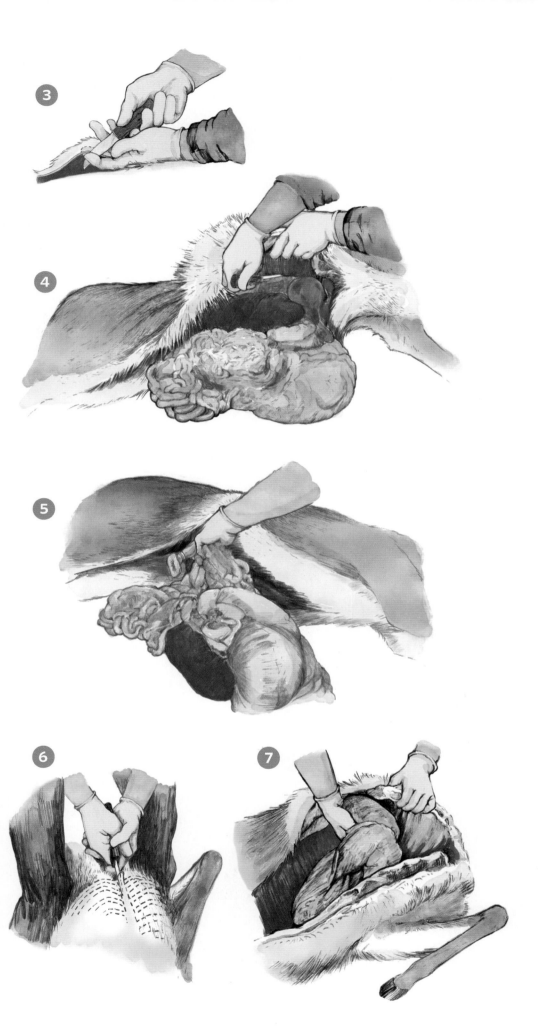

3. Withdraw the knife and insert two fingers into the cut. Using your fingers as a guide, cut the belly wall along the midline as far back as the pelvis.

4. Now lay the deer on its side with its belly facing downhill. Hold the belly wall open with one hand, and with the other hand or a knife break down the attachments of the insides under the back.

5. Reach up into the pelvis and pull out the bung and intestinal tract, including the bladder. Go back around the rear of the deer and, with your knife, ream the inside of the pelvis to remove all glandular tissue that failed to come out with the bung.

6. Split the breastbone from the rear to the front and from the inside out. Cut the trachea and esophagus across the lower neck and loosen them from the neck tissues.

7. Cut the skirt parallel to the belly wall and pull out the heart, lungs, and trachea. If your knife won't cut the breastbone, cut the skirt, and, reaching in with your knife, cut the lungs and heart loose.

8. Roll the deer onto its belly on a clean spot. If there are two of you, one should take the horns (or ears), the other the tail, and "stand him up and shake him" to get all the blood out of the body cavity. If you are alone, lift one end at a time, starting with the head. In warm weather, hang and skin the deer immediately and find a cooler in which to put the meat for 24 to 48 hours before you cut and freeze it.

SCOUT
FOR
DEER

The day that you hunt should not be the first time you visit the land you'll be hunting on. Satellite maps can help you size up an area before hunting, but they can't completely take the place of being out there on foot to see where the deer and their food sources are. Regular visits to your intended hunting ground will help you understand the area better. Scouting can be enjoyable and is comparable to the proverbial day at the park. Pack a picnic; bring a camera and binoculars. Once you have identified food sources and travel routes that the deer in the area are using, you can start looking for good sites where you can hide or set up a tree stand from which to ambush deer.

✳ As you walk around, look carefully for footprints and scat.

✳ You might be able to identify bedding areas, which will be oval-shaped depressions in tall grass or brush, with scat and cloven footprints nearby.

✳ Pay attention to what types of trees you see. Oak trees are going to drop acorns that are an important source of food for deer when hunting season starts.

✳ Any regularly mown grass or hayfield will also serve as a food source and gathering area in fall and winter. Try walking along the edges of any fields to look for deer trails where deer will be entering the area.

Look for Funnels

Natural and man-made features of the landscape can function as "funnels," relatively narrow trails and passages that deer are likely to pass through. Look at a satellite map and identify the bedding areas of thick cover, then look for sources of water and food. Draw lines between these points while keeping them close to the kind of cover whitetails prefer. Examine the topography along those lines you have drawn. Look for a spot where you can set up a good, safe shot that isn't directed toward a road or house. That is going to be a very good place to look for deer. Other features that can function as a funnel are a mountain pass, a wadable area along an otherwise deep river, and a gap in a fence.

Deer scat and footprints are easy to identify. The relative freshness of either is an indicator of how recently a deer has passed by.

[Adapted from *The Beginner's Guide to Hunting Deer for Food* by Jackson Landers]

Since fish is so perishable, you should clean your catch as soon as it is caught (the entrails must be removed a maximum of 2 hours after the catch). Always use a sharp knife. To begin, thoroughly wash the fish to remove grime and slime and let it dry for a few minutes.

CLEAN A FISH

1. If you intend to skin your fish, there is no need to scale it. (Trout need to be neither scaled nor skinned; the grilled skin is delicious.) To scale a fish, first mist it lightly. Then, holding down the tail, use a fish scaler or sturdy knife to scrape the scales from tail to head, including around the pectoral fin and up to the gills.

2. Cut off the head by slicing down behind the gills at an angle.

3. Slice horizontally along the belly and remove the innards. Clip or cut off the fins, and be careful: some fish, catfish and bluegills especially, have spiny, sharp fins.

4. Remove the kidney line (the black line adhering to the underside of the spine) using a teaspoon or the back of your thumbnail. Wash carefully.

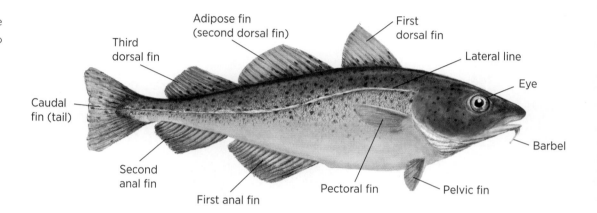

Third dorsal fin

Adipose fin (second dorsal fin)

First dorsal fin

Lateral line

Eye

Caudal fin (tail)

Barbel

Second anal fin

First anal fin

Pectoral fin

Pelvic fin

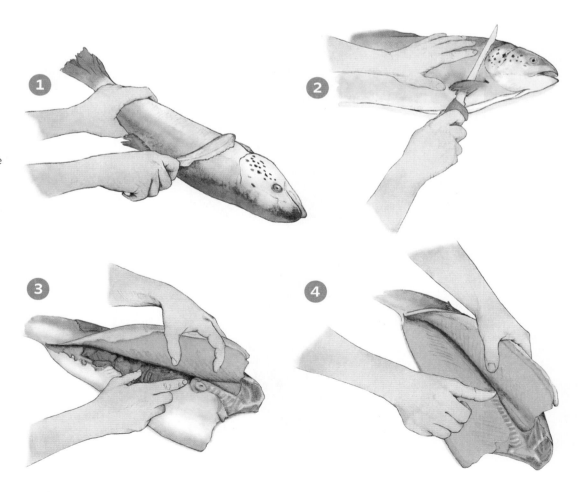

SHUCK AN OYSTER

Oysters are pretty much the only animals in the Western world that are commonly eaten alive. By law, oysters in the shell must be sold alive. Keep the oysters cold and buy them the day you plan to shuck them, if possible. When you buy them, make sure they are clamped shut and smell fresh and salty. Don't suffocate them in plastic, and discard any oysters that have opened.

Step 2

Step 3

Step 4

Prying the shells open can be intimidating but needn't be. Don't panic. Shucking is not that hard. You'll need heavy rubber or mesh gloves, an oyster knife (the best are slightly curved on top) or a flat-head screwdriver, and an old kitchen towel or rag.

1. Rinse the oysters under cold water and scrub well with a stiff brush to remove dirt. Use a knife to remove any barnacles that might get in the way of slurping.

2. Place an oyster in the center of the kitchen towel (or, if doing this outside, you can omit the towel) and hold it down with your hand. Insert the tip of the knife into the hinge (it's indented, where the shells come together, and no two hinges are alike) and jimmy open the shell.

3. Run the knife around the edge to loosen the oyster, taking care not to dump the liquid — it's delicious, and contributes to the salty brininess of the experience.

4. Discard the top shell, and cut the muscle holding the meat to the shell so you can slurp it. (Don't rinse the oyster.) Set it on a bed of ice if you aren't eating it immediately.

[Adapted from *Fresh Fish* by Jennifer Trainer Thompson]

A bad day of clamming is still a great day. It's you, the wind, the water, maybe a friend, and intense digging. It's clams squirting back at you when you least expect it. There's something timeless about a vast stretch of untouched beach.

DIG
CLAMS

To go clamming, you don't need much more than a sense of adventure and the following:

* A shellfish permit

* A clam rake (a spoon or garden hoe will do in a pinch)

* A basket or bucket (a beach towel will work if you're unprepared)

1. Get a permit if necessary. Tidal flats are a public resource and can be harvested by anyone with a shellfish permit. You can usually get a temporary one — or at least get the skinny on it — at the local town hall. If you're a vacationer or nonresident, expect to pay twice what a local would pay for your license.

2. Before cooking, discard any clams that are opened.

3. Hard-shell clams just need to be rinsed off before being cooked or served, but soft-shell clams (steamers) should be rinsed several times under cold water and then immersed in seawater or salted water (a tablespoon of salt for every quart) for at least an hour to remove any sediment before being cooked.

Storing Fresh Clams

If you're not cooking for a few hours, it's convenient to leave the clams in a bucket of salt water in a cool place, and they can stay there for up to 8 hours. If the water gets murky, feel free to change it — the clams are simply discharging their sand and grit. Don't keep clams submerged in water for longer than 8 hours. If you aren't cooking them until the next day, take them out of the water and store them in the refrigerator or on a bed of ice in a cooler.

[Adapted from *Fresh Fish* by Jennifer Trainer Thompson]

KNIT A HAT
WITHOUT A
PATTERN

One of the best things about hats (and there are many) is the way that one can be knit, spur of the moment, with no pattern and very little planning. If you have yarn and the needles that go with it, you can have a hat.

TOOLS AND MATERIALS

- Yarn (your choice)
- Needles (use straight or circular, but if you choose to knit in the round, you'll need a set of more or less matching double-pointed needles to finish the top of the hat when the stitches won't fit around the circular anymore)
- Measuring tape
- Darning needle for sewing up

1. Knit a swatch and find out how many stitches to the inch you're getting with the yarn and needles you have chosen.

2. Measure around the head of the recipient, or use a head size chart to make an educated guess. Multiply the number of inches around the head by the number of stitches to the inch.

3. Cast on the calculated number if you're knitting in the round or the calculated number plus two stitches (for the seams) if you're going back and forth.

4. Knit either around and around or back and forth (or do ribbing, or whatever you like) until the hat is long enough to reach the crown of the head. When in doubt, knit longer. A hat that's too long can be folded up.

5. When you reach the crown, you have three choices. Which one you opt for has a lot to do with your personality and how close you are to the deadline for the hat.

✳ **QUICK AND DIRTY/ CHRISTMAS EVE SOLUTION:** Do nothing. Knit to the top of the head, work an extra inch, then thread the yarn through the working stitches and gather them up tight. Sew the seam (if you have knit flat). This makes a hat with a fetching gathered top and works best if you've used yarn that isn't too bulky.

✳ **A LITTLE MORE TIME AND EFFORT:** For the next round (or row), knit two stitches together every three or four stitches. Work one row plain, then work one row with a decrease every other stitch. Work another row plain, and on the last row (or round), knit two stitches together all the way across. Gather up the remaining stitches, and you're done.

✳ **TYPE-A SOLUTION:** Count your stitches. Choose a number between 5 and 10 that divides into your total. For example, if you have 80 stitches in your hat, 8 is a good choice. Now work a row decreasing in groups of eight (or whatever your number is): knit six, knit two together — that's eight. Work the next row plain (with no decreases), then, on the next row, make the group of stitches one less: knit five, knit two together. Work a row plain, then knit four, knit two together, and so on. Carry on in this ever-diminishing way, alternating a row of decreases with a row of plain knitting, until you are knitting two stitches together all the way across the row. Gather up the remaining stitches. The decreases will spiral elegantly around the crown of the hat.

[Adapted from *Knitting Rules!* by Stephanie Pearl-McPhee]

KNIT A SCARF THAT RECORDS THE WEATHER

When was the last time you lay on the grass and watched the clouds drift by? It's surprisingly easy to forget to look up and appreciate the colorful show that swirls above our heads at every moment. This project asks you to keep an eye on the weather and to track its comings and goings more closely than usual. Each day, you will knit a stripe in colors that match the particular day's sky, slowly creating your own wearable weather report.

PREPARE YOUR PALETTE

First, gather balls of laceweight yarn that correspond to the various colors of the daytime sky: bright blue, light blue, white, light gray, and dark gray. Using laceweight yarns means you can use the strands doubled so that you have more color options for illustrating the sky. (Using US 3 needles, you'll get a gauge of about 7 stitches to an inch.) For example, on a partly cloudy day you might select white and light blue. For a thunderstorm, you might combine light gray and dark gray. And for a pure bright blue sky, you might choose to knit the stripe with two bright blue strands. Make two separate balls of some colors (probably just the blues) so you'll have the option for the latter. Feel free to add your own flourishes; for example, on rainy days, you could consider knitting clear glass beads into your scarf.

At What Hour?

You might want to observe the sky at the same time each day. Or you might want to wait until each evening and reflect on the essence of that day's weather as a whole. For example, even if a bright blue sky prevailed for most of the day, you might still choose gray yarns to represent the booming thunderstorm that suddenly swept through town in the afternoon.

CHECK THE WEATHER AND START KNITTING

1. Begin your scarf by choosing the two-strand color combination that best represents the weather on the first day of your project. Treating these two strands as one, cast on 40 stitches.

2. Then, day after day, observe the sky, select the two colors that express its essence best, and add a stripe to your scarf by working two rows in garter stitch with those yarns.

3. Continue for a year. When you're done, bind off and weave in the loose ends.

Oakland

Santa Fe

Copenhagen

Seattle

[Adapted from *Knit the Sky* by Lea Redmond]

Some beginners enjoy learning "needle-less" knitting, a.k.a. finger knitting. It's easiest to learn if you use bulky yarn. Use the finished product as a belt, a strap, or even a fun, skinny scarf. When knit with a nonstretchy yarn, such as cotton, it could be used as a pet toy or collar.

FINGER KNIT

1. **CAST ON.** Hold your left hand with your palm facing you. Lay the yarn tail between your thumb and index finger. Wrap the yarn counterclockwise around your index finger, then behind your middle finger, over your ring finger, and behind your little finger. Continue winding by going back the way you came but now wrapping over your little finger, behind your ring finger, over your middle finger, and under your index finger. Repeat this same pattern out to your little finger and back to your index finger, this time placing the yarn just above the first wrap. Don't wrap too tightly, and don't let the strands of yarn overlap one another.

2. **KNIT.** Beginning at your little finger, lift the bottom strand of yarn up and over the top strand and off the tip of your finger (the top strand stays put). Do the same on each of your other fingers in order (ring, middle, index). For subsequent rows, beginning at your index finger, wrap each finger one more time (out and back) as you did to cast on. Once again, pass the bottom strand up and over the top strand and each of your fingertips in turn. If you have to lay down your knitting before it's complete, slide it onto a pencil or other "stick."

3. **BIND OFF.** When your knitting is as long as you want it, stop wrapping after you've passed a whole row off your fingers. (The yarn is at the left, next to your index finger, and each finger has only one strand of yarn on it.) Lift the loop off your little finger and place it on your ring finger. Lift the bottom strand over the top strand and off your finger, then move the loop off your ring finger onto your middle finger. Repeat this sequence with each finger until only the index finger holds a loop. Cut the tail and draw it through that loop, and pull snugly to fasten. Fasten off the beginning tail as well.

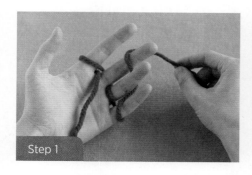
Step 1

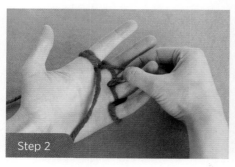
Step 2

Step 3

[Adapted from *The Knitter's Life List* by Gwen W. Steege]

A hellstrip is that area between the street and a sidewalk that is usually planted with grass or inundated with weeds, and you're never sure if *you* should mow it or if the city takes care of it. Why not replace the grass and weeds with a meadow planting? These meridians or sidewalk planting strips are the perfect spot for some tough meadow plants like the ones below. Once you've confirmed that you're responsible for this area (check with your local department of public works), ask whether there are any height restrictions for plants in the hellstrip.

MAKE YOUR HELLSTRIP HEAVENLY

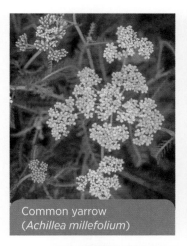
Common yarrow
(*Achillea millefolium*)

Little bluestem
(*Schizachyrium scoparium*)

California poppy
(*Eschscholzia californica*)

Beardtongue
(*Penstemon digitalis*)

Evening primrose
(*Oenothera* species)

Deerhorn clarkia
(*Clarkia pulchella*)

New England aster
(*Symphyotrichum novae-angliae*)

Lavender
(*Lavandula angustifolia*)

Sweet alyssum
(*Lobularia maritima*)

Gazania
(*Gazania rigens*)

Eastern red columbine
(*Aquilegia canadensis*)

Blue grama
(*Bouteloua gracilis*)

[Adapted from *Mini Meadows* by Mike Lizotte]   **177**

CREATE AN
EDIBLE DRIVEWAY
HEDGE

Turn your driveway into an edible landscape by lining it with fruiting hedges that will provide beautiful flowers followed by delicious fruit. Nanking cherry, saskatoon, and red currant are a few good choices, along with alpine strawberries for ground cover.

Before ripping out your forsythia hedge or planting a fruiting line, consider some practicalities:

* Don't plant too densely or allow spreading plants to grow too densely, especially in sites with less than full sunlight, or the plants will shade themselves out of productivity and become more prone to diseases.

* Where winter brings snow and ice, room is needed along at least one side of a driveway to pile snow. And if you ever use salt to melt ice on your driveway, choose fruiting shrubs that are most salt tolerant; these include beach plum, goumi, rugosa rose, and currants.

* Hedges often look best when they are uniform, which means limiting them to a single species, and perhaps even a single variety. Just a warning: That could be a lot of fruit, and all at one time.

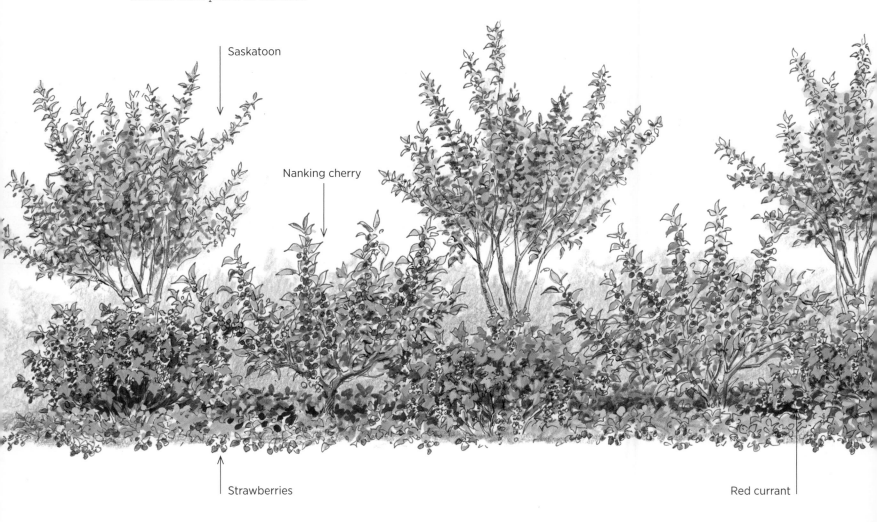

Saskatoon

Nanking cherry

Strawberries

Red currant

[Adapted from *Landscaping with Fruit* by Lee Reich]

Depending on numerous factors, including soils, light, and your personal preferences, lawn grasses are not always the ideal plants for all parts of the landscape. Here is just a sampling of alternative plants for special landscape situations. No mowing required!

LEARN HOW TO
NEVER MOW
AGAIN

ASARUM CANADENSE

Wild ginger, with its glossy, evergreen, heart-shaped leaves, makes a stunning planting under trees, and it grows best in areas where leaves have long been left to decay. It is not related to the common ginger, though it does have an edible root. Look also for *A. caudatum*, *A. shuttleworthii*, and especially *A. europaeum*, which are similar.

* **SOILS:** Rich, acid
* **ZONES:** 3–7
* **LIGHT:** Light to moderate shade
* **SPECIAL FEATURE:** Good for growing under trees

DIANTHUS SPECIES

A common resident of perennial flower gardens, this creeping plant doubles as a dynamite grass substitute on a mostly sunny slope. Tolerant of heat and humidity, dianthus also holds its foliage all winter, even in a northern climate. Shear it back after the first bloom and it will reliably bloom a second time.

* **SOILS:** Wide range
* **ZONES:** 3–8
* **LIGHT:** Full sun to moderate shade
* **SPECIAL FEATURE:** Holds slopes

Continued on next page

Dianthus 'Pixie'

[Adapted from *The Organic Lawn Care Manual* by Paul Tukey] 179

FERNS

Too numerous to mention just one species, ferns are nature's most common plants for the forest floor. We should take the hint! You can find ferns for every climate, ferns for food, and ferns with colorful fronds. Many are evergreen, drought tolerant, and well behaved.

* **SOILS:** Wide range
* **ZONES:** Vary
* **LIGHT:** Light to heavy shade
* **SPECIAL FEATURE:** Good for growing under trees

GENISTA PILOSA

Becoming popular in the Pacific Northwest, this low-growing shrub appears at first to be a member of the juniper family, but when the plant drapes itself in stunning pea-sized yellow flowers in spring, you'll know it's something quite different. Highly drought tolerant, it can take the heat.

* **SOILS:** Wide range
* **ZONES:** 5–9
* **LIGHT:** Full sun to light shade
* **SPECIAL FEATURE:** Holds slopes

GERANIUM 'ROZANNE'

This drought-tolerant perennial geranium has purple flowers that appear from June until well after the first frost. The plant needs scarcely any attention once it's established.

* **SOILS:** Wide range, except wet
* **ZONES:** 5–9
* **LIGHT:** Full sun
* **SPECIAL FEATURE:** Tolerates poor soils

ISOTOMA FLUVIATILIS

Commonly known as blue star creeper because of its proliferation of small blue flowers from spring into summer, this evergreen plant stays low to the ground. It is ideal for pathways around rocks or at the edge of a driveway because it can withstand daily foot traffic. It will require a bit more shade in warmer climates.

* **SOILS:** Wide range
* **ZONES:** 5–9
* **LIGHT:** Full sun to partial shade
* **SPECIAL FEATURE:** Good for areas with foot traffic

Sedum rupestre

SEDUM SPECIES

More than 300 species of plants belong to the sedum family, which is one of the toughest on the planet. Many flower with amazing vibrancy; others have succulent foliage and look like desert tropicals. Many gardeners plant multiple species together.

* **SOILS:** Wide range
* **ZONES:** Vary
* **LIGHT:** Full sun to light shade
* **SPECIAL FEATURE:** Tolerates poor soils

THYMUS CITRIODORUS

Lemon thyme will stay evergreen all winter long in Maine yet also grow in Florida and Texas. It has a pleasant aroma and will spread quickly once established.

* **SOILS:** Wide range
* **ZONES:** 4–10
* **LIGHT:** Full sun to moderate shade
* **SPECIAL FEATURE:** Good in drought and heat

TIARELLA CORDIFOLIA

This plant forms a snowy carpet when it flowers in spring. The handsome heart-shaped foliage is attractive all summer, with good color in autumn in northern areas.

* **SOILS:** Well drained, rich
* **ZONES:** 3–10
* **LIGHT:** Moderate shade
* **SPECIAL FEATURE:** Good for shade

VIOLA LABRADORICA

One of the many violets that can be a gardener's friend or foe, this member of the family is highly useful in shady areas under trees and can tolerate reasonable foot traffic. In locations where Labrador violet really takes hold, you may need to take steps to keep it in check.

* **SOILS:** Wide range
* **ZONES:** 2–6
* **LIGHT:** Moderate to full shade
* **SPECIAL FEATURE:** Good for areas with foot traffic

YUCCA FILAMENTOSA

Though not a ground cover, the incredibly versatile yucca provides a tropical flair to any garden, even in the North. Normally around 2 to 3 feet tall, all the sword-shaped, rigid leaves arise from a central point in a rosette. In summer, the plant produces a flower stalk that often grows 4 feet or more.

* **SOILS:** Poor
* **ZONES:** 5–10
* **LIGHT:** Full sun to moderate shade
* **SPECIAL FEATURE:** Good in drought and heat

FIND YOUR WAY AROUND THE NIGHT SKY

Learn to identify the Big Dipper, and you'll quickly learn to find your way around the night sky. The Big Dipper is a starry signpost that points to the North Star, Polaris, and to many other stars and constellations.

Cassiopeia (the queen) is on the opposite side of Polaris from the Big Dipper. All through the night, Cassiopeia and the Big Dipper spin slowly around Polaris.

Next to Cassiopeia is **Cepheus** (the king), a much fainter constellation. And wrapping around the Little Dipper and between all of these constellations is **Draco**, the dragon.

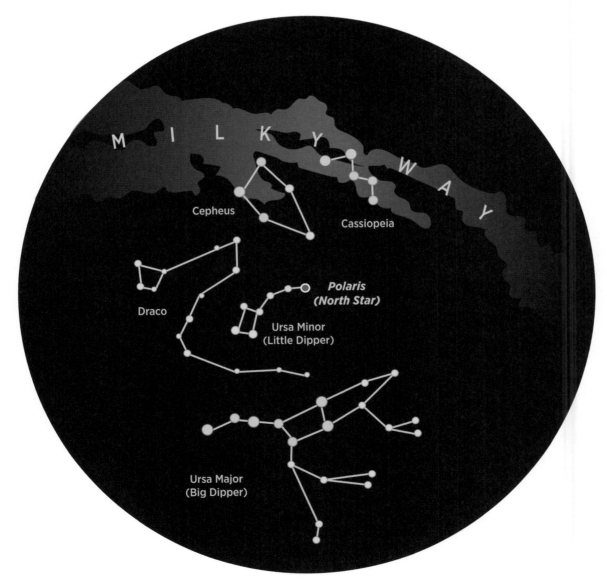

MILKY WAY

Cepheus

Cassiopeia

Draco

Polaris
(North Star)

Ursa Minor
(Little Dipper)

Ursa Major
(Big Dipper)

[Adapted from *Sky Gazing* by Meg Thacher]

STARRY SIGNPOST

You can use the other stars in the Big Dipper to find **Pegasus** (the flying horse), **Auriga** (the chariot driver), and **Gemini** (the twins).

The handle of the Big Dipper makes an *arc* to **Arcturus**, the brightest star in the constellation Boötes. From Arcturus, *speed* on to **Spica** (*speak*-uh), the brightest star in the constellation Virgo.

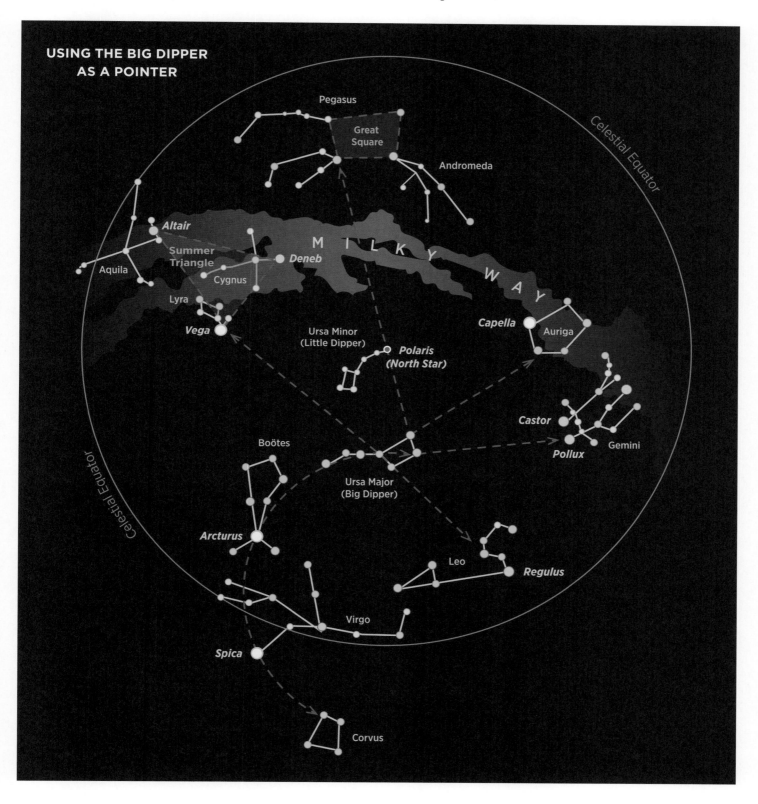

USING THE BIG DIPPER AS A POINTER

Pegasus

Great Square

Andromeda

Celestial Equator

Altair

Summer Triangle

M I L K Y

W A Y

Aquila

Deneb

Cygnus

Lyra

Vega

Ursa Minor (Little Dipper)

Polaris (North Star)

Capella

Auriga

Castor

Gemini

Pollux

Celestial Equator

Boötes

Ursa Major (Big Dipper)

Arcturus

Leo

Regulus

Virgo

Spica

Corvus

MAKE SILKY-SMOOTH SHAVING CREAM

Keep this cream on hand for silky-smooth skin and a close shave. Be careful in the shower when you're using it, as it can make the floor of the shower slippery. In a tub, an antiskid mat can be helpful. Store this cream in a cool, dry place, and try to keep water out of the jar to preserve its freshness.

INGREDIENTS

¼ cup coconut oil

¼ cup shea butter

1. If the coconut oil is solid, melt it in a microwave or a double boiler.

2. Combine the coconut oil and shea butter in a bowl. Using an electric mixer, whip until light and fluffy, about 2 minutes.

3. Scrape the cream with a spatula into a glass jar with a lid.

Step 1

Step 2

Step 3

[Adapted from *Girls' Home Spa Lab* by Maya Pagán]

This aftershave tonic smells delightfully spicy. When strained, it can also be used as a scented hair rinse or scalp cleanser for oily or normal hair (avoid use on blond or bleached hair, as it may temporarily stain).

MAKE A NATURAL
AFTERSHAVE
TONIC

INGREDIENTS

- 1 cup plain vodka

- 1 cup witch hazel

- 1 sprig fresh peppermint or spearmint

- 1 sprig fresh rosemary

- 1 cinnamon stick

- 10 whole cloves

  Peel of 1 medium lemon, cut into thin strips

  Peel of 1 medium orange, cut into thin strips

- 1 teaspoon vegetable glycerin

- 10 drops sweet orange or cardamom essential oil

1. Combine all the ingredients in a 1-pint or slightly larger jar. Screw on the lid and label and date the jar. Set in a dark, cool cabinet to steep for 2 weeks, shaking the jar vigorously every day.

2. After 2 weeks, strain the liquid through a fine strainer lined with cheesecloth, muslin, or a coffee filter to remove all particulate matter. Pour into storage containers. (You can add fresh citrus peels or spices to the storage containers for aesthetic appeal, if desired.) Label and date. For maximum freshness and potency, use within 6 months. Store in a dark, cool cabinet.

TO USE: Shake well before each application. Saturate a cotton ball or pad, and apply to your face and neck after each shave, or just splash some on with your hands. To help prevent ingrown hairs, apply the tonic similarly to any other area you might shave — legs, underarms, bikini area, and so on. Be aware, it will sting a bit! Use daily. Follow with moisturizer.

[Adapted from *Pure Skin Care* by Stephanie L. Tourles]

PLANT A TREE (OR SHRUB)

Many of the techniques for planting a tree or shrub are the same no matter whether it's been put up in a container, balled and burlapped, or shipped bare-root. The following instructions are for planting a balled-and-burlapped tree.

1. Using colored chalk, spray paint, or a garden hose, mark a circle at least two or preferably three times the diameter of the rootball, container, or bare-root system. If you want your circle to be absolutely symmetrical, put a bamboo stake at the center, tie a piece of string the length of the radius to it, and measure your circle by moving the string around the stake. Lift the sod inside the circle with a flat-edged spade or sod lifter (use it to patch bare spots in your lawn).

2. Measure the depth of the rootball with a yardstick or tool handle. Use a shovel to dig a hole almost as deep as the rootball, setting the soil you remove on a mat at the side of the hole. As a safeguard against planting the rootball too deep, check the root collar (where the trunk meets the roots) to determine the actual depth of the rootball.

3. Rough up the sides and base of the hole with a hand rake so that roots can penetrate more easily. (The shovel, pushed against surrounding soil, may have glazed the hole, which would slow the root system's expansion.) In heavy clay soil, add a *little* compost or peat moss — it should make up no more than 10 to 15 percent of the total backfill. Plants establish better in well-drained, amendment-free, native soil.

4. Put the plant in a wheelbarrow to bring it to the planting hole. If you don't have a wheelbarrow, support the rootball from below when you carry it. Do not carry the plant by its trunk. Take the tree or shrub to firm ground at the edge of the planting hole, then carefully set the plant in the center of the hole.

5. Open the burlap and remove it. If a crumbly or damaged rootball makes that impossible, cut away the burlap from the top and sides of the rootball once you've situated it in the hole. Equally important, if there's a wire cage, use wire cutters to remove as much of it as possible.

6. Lay a yardstick or tool handle across the hole to check that you are not planting too deep. The trunk flare should be at or just above ground level. Never bury the flare. There should be no space between the handle and the top of the rootball. Carefully adjust the soil level at the bottom of the hole if needed, while supporting the rootball.

7. Clip off any ragged or frayed roots that are exposed. These roots may have been torn in the process of digging up the plant at the nursery. Roots with fresh, smooth cuts will close up better than rough breaks once planted.

8. Add the soil back into the hole until it is half full. Be sure that the trunk flare and top of the rootball stay at or just above ground level. Tamp the soil gently with your foot, then water it in. The soil will settle. Continue to add soil until you have filled the hole, tamping as you go.

9. Make a ridge of soil around the periphery of the hole. This creates a bowl that will retain both rainfall and irrigation water so they can nurture the new tree. Water the plant thoroughly, adding a little more topsoil if the soil settles noticeably around the rootball after watering. Slow watering is better than strong hosing. Too much water too fast can ruin the soil's minute air pockets, from which roots absorb the air they need.

10. Staking is rarely necessary, except on windy or exposed sites, and should be removed after a year. Here, a flat, flexible band loops the trunk at the lowest branch so the treetop can still move. The band attaches to a 2×2 wooden stake angled and pounded 18 inches deep into virgin soil in line with the prevailing wind. Flag the stake and band to prevent people from tripping over them.

[Adapted from *The Homeowner's Complete Tree & Shrub Handbook* by Penelope O'Sullivan]

Step 2a

Step 2b

root collar

Step 3

Step 4

Step 5

Step 6

Step 7

Step 8

Step 10

REJUVENATE
A SHRUB

When you have an upright shrub that doesn't flower or color up as it did in the past, or one that looks overgrown, weak, congested, or straggly, it may be a candidate for renewal pruning. Drastic renewal is easy: simply cut down the whole shrub, leaving about 6 inches of stem at the base. However, it's not suitable for every shrub.

If you worry that whacking back a shrub in this way will cause a big hole in your view, you don't have to be quite this extreme. Spread the rejuvenation over 3 or 4 years, cutting back one-quarter to one-third of the branches each year. Start in early spring before new growth begins, clipping the oldest, biggest branches first, then the weak and ugly stems. Repeat the process each year until the shrub has been renewed.

Gradual Renewal Pruning

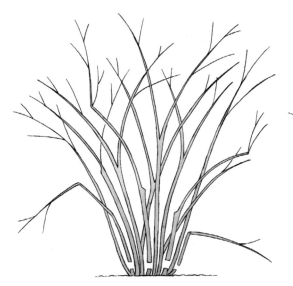

YEAR 1: Remove one-quarter to one-third of branches.

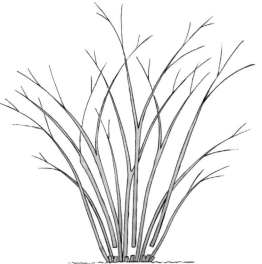

YEAR 2: Remove another one-quarter to one-third of branches.

Drastic Renewal Pruning

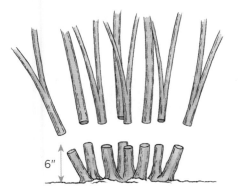

6"

[Adapted from *The Homeowner's Complete Tree & Shrub Handbook* by Penelope O'Sullivan]

When to prune a flowering shrub depends upon your intention. For their health, remove dead or injured branches any time. Shape deciduous plants when they are bare. In general, for more flowers, trim summer and fall bloomers when they are dormant, and trim spring bloomers after they flower, before new buds form.

PRUNE A FLOWERING SHRUB

Depending upon the shrub, you may not want to stop pruning it after 3 to 4 years of renewal pruning. For example, pruning a quarter of your forsythia stems down each year could keep blooms abundant and excessive growth under control.

Prune after Blooming

Deutzia gracilis 'Nikko'

Kerria japonica 'Golden Guinea'

Rhododendron periclymenoides

Prune when Dormant

Nandina domestica 'Fire Power'

Symphoricarpos species

Rhododendron 'Koromo-shikibu'

[Adapted from *The Homeowner's Complete Tree & Shrub Handbook* by Penelope O'Sullivan]

GROW A
LEMON TREE
INDOORS

Every household, especially those inclined toward culinary delight, ought to grow its own lemon tree. You can even grow one in a hanging basket. It's not unusual for a tree growing in a 12-inch basket to bear 30 or more lemons. In general, lemons are easy to care for and fast growing. The fruits can be left on the tree for harvesting throughout the year.

SOIL: Plant the tree in well-drained potting mix in a pot or hanging basket.

LIGHT AND TEMPERATURE: Place the tree in a spot that receives full sun and maintains a year-round temperature of at least 50°F/10°C for Ponderosa lemons and at least 65°F/18°C for Meyer lemons. If the temperature dips lower than that, reduce watering and fertilization to minimize the chance of root rot.

FERTILIZING: Fertilize weekly or every other week throughout the active growing season as long as temperatures are warm. Reduce or stop in winter.

PRUNING: Prune at any time of the year to maintain the tree's form and size. For the least disruption to fruiting, wait until the spring flush of flowering is complete to head back plants.

Which Lemon Variety?

THE MEYER LEMON is famous for its essence, flavor, and many uses; it's like having an old friend in the kitchen. Plants will grow almost continuously under warm conditions and high light; therefore, the upright, spreading branches need to be pruned back to maintain a dense, well-branched specimen. Prune young plants to create strong scaffolding that will bear the weight of plentiful fruits when the plant matures. Meyer is thought to be a hybrid between a lemon and a sour orange. The fruit will produce almost twice as much juice as the common table lemon and has a distinct rich flavor.

THE PONDEROSA LEMON is extremely vigorous and bears fruit easily. The fruits are strong, flavorful, and quite acidic, making them great for baking and cooking. Since each fruit is large, sometimes reaching up to 5 pounds, pay special attention to shaping the young plant to create a full, well-branched specimen able to hold the heavy weight. Limbs left unpruned may tear under the strain of the heavy fruits. Ponderosa is a hybrid between a lemon and a citron.

Meyer lemon

[Adapted from *Growing Tasty Tropical Plants in Any Home, Anywhere* by Byron E. Martin and Laurelynn G. Martin]

What better way to reuse an old tire than an old-school tire swing? All you need is a regular tire (not heavy duty), about 50 feet of 1½-inch rope, a length of old hose or tubing (to protect the tree from rope burn), and a couple of well-tied bowline knots. Be sure to choose a branch that is at least 6 inches in diameter, and drill a drainage hole in the bottom of the tire so that rain doesn't collect in it.

HANG A TIRE SWING USING A BOWLINE KNOT

Tie one end of the rope to the tree branch and the other end to the tire so that it hangs as far off the ground as you like.

How to Tie a Bowline Knot

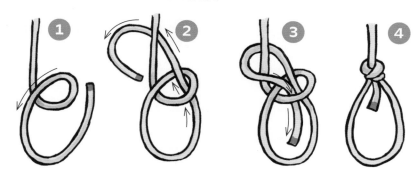

[Adapted from *Backyard Adventure* by Amanda Thomsen]

MAKE A HEAVENLY HAMMOCK
(AND LEARN ANOTHER KNOT)

Make this flat hammock out of practical or decorative fabric for a lovely addition to your deck or backyard. Use coated canvas or naturally water-repellent nylon to keep the hammock dry so you can use it all spring and summer, and even shortly after a rain shower.

MATERIALS

- One 90″ × 36″ piece of heavy fabric (such as canvas or pack cloth)
- Sewing thread, preferably nylon upholstery thread, for strength
- Two 36″-long × 1½″-diameter dowels
- Two 2- to 3-yard lengths of rope (for cotton rope, at least ⅜″ thick; for nylon rope, as small as ¼″)
- Two heavy-duty 2½″ stainless steel rings
- Heavy rope (for hanging)

1. Hem the 90-inch sides of the fabric by turning 1 inch under twice, and topstitch close to the inside turned edge.

2. Turn and press under 1 inch at each shorter end; make a 5-inch fold and stitch it down close to the turned-under edge and again ¾ inch in from that.

3. Drill holes 1 inch in from both ends of the two dowels, and insert them into the hammock casings created by the 5-inch folded ends.

4. Using the 2- to 3-yard lengths of rope, make a lark's head knot over each ring.

Lark's Head Knot

A. Hold a loop behind the metal ring.

B. Pull the lower ends through the loop.

C. Pull down.

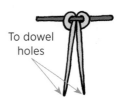

To dowel holes

D. Tighten.

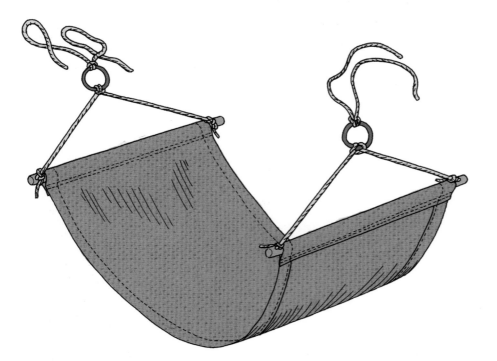

5. Thread each end of the rope of one of the rings through the holes at either end of one of the dowels. Loop the rope around the dowel and tie a bowline knot.

6. Repeat step 5 with the other knotted ring and dowel, and knot so that the ends won't pull back through.

7. Hang the hammock from ropes attached to the steel rings and tied to trees.

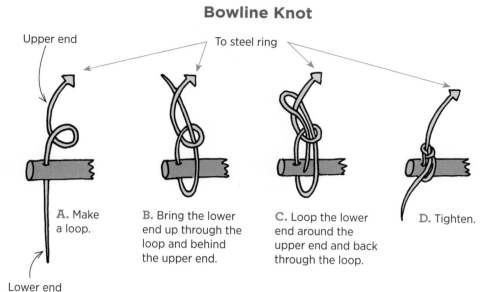

Bowline Knot

Upper end — To steel ring

A. Make a loop.

B. Bring the lower end up through the loop and behind the upper end.

C. Loop the lower end around the upper end and back through the loop.

D. Tighten.

Lower end

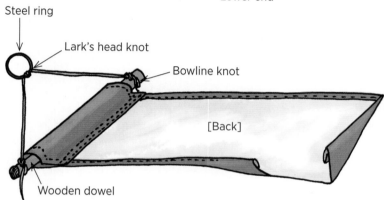

Steel ring

Lark's head knot

Bowline knot

[Back]

Wooden dowel

Finding or Making Extrawide Fabric

Extrawide cloth can be difficult to find in fabric stores. It is sometimes available through boat supply catalogs or specialty fabric houses. If you are unable to find what you are looking for, you can make a piece of fabric large enough for a tarp by piecing together two widths of fabric. Cut a 6-yard length of 36" wide fabric into two 3-yard lengths. Lay the two lengths of fabric on top of each other, right sides together, and, using a 1" seam allowance, stitch them along the length of the selvage. To "fell" the seam for added security, trim one side of the seam allowance to ½". Fold the other side over and around the shorter seam allowance, and stitch the seam allowances down at ⅛" from the edge, and again at ⅜" in from the edge. You have now created a double-needle, flat-felled seam and made a piece of fabric that is twice as wide as you had before.

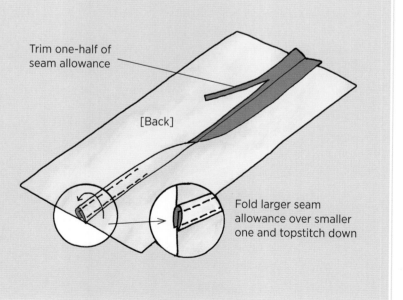

Trim one-half of seam allowance

[Back]

Fold larger seam allowance over smaller one and topstitch down

BUILD A TIN CAN STOVE

You can build a top-loading, updraft stove out of a coffee can (or any other tin can, preferably unlined) and some hardware cloth (metal mesh). The fuel can be almost any dry biomass, from twigs or wood pellets to cherry pits or dry corncobs. Try different fuels and experiment with can sizes and air-hole diameters. It may take some trial and error, but the materials are inexpensive, and the project takes only about 15 minutes.

1. **MAKE THE BOTTOM AIR INLETS.** Remove any paper from the empty can. Turn the can upside down and drill or punch eight evenly spaced ⅛-inch holes around the perimeter of the bottom lid, about halfway in from the edge, and make one hole in the center; these are the primary air inlets to support fuel combustion.

2. **MAKE THE SIDE AIR INLETS.** Position the can with the open end up and mark a line around the perimeter of the side, about one-third of the way down from the top. Drill eight evenly spaced ¼-inch holes along this line; these are the secondary air inlets and will provide oxygen to burn the pyrolysis gases before they leave the stove.

3. **ADD THE FUEL SCREEN.** Cut a square piece of ¼-inch hardware cloth or similar metal mesh the same width as the interior diameter of the can. Bend down the edges of the mesh so that it will fit inside the can and create a shelf that will suspend the fuel about ½ inch above the bottom air inlet holes.

4. **FIRE UP THE STOVE.** Set the stove on top of a fireproof surface that allows air to enter the primary air inlets on the bottom of the can; an open barbecue grill works well. Fill the can about one-third full with dry biomass. Put some paper or tinder on top of the biomass and light it from the top. After a few minutes, the biomass should start to burn from the top down. It may be a bit smoky at first. Then you'll see blue flames appear at the inside of the secondary air inlets; these are the pyrolysis gases being burned with the addition of more oxygen.

5. **TIME TO COOK!** Balance two pieces of angle iron on top of the stove to rest a pot on for cooking. A more stable design would be to cut a notch halfway through the center of two 1-inch-tall pieces of thin metal bar stock, slide the bars together, and lay that frame across the top of the can. Allow 1 to 2 inches of space between the top of the can and the bottom of the pot.

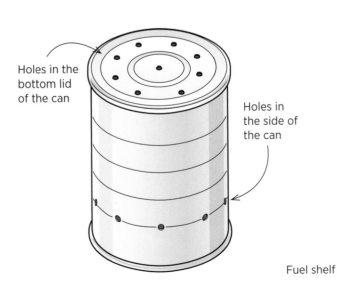

Holes in the bottom lid of the can

Holes in the side of the can

CUTAWAY VIEW

Fuel shelf

[Adapted from *The Homeowner's Energy Handbook* by Paul Scheckel]

Many easy-to-use knife sharpeners grind away too much of the blade. An alternative is to sharpen the old-fashioned way: with a whetstone. Whetstones can be made of diamond, quarried stone, or synthetic materials (the least expensive), and they may be cleaned or lubricated with either water or mineral oil, but it is not necessary to use either.

A sharpening steel can make a sharp blade sharper. However, you'll need a honing steel to make a dull blade sharper.

SHARPEN
AND HONE
A KNIFE

SHARPENING

1. **POSITION THE WHETSTONE AND KNIFE.** Position the whetstone on a dampened cloth or paper towel on a flat work surface, coarse grit facing up. The cloth will keep the stone from moving. Hold the knife so that the cutting edge meets the stone, point-first, with the cutting edge meeting the stone at an approximate 20-degree angle. You can stick a ¼-inch binder clip on the knife to keep the knife at the proper angle. Stabilize the blade with your hand.

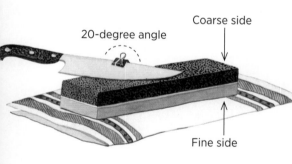

20-degree angle

Coarse side

Fine side

2. **SLIDE THE KNIFE ACROSS THE STONE.** Using moderate pressure, slide the blade forward across the whetstone, covering the entire length of the blade and keeping the angle of the blade relative to the stone at a constant 20 degrees. Repeat about 10 times, then turn the knife over and give the other side of the blade 10 strokes on the whetstone.

3. **REPEAT ON THE OTHER SIDE OF THE WHETSTONE.** Turn over the whetstone so that the fine-grit side is facing up. Repeat the 10 strokes at a constant 20-degree angle on each side.

HONING

1. **STEADY THE HONING STEEL.** Holding the handle of your honing steel, point the steel straight down and rest its tip on a flat work surface. Hold the knife in your dominant hand, with the sharp edge of the blade touching the steel, and position the blade so that it rests at a 20-degree angle to the steel.

2. **DRAW THE KNIFE ACROSS THE STEEL.** Starting with the heel of the knife (the part closest to the handle), draw the blade downward along the steel toward the counter, maintaining light pressure and pulling the handle back toward you so that the entire length of the blade, from the heel to the tip, comes in contact with the steel. As the edge of the blade makes contact with the steel, you should hear a light ringing sound. If you hear a grinding sound, either you are using too much pressure or your angle is wrong.

3. **ALTERNATE SIDES AND REPEAT.** Repeat the same motion on the other side of the knife blade, using the opposite side of the steel. Repeat four or five times on each side. Wipe the knife with a dish towel afterward to remove any steel dust.

[Adapted from *The Backyard Homestead Book of Kitchen Know-How* by Andrea Chesman]

CUT UP A CHICKEN

The key to successfully breaking down a chicken is cutting through the joints (easy), not the bone (hard). Finding the joints is all about locating articulation. When you first start breaking down chickens, don't be afraid to move the joints with one hand while feeling around with the other — wiggle the wing, shake the drumstick, shimmy the thigh. The goal is to find that place where the joints meet so that you can identify the space between them. That's where you want to cut.

Use a 5- to 6-inch boning knife for everything except cutting through the joints and splitting the breast, which are easier to do with an 8- to 10-inch chef's knife. It's easiest to remove the backbone with heavy-duty kitchen shears.

1. **REMOVE THE WINGS.** Place the chicken on its side on your cutting board. Gently pull the wing away from the body. Without going too deep, stick the tip of your knife into the hollow where the wing meets the breast and cut around the joint, releasing the wing. Repeat with the other wing.

    If you're going to cook the wings, use your chef's knife or kitchen shears to cut off the wing tips (which are great for making stock), and then to cut through the joint connecting the remaining part of the wing.

2. **REMOVE THE LEG QUARTERS,** which are the connected drumstick and thigh on each side.

    A. Make sure the chicken is breast side up. Gently pull a leg away from the body and use the tip of your knife to cut into the excess skin (just the skin!) between the leg and the body. Be careful not to cut very deeply.

    B. Put the knife down, grab the leg with your dominant hand, and stabilize the chicken with your other hand. In one swift, easy motion, twist the leg away from the body and down toward the cutting board to pop the drumstick joint out of its socket. This should happen pretty easily. Repeat this process with the other leg.

    C. Now you can make your final cuts to release the leg quarters: one at a time, holding each leg away from the body, cut through the joints you just popped and the skin, too, in order to fully release them.

3. **IF YOU WANT, SEPARATE THE DRUMSTICKS AND THIGHS.** To find the joint between the leg and thigh, flip each leg quarter over and look for the fat line between where the drumstick and thigh meet. That's exactly where you'll want to cut.

    To double-check that you're in the right place, move the drumstick back and forth with one hand while your other feels around for the joint. Once you're sure that you've found it, cut straight down. Your knife should cut easily into the space between the joint where the bones meet. If you meet a lot of resistance, you're not in the right spot.

4. **REMOVE THE BACKBONE.** By now you're left with just the body of your bird. Prop up the chicken so it's resting on the neck flap, with the large cavity opening facing upward. You'll see a vertical line of fat on each side of the carcass between the rib cage and the breast; this is where you want to cut, with either a very sharp chef's knife or your kitchen shears. Follow the fat line all the way down, through the ribs. If it helps, you can use your hands to snap the backbone and then continue cutting. Once you cut the backbone free, you'll be left with a whole breast.

5. **SPLIT THE BREAST.**

    A. Flip the breast over so it is skin side down and find the wishbone, which is the only bone that you have to cut through in order to split the breast (the rest is cartilage). Crack it by pressing down hard with your knife, then flip the breast over.

    B. Starting from the split wishbone, use your chef's knife to cut straight down the middle of the breast, splitting it into two even pieces.

There. You did it.

[Adapted from *Winner! Winner! Chicken Dinner* by Stacie Billis]

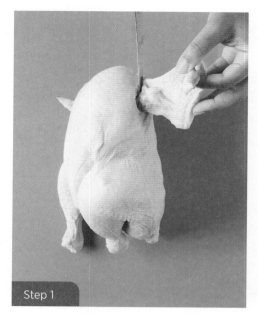

Step 1

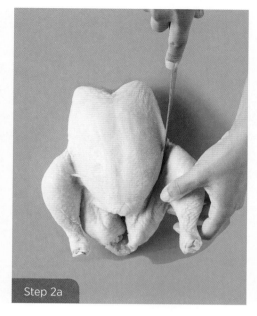

Step 2a

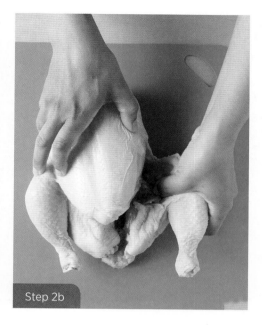

Step 2b

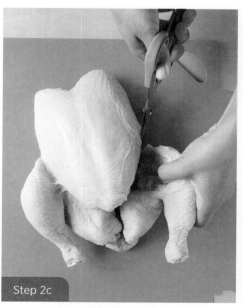

Step 2c

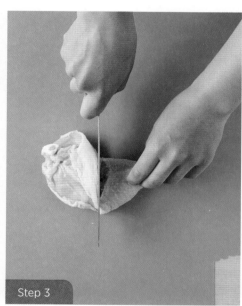

Step 3

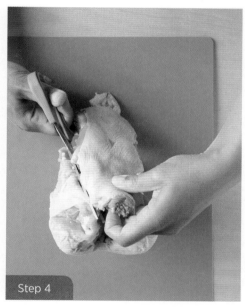

Step 4

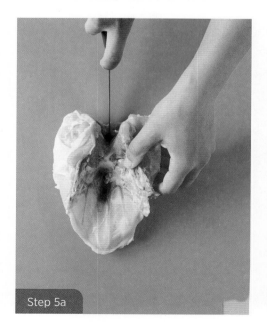

Step 5a

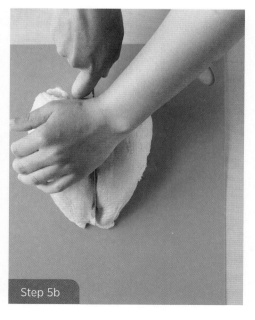

Step 5b

Going Skinless

Once you break your whole bird into pieces, you can make any of the pieces skinless by simply pulling the skin off with your fingers. Any "film" left on the chicken — technically called fat cap — is okay to eat. Tasty, even.

CARVE A
TURKEY

Don't wait until holiday dinners to learn how to carve a turkey. These tips will give you the skills to impress your guests. Allow 15 to 30 minutes between roasting and carving. This gives the juices time to be absorbed.

1. **REMOVE THE DRUMSTICK AND THIGH.** To remove the drumsticks and thighs, pull each leg away from the body. The joint connecting the leg to the hip often snaps free or may be severed easily with the point of a knife. Cut the dark meat completely from the body by following the body contour carefully with the knife.

2. **SLICE THE DARK MEAT.** Place the drumsticks and thighs on a cutting surface and cut through the connecting joint. Both pieces may be individually sliced. Tilt the drumsticks to a convenient angle, slicing toward the table.

3. **SLICE THROUGH THE THIGHS.** To slice the meat from a thigh, hold it firmly on a cutting surface with a fork. Cut even slices parallel to the bone.

4. **REMOVE THE BREAST MEAT.** Slice off half of the breast at a time by cutting along the keel bone and rib cage with a sharp knife.

5. **SLICE THE BREAST.** Place the halved breast on a cutting surface and slice evenly against the grain of the meat. Repeat with the second half of the breast when additional slices are needed.

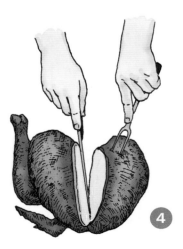

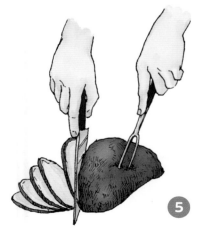

[Adapted from *The Backyard Homestead* edited by Carleen Madigan]

Peeling tomatoes is a prerequisite for making tomato sauce, since the skins won't break down in the sauce and also contain a lot of flavonols, which impart a bitter flavor. The task doesn't have to be an onerous one, however. Here's an easy way to do it.

PEEL A TOMATO
THE EASY WAY

1. Fill a large saucepan two-thirds full of water and bring to a boil. Meanwhile, using a sharp serrated knife, cut a very shallow X on the bottom of the tomatoes.

2. Using a strainer or tongs, lower the tomatoes into the boiling water. Count to 20, remove the tomatoes, and place them in a bowl or on a cutting board. After a minute or so, you'll notice that the skins have shriveled and loosened near the cuts.

3. When the tomatoes are cool enough to handle, peel off and discard the skins before proceeding with your recipe. Note that some cooks place the tomatoes in a bowl of ice water as they come out of the boiling water to help stop the cooking.

Step 1

Step 2

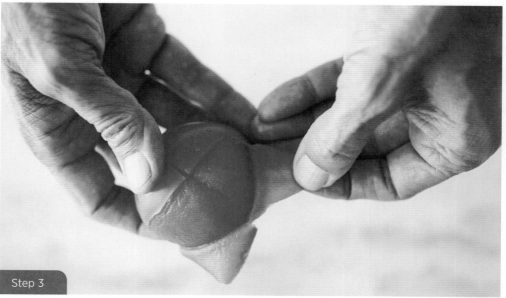
Step 3

[Adapted from *The Harvest Baker* by Ken Haedrich]

SAVE TOMATO SEEDS

The best time to save seeds from your open-pollinated tomato varieties is when the first tomatoes ripen. Use the first ripe tomatoes for seed saving to reduce the chances that the bees will have worked the flowers and cross-pollinated the seed in the tomato. For consistent results, make sure the seeds you are saving come from tomatoes that are true to type, meaning they match your expectations from either the description or past experience.

By fermenting the seeds, you will remove any pathogens on the seed surface, and below or in the surrounding seed gel. The seeds end up clean, attractive, and easy to package and store. Just be sure you don't ferment them for too long and end up sprouting the seeds!

1. Note the variety of the tomato and write it on a cup, along with the date. Cut the tomato in half and squeeze each half over the labeled cup to capture the seeds and gel. If the pulp in the cup is very thick or dry or can't be swirled, add just a bit of water. Check your knife and cutting board to make sure no seeds are present, and then move on to the next variety.

2. Once you have saved seed from all of the varieties you are working with, move the cups to a place where they can sit undisturbed to ferment for a few days, out of the sun. The smell will be pretty bad, so outdoors in a protected place or a garage works well. Cover the cups loosely with a paper towel. The paper towel should help keep flies that are attracted to the fermentation from laying their eggs in the pulp.

3. If the conditions are very warm (85°F/29°C or higher during the day), check the cups of fermenting pulp on the second day. If the weather is cooler, it could take up to 5 days for the fermentation to take place and the fungal layer to form. Once the pulp starts to ferment (indicated by an offensive smell and the presence of a layer of white, or occasionally black, fungus), it's time to rinse the seeds.

4. Remove the paper towel and bring the cups of fermented tomato pulp to a sink. Add water to each of the cups to within 1 inch of the top, then stir each cup a few times (be careful that seeds from one cup are not introduced into the next). Allow the contents to settle for a few minutes. The good seeds will sink to the bottom of the cup, and fungal material and other solid debris will float.

5. Gently tip the cup over the drain and pour off the floating debris. The cup contents can be quite concentrated, viscous, and opaque at this point, so be very careful to not allow any seeds to escape along with the upper debris. Add more water, swirl again, and pour off more floating nonseed material. Repeat until you have a cup of clear water and settled seeds.

6. Pour the material through a fine sieve (make sure the mesh is sufficiently small to capture the seeds). With the back of a spoon, push the seeds against the sieve under a stream of water to ensure that any remaining nonseed solids rinse through. Take a cloth and push against the seed mass from the outside of the sieve to wick away excess water.

7. Label a paper plate with the variety, scrape up the seeds into a mass with a spoon, and press them onto the plate in a single layer. Store the plates of clean, spread, labeled seeds in one layer in a place where they can air-dry. After a week, the seeds should be sufficiently dry for final storage.

[Adapted from *Epic Tomatoes* by Craig LeHoullier]

Step 1

Step 2

Step 3

Step 5

Step 6

Step 7

Storing Seeds

The main enemy of tomato seeds is moisture. Any seed storage option should take this into consideration. Screw-top glass or snap-top plastic vials work well. Seeds are surprisingly durable; even when exposed to all sorts of temperature changes, they can still germinate well after 12 or even 14 years. Tomato seeds will remain viable even longer if stored in the freezer, in a vial with a small packet of silica gel. Just be sure to allow the seed containers to reach room temperature before opening them.

GROW VEGETABLES VERTICALLY

Creative gardeners with limited space are always experimenting with ways to grow food up, and some of their solutions are nothing short of inspiring. While trellising remains the most common method of vertical crop production, here are some other ideas for growing food in spaces you may have never thought possible. Whether you have a full garden, a strip of an alley, an apartment balcony, or just a windowsill, you can grow up.

◀ An A-frame with a couple of narrow raised beds increases your growing space considerably. Wider beds provide space for a different crop in front of the vines, or use the shaded space between for a bed of spinach while the vines establish themselves.

▲ Use ready-made stock panels to create strong support systems for a variety of plants. The openings must be large enough to admit your hand for easy harvesting.

▲ A series of wire mesh panels set in a zigzag pattern makes for easier picking come harvesttime.

▲ A cloth shoe bag takes up little room while producing a variety of greens and herbs.

[Adapted from *Vertical Vegetables & Fruit* by Rhonda Massingham Hart]

◀ Create your own stacking pot sculpture by anchoring a pipe and threading each pot over the pipe, so that the pipe passes through the hole in the bottom of the pot. Tip each pot at an angle away from the one beneath it for a planting system that only looks helter-skelter. The pots rest against each other while their weight holds them in place.

▲ An old pair of jeans or shorts can be pressed into service with some sturdy sewing and a plastic liner.

▶ Stack cinder or landscape blocks in a crisscross fashion so that empty pockets protrude at intervals. Set trailing plants in the top and let the vines cascade, or include a trellis at the back of the shelves for them to climb up.

▲ Stacking a couple of hanging baskets over each other doubles your available vertical space on a porch or balcony.

◀ An old swing set can be given a new lease on life as a support for bean vines.

MAKE EASY, PERFECT PIECRUST

This pie dough is wonderfully versatile and can be used for both sweet and savory pies. It has great flavor and a flaky texture, and it is easy to handle. Once you're comfortable making this dough with all butter, try replacing 2 tablespoons of the butter with 2 tablespoons of shortening or lard. Those fats will make the dough more tender and less prone to shrinkage.

MAKES ONE 9- TO 9½-INCH STANDARD OR DEEP-DISH PIE SHELL

INGREDIENTS

- 1½ cups all-purpose flour, plus more for dusting
- 1½ teaspoons cornstarch
- ½ teaspoon salt
- 10 tablespoons (1¼ sticks) cold unsalted butter, cut into ½-inch cubes
- 2 teaspoons white vinegar
- Scant ⅓ cup cold water

1. Combine the flour, cornstarch, and salt in a large bowl. Scatter the butter cubes on a large flour-dusted plate. Measure the vinegar into a 1-cup glass measuring cup. Add just enough cold water to equal a scant ⅓ cup. Refrigerate everything for 10 to 15 minutes.

2. Transfer the dry ingredients to a food processor. Add all of the butter, then pulse the machine six or seven times, until the butter pieces are roughly the size of small peas. Pour the vinegar-water mixture through the feed tube in a 7- to 8-second stream, pulsing the machine as you add it. Stop pulsing when the mixture is just starting to form larger clumps.

Step 2a

Step 2b

Step 2c

Step 2d

[Adapted from *Pie Academy* by Ken Haedrich]

3. Turn the dough out onto your work surface and pack it into a ball. Put the dough on a sheet of plastic wrap and flatten it into a ¾-inch-thick disk. Wrap the disk and refrigerate for at least 1 hour before rolling. You can also freeze the dough at this point; just slip the wrapped disk into a plastic freezer bag, freeze for up to 2 months, and thaw overnight in the refrigerator before using.

Recipe for Success

If you're going to double the recipe for a double pie crust, you need a food processor with at least a 12-cup capacity.

Don't start pulsing the machine until you have the measuring cup of vinegar-water poised above the feed tube. Start pulsing as soon as you start pouring.

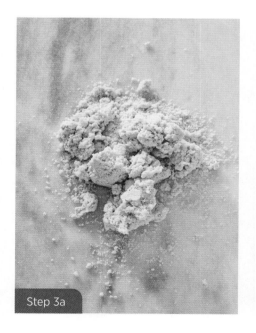

Step 3a

Step 3b

Step 3c

MAKE A LATTICE-TOP PIE

A lattice top can give your pie an especially attractive and folksy appeal. Lattice tops can be quite fancy, with multiple strips running in all directions, but a good place to start, if you're a beginner, is with the basic lattice here.

1. Start with a double-crust dough recipe and divide the dough into equal pieces. Or make two single-crust dough recipes. Either way, roll out one of the disks and line the pie pan with it, letting the excess dough drape over the edge of the pan.

2. Roll out the other dough half into the best rectangle you can manage, roughly 12 inches long and 11 inches wide. Using a pastry wheel, pizza cutter, or paring knife, and a ruler for a guide, cut the pastry into lengthwise strips 1¼ inches wide. (Each strip, in other words, will be about 12 inches long and 1¼ inches wide.)

3. Turn the pie filling into the pie shell, taking care to smooth over any pieces of fruit that jut up, like apples and other larger pieces of sliced fruit; the fruit's edges could tear the lattice. If you're dotting the top of the fruit with butter, do it now.

4. Lay five of the pastry strips vertically across the pie. Fold back strips 2 and 4 a little more than halfway, then lay another strip horizontally across the center of the pie.

5. Unfold the folded dough strips, then fold back strips 1, 3, and 5.

6. Lay another perpendicular strip across the pie.

7. Unfold strips 1, 3, and 5 over the second strip. Fold the other ends up over the perpendicular strip and lay another strip across the pie.

8. Unfold strips 1, 3, and 5 to form the final lattice.

9. Trim the strips and overhang evenly all around the pie, leaving a ½- to ¾-inch overhang, then pinch the excess dough into an upstanding ridge. Flute or crimp the edge as desired, then proceed to bake the pie according to the recipe instructions.

[Adapted from *Pie Academy* by Ken Haedrich]

Step 2

Step 3

Step 4

Step 5

Step 6

Step 7

Step 8

Step 9

LEARN FIVE FUNKY
CHICKEN COOP DESIGNS

These unconventional chicken coop designs treat the chicken coop like the hybrid structure it is — part outbuilding, part outdoor furniture, part sculpture. They are also completely functional, sometimes serving multiple purposes at once.

▲STOOP COOP

Is it possible for a chicken coop to be a gathering place? Instead of a utility structure in exile, what if a coop could be a place to commune, hang out, and even sit on?

▲CHICK-IN-A-BOX

This coop features a butterfly roof and post-and-beam-style joinery. The roof is angled such that rainwater is collected and funneled down to the chickens to drink.

[Adapted from *Reinventing the Chicken Coop* by Kevin McElroy and Mathew Wolpe]

►KIPPEN HOUSE GARDEN-ROOF CHICKEN COOP

If you lack the space for a garden *and* chicken coop, why not have two in one? This coop has a garden bed for a roof, which also acts as an insulator that helps keep the coop interior cool in summer and warmer in winter.

▲SYM

SYM is much more than a chicken coop; it's a symbiotic urban farming system. It sits above two worm compost bins that are fertilized directly by the chickens' manure. The chickens can eat insects that are naturally attracted to the compost and come in through the mesh floor, as well as worms taken from the bins and fed to them. The rooftop collects rainwater.

►COOPSICLE

The floor of this tree-house-inspired coop sits 48 inches off the ground, allowing for easy human access and cleaning. The spiral staircase leads to the coop through a hatch door cut into the floor.

IDENTIFY 10 NATIVE POLLINATORS

Many insects do the work of pollination, but none so much as our native bees. These insects are vital to a large majority of fruit and vegetable crops that we eat. They also keep plant communities healthy and productive and support the wide range of wildlife that feeds on seeds and fruits. Humans can support these important pollinators by planting a variety of flowering plants (see page 253) and preserving habitat, large and small. Here are some native pollinators to keep an eye out for.

ANDRENA: MINING BEES

Andrena bees are frequently encountered by gardeners because of their habit of nesting in lawns, typically in sandy soil near or under shrubs.

AGAPOSTEMON: GREEN SWEAT BEES

A fast-moving metallic green blur over summer flowers is probably an *Agapostemon*, a genus widespread across North America. They dig deep, vertical burrows in flat or sloping soil.

HALICTUS: SWEAT BEES

Halictus are called sweat bees because they are attracted to human sweat and drink it for its salt content. They are important pollinators of crops such as hybrid sunflowers and watermelon.

HOPLITIS: MASON BEES

Hoplitis are called mason bees because they construct walls to separate the brood cells in their nests. They visit a wide variety of flowers, many favoring plants in the pea, mint, and figwort families.

ANTHIDIUM: CARDER BEES

Anthidium are called carder bees because they "card" or comb cottony down from hairy leaves and use the down to construct brood cells. It's easy to know if carder bees have nested in a tunnel: it's plugged with a tuft of hairs.

MEGACHILE: LEAFCUTTER BEES

Megachile cut pieces of leaves or petals with which to construct their brood cells. Some species specialize on certain plants such as those in the aster and pea families.

[Adapted from *Attracting Native Pollinators* by The Xerces Society]

PEPONAPIS:
SQUASH BEES

Peponapis species all specialize in gathering nectar and pollen from flowers of squash plants, including pumpkins, watermelon, squashes, and gourds. They forage early in the morning when squash flowers open and mate inside the flowers, and males even shelter overnight in them.

SVASTRA:
SUNFLOWER BEES

Svastra females have large scopae that cover the lower half of their rear legs, making it look like they are wearing shaggy legwarmers. Many species are associated with sunflowers, while others specialize on the evening primrose family and one on cactus.

ANTHOPHORA:
DIGGER BEES

Anthophora visit a wide variety of flowers and have very long tongues that enable them to drink nectar from deep flowers. One species has been shown to be an important pollinator of cherry tomato crops.

BOMBUS:
BUMBLEBEES

Bumblebees are among the most easily recognized and best-loved bees. They nest in colonies in small cavities such as abandoned rodent burrows and grass tussocks. They are important pollinators of crops as diverse as tomatoes, watermelons, and blueberries.

HIVE A
NEW COLONY
OF BEES

Package bees are seriously stressed out. Besides having been shaken out of their home into a strange box with an unfamiliar queen, they have been bounced and banged around, often over long distances. Be kind to them, and get them into a hive as soon as possible. If the day that you pick them up is cold or rainy, keep the box in a cool, dark, dry place while you wait for better weather.

1. Assemble your tools, light your smoker, and don your veil. You can try working without gloves, but have them near, in case you decide you want them. You probably won't need to calm your bees with smoke on day one but lighting it is good practice.

2. Remove the outer and inner covers and feeder from your assembled hive. Also remove the four center frames from your hive body.

3. Fill the feeder with sugar syrup and set it aside. *Tip:* If you lightly spritz some sugar syrup on the bees through the metal grate of the package box, the ones that get misted will be less likely to fly when you pour them into the hive body.

4. Set the package close to your open hive. Using your hive tool, pry the lid off the top of the box, which will reveal the queen cage and feeder can. The bees have been eating sugar syrup from this can as they journeyed to their new home. Remove the queen cage. Some bees will escape from the box. Keep calm and carry on.

Step 1

Step 2

Step 3

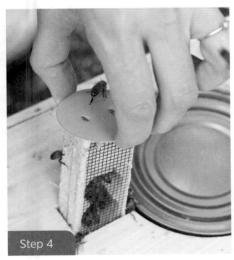
Step 4

[Adapted from *Homegrown Honey Bees* by Alethea Morrison]

5. Inspect the queen cage and make sure the queen is alive. If she is not alive (this is rare), contact your supplier immediately and schedule a hasty replacement.

6. Using pliers, remove the feeder can. Quickly set the wooden lid back on the top of the box to cover the now-exposed holes. *Tip:* Fewer bees will escape if you give the box a sharp thump on the ground before removing the syrup can.

7. Peel back (but don't remove) the metal disk with your pliers to reveal a hole in the queen cage that is plugged with sugar candy. Keep one side of the disk attached to the cage.

8. Wiggle a nail through the candy plug, being extremely careful not to impale or stab the queen. The bees will eat through the candy to release the queen, and this hole gives them a head start. Set the queen cage aside for a moment. If it's cool outside, put her in a shirt pocket to keep her warm.

9. Pick up the package box and give it one solid slam on the ground to knock the bees to the bottom. Don't be timid. You want them to lose their footing for the critical next step.

10. In one steady motion, remove or let the lid fall off, turn the box over, and pour the bees into the center well of your hive body. Shake and tilt the box to dump out as many as you can.

Continued on next page

Step 5

Step 6

Step 7

Step 8

Step 9

Step 10

11. Prop the package box so the opening faces the hive entrance and the remaining bees can easily find their way in. The lemony pheromone smell of the others will lure them home.

12. Gently reinsert the center frames in the hive body. Work slowly and carefully so you don't crush the bees. The frames will settle as the bees move.

13. Insert the queen cage between two frames that are closest to the center of the box. Rest the metal disk on the tops of the frames, so the cage is hanging in the hive. Be sure worker bees have access to the screened sides of the cage.

14. Replace the inner cover, the feeder filled with syrup, and, finally, the outer cover. Insert the entrance reducer to protect your new colony from robber bees.

Step 12

Step 11

Step 13

entrance reducer

Step 14

Swarming is a process by which one colony of bees becomes two. If you're a beekeeper, collecting a swarm is a free way to increase your production. Swarms collected in summer are far less likely to succeed than those collected in spring because the scarcity of nectar-producing plants makes it difficult for the colony to build stores and population sufficient to ensure a successful first winter. Although swarms of bees do not usually sting, they can if they're hungry or on the defensive. In regions where Africanized honey bees are established, collecting swarming bees is discouraged, if not illegal.

CAPTURE A
SWARM
OF BEES

A classic swarm clusters temporarily while scouts find a new nest.

The swarm is shaken off the tree so it falls into a box below.

The box is covered with a screened top and is now ready to be moved elsewhere.

[Adapted from *Storey's Guide to Keeping Honey Bees* by Malcolm T. Sanford and Richard E. Bonney]

FIX A FLAT BICYCLE TIRE

Changing a tire may sound complicated, but it's not overly difficult and is an essential skill. It will take the average rider 15 minutes or so to change a tire, but with practice it can take only a few minutes. And the feeling of accomplishment is significant as you resume your ride on a tire that you've repaired yourself at roadside.

1. Disengage the brakes.

2. Remove the wheel from the bike.

3. Use a tire lever to disengage the tire and tube from the rim of the wheel. Road bike tires are a bit more difficult to change than mountain bike tires. To fully disengage the bead, you'll probably need to use more than one tire lever. In either case, once the bead is totally free, the tube should be accessible and you shouldn't need to remove the tire completely from the rim.

4. Determine the cause of the flat. Use a pump to inflate the tube until it's bigger than the wheel. You should be able to hear or feel where the air is coming out. Remove any foreign object before repairing or replacing the tube.

5. Repair the tube using a patch kit (they usually come with instructions), or pull out the tube and replace it.

6. Reinstall the tire and tube on the wheel. Pump up the tube a little so it has some shape and stuff it back into the tire. Using your thumbs, push the tire bead back into the rim. If you need to use the tire lever to reengage the bead, use the flat end of the lever, not the J-hook.

7. Inflate the tube.

8. Reinstall the wheel on the bike.

9. Reengage the brakes.

10. Hop on your bike and go.

Mountain Bike
The hooked end of the lever grabs the bead.

Slide the tire lever between the rim and the bead. When you've worked the lever all the way around the tire, the tube will be easily accessible.

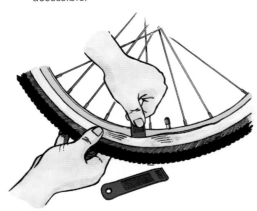

Road Bike
First, slide the lever between the rim and the bead. Pivot the lever away from the rim and toward the spokes, bringing the bead of the tire with it.

Hook the J of the tire lever onto one spoke of the wheel to hold the lever in place. Engage the bead with the second tire lever a few inches farther along the rim and again pivot the lever to shift the bead to the outside of the rim. Slide the second lever along the rim to free the rest of the bead.

Use a third lever if the bead is too tight to budge. When the bead is totally free, you'll be able to pull out the tube.

[Adapted from *Bikes, Scooters, Skates & Boards* by Neil Bibbins]

If the chain falls off your bike's chainring or cassette, you can't pedal anywhere. Almost all cyclists encounter this problem at one time or another. Repositioning the chain on the chainring or rear cassette is usually simple, but the approach will vary somewhat depending on whether the chain fell off in the front or in the back.

PUT YOUR BIKE CHAIN BACK ON

FRONT CHAINRING

1. Move the front shifter to the lowest gear position.

2. Kneeling next to the bike, push the bottom of the rear derailleur cage forward with your left hand to create slack in the chain.

3. Ease the excess chain forward with your right hand, and wrap it around the smallest chainring.

4. Lift up the rear end of the bike and slowly rotate the pedals forward to seat the chain on the proper gear. You're back in business.

5. If the chain is jammed against the frame, try to free the chain by gently lifting it, or visit the bike shop.

REAR CASSETTE

1. Try to free the chain from its resting place by gently lifting it. If the chain is stuck between the cassette and the frame, loosen the quick release to help free it.

2. Remove the chain from the front chainring to generate some slack.

3. Pull the chain back, ease it over the rear cassette, and jiggle the pedals slightly to seat the chain.

4. Push the rear derailleur forward to create some slack, and ease the chain forward onto the smallest front chainring.

5. Lift up the rear end of the bike and slowly rotate the pedals forward to ensure that the chain is properly seated. If it turns, you're ready to roll.

SINGLE-SPEED BIKE

1. Use an adjustable wrench to loosen the rear wheel's axle nuts, and slide the wheel forward to generate some slack in the chain.

2. Wrap the chain around the front and rear gears, making sure that the chain is fully seated on the teeth.

3. Slide the wheel back to its proper position, ensuring proper chain tension, and tighten the nuts just enough to hold the wheel in place. (Chain tension is correct when there is about ½ inch of play in the middle of the chain.)

4. Check to be sure the wheel is straight in the frame, then tighten the nuts securely.

5. Check the tension of the chain and the alignment of the wheel one last time before riding. It might take a few attempts to get it just right, but it's important to make sure that the tire doesn't rub against the frame.

Create slack in the chain by pushing the rear derailleur cage forward.

Try to free the chain by gently lifting it.

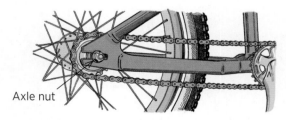

Axle nut

Loosen the axle nuts and slide the wheel forward.

[Adapted from *Bikes, Scooters, Skates & Boards* by Neil Bibbins]   **217**

Large ceramic pots for plants can be expensive, and plastic pots just aren't that attractive. So why not make your own? Hypertufa looks like concrete, but it's much lighter. Instead of mixing cement with sand and gravel to make concrete, you mix it with lighter material such as peat moss (other common ingredients are perlite and vermiculite). The simple recipe below mixes cement with potting soil. You also need two clean plant pots to use as a mold, one small enough to fit inside the other.

MAKE LARGE GARDENING POTS WITH HYPERTUFA

1. Spray the parts of the pots that the hypertufa will touch with cooking spray (or brush with cooking oil). This prevents sticking and makes it easier to slide the molded hypertufa out of the pots once it is dry.

2. Mix together equal parts of potting soil and Portland cement. Add enough water so that the mixture is completely wet, but not soupy.

3. Put about 1 inch of hypertufa at the bottom of the larger pot. This will be the bottom of your hypertufa pot.

4. Put the smaller pot on top of the layer of hypertufa, and center it so that there is equal space all around the sides. Use a trowel to fill up that space with your hypertufa mix. The idea is to make sure there are no big air pockets. But you don't want to pack it down too much, or the mix will be too dense. Fill to the top of the pot and smooth out the top edge.

5. Cover the whole setup with a sheet of plastic and put it in a dry, shady spot. Wash the container and tools you used quickly, before the hypertufa dries on them.

6. Let the hypertufa sit in the pots for at least a week to dry. When it's ready, peel the inner pot away from the sides and pull it out.

7. Turn the larger pot over and push gently from the bottom. Your new hypertufa pot should slide right out! Drill a hole in the bottom for drainage.

Step 4

Step 7

[Adapted from *Gardening with Emma* by Emma Biggs and Steven Biggs]

GROW PLANTS FROM SEED

If you're trying to get the most vegetables for the least amount of money, starting plants from seed is the way to go. You can place your seed flats on a sunny windowsill, but you'll consistently get the best results if you use fluorescent grow lights. It is easy to maintain the proper temperature and light conditions with grow lights, so the plants need less attention.

Tips: Keep the soil at whatever temperature is recommended on the seed package; it's usually between 70°F and 80°F/21°C and 27°C. It's a good idea to use a nursery heating mat (the kind sold for seed starting) with a thermostat beneath the seed flats to provide proper temperature evenly.

Don't use commercial potting soil to start seeds. It is good for repotting houseplants, but because it is usually not sterilized, it is likely to contain soil bacteria and possibly weed seeds. Instead, use a commercial soilless medium, such as Pro-Mix.

1. Soak the seed-starting mix in your flats thoroughly with slightly warm water until it is completely moist. Spread the seeds over the top of the mix as sparsely as possible. Sowing them in rows will make them easier to transplant later. Although it is difficult not to spread seeds, especially the tiny ones, too thickly, they grow much better if they are not crowded.

2. Cover the seeds with a thin layer of fine vermiculite, unless your planting directions say to cover the flat with a sheet of glass or plastic. Vermiculite keeps the soil from crusting and helps discourage damping-off.

3. Label each flat with the name of the seeds and the day they were sown.

Step 1

Step 2

Step 3

[Adapted from *The Flower Gardener's Bible* by Lewis and Nancy Hill]

4. Set the flats under grow lights, and leave the grow lights on 24 hours a day until the seedlings are well started. Water at least once each day, using a gentle spray that will not hurt the delicate seedlings. The water should be at room temperature or slightly warmer to avoid chilling the seedlings. Try to give them enough, but not too much. Overwatering and cool temperatures are the primary causes of seedling failure.

Step 4

5. In 3 to 4 weeks, once the seeds have sprouted and are growing well, gradually lower the heat to 65°F/18°C. Reduce the amount of time the seedlings spend under grow lights to about 12 hours daily, or set the seedlings in a sunny window during the day. Apply a liquid fertilizer once a week, but at only half the strength recommended on the label.

6. As soon as the seedlings have developed their first set of true leaves, transplant them to flats or small pots that are filled with soilless mix. Space them 2 to 3 inches apart in the flats, or one seedling to each pot. If you have a large number of seedlings you may prefer to transplant them into a prepared outdoor bed as soon as it is warm enough.

Step 5

10 Easy Vegetables to Grow from Seed

1. Lettuce
2. Bush beans
3. Summer squash
4. Kale
5. Cucumbers
6. Spinach
7. Pumpkins
8. Beets
9. Swiss chard
10. Carrots

Step 6

GROW AN AVOCADO TREE FROM A PIT

Avocados are surprisingly easy to grow at home. To begin, wash off an avocado pit and remove the brown skin, if you can, using your fingernail or a knife. (This helps germination but isn't essential.) You have several options for sprouting: you can sprout the pit directly in potting mix, use toothpicks to submerse it in water, or wrap it in damp paper towels. With three avocado pits, you can try all three methods and see which works the best!

OPTION 1: PLANT IT

The easiest method is to simply fill a jar about three-quarters full with potting mix and then sink the pit (pointy end up) into the soil. Leave about one-third of the pit uncovered, as avocados need light to germinate. Water it well, cover the jar with a plastic sandwich bag, and place it on a sunny windowsill. Remove the bag when a sprout appears.

OPTION 2: SOAK IT

To see more of what is going on, insert three toothpicks into the pit's upper half, each pointing slightly upward, then suspend the pit in a jar filled with water, with the toothpicks supporting it on the rim. The pit should be about half covered by the water. Place the jar on a sunny windowsill and keep an eye on the water level so the pit does not dry out.

OPTION 3: WRAP IT

Wrap the pit in damp paper towels, place it in a sealed plastic ziplock bag, and set it on a warm, sunny windowsill. Check the pit weekly to make sure the towels are moist.

Avocado pits can take several weeks or longer to germinate, but eventually the pit will crack and a sprout will emerge. If you used the toothpick or paper towel method, transplant the germinated pit to a jar or small pot filled with potting mix, keeping at least half an inch of the pit above the soil line. After another few weeks, the sprout should grow taller and eventually produce leaves. Keep the soil moist and be patient!

Where Are the Avocados?

Given the right conditions, avocado trees started from pits can grow to be quite large, but they rarely produce fruit. Commercial growers instead rely on trees that have been grafted, meaning the roots from one variety of avocado have been joined to the trunk and branches of another variety known to produce fruit.

[Adapted from *Mason Jar Science* by Jonathan Adolph]

There truly is nothing like a nuzzling baby goat. The best (and easiest) way to train a kid goat to bottle-feed is the following method. Use a nipple that the kid likes, such as the Pritchard nipple. A nipple designed for human infants may also work. Measure the amounts you offer your kid and feed uniform meals at evenly spaced intervals. Kids require 15 to 20 percent of their body weight in milk or formula daily. Be sure to wash the bottle and nipple thoroughly after each feeding.

BOTTLE-FEED
A BABY GOAT

1. Sit cross-legged on the floor with the kid tucked between your legs and facing away from you, his front legs straight and his butt on the ground.

2. Cup your left hand under his jaw and open his mouth. Insert the nipple with your right hand, then balance and steady it with the fingers of your left hand, with the left palm still under his jaw. This way he's less likely to spit out or otherwise lose the nipple.

3. Hold the bottle at mama-goat height (this height will vary by breed). Encourage him to lift and tip back his head. Kids function as single-stomached animals rather than ruminants until they begin nibbling dry food, usually around 2 to 3 weeks of age. When your kid's head is up and back, a band of muscle tissue closes and, bypassing his undeveloped rumen, directs milk straight from his mouth to his abomasum (the only stomach compartment containing digestive enzymes). However, don't let milk pour into his mouth; if he can't swallow the milk fast enough, it might spill into his lungs. Hold the bottle as level as possible while still keeping fluid in the bottle cap and nipple.

4. If your kid won't nurse, place a towel over his head while you are feeding him; this simulates the darkness of a doe's underbelly. Or squeeze a little fluid from the nipple and use it to dab milk on his lips; give him a taste but don't shoot a stream into his mouth.

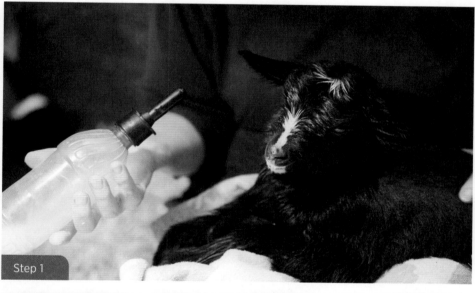
Step 1

Step 3

[Adapted from *The Backyard Goat* by Sue Weaver]   **223**

CLIP A CAT'S CLAWS

If you have a kitten, start right away touching her paws and lightly pressing on her pads to expose her claws on a regular basis. Do it in a fun way, for just a few seconds at a time at first, and always dole out some delicious treats. This will make nail-trimming sessions more pleasant for the both of you. Also be sure to talk calmly to your cat while trimming her nails. A mellow older cat might be willing to learn how to have her nails trimmed, but for a feisty cat, it may be safer to have the nail trimming done by a veterinary technician during a health visit or by a professional groomer.

Home Paw-dicure

Nail trimming at home is easier if one person holds the cat while the other uses the clippers. If your feline is receptive, give it a try. Set out the grooming tools in the bathroom or other enclosed space so your cat can't escape. You will need a thick towel, nail clippers, and styptic powder in case you accidentally cut a nail too short and it bleeds. Don't forget some treats!

3. **SNIP JUST THE TIP OF THE CLAW** — the clear, white part. The pink area is called the quick and is where the vein that runs through the claw ends. It will bleed if cut.

4. **WHEN YOU'RE DONE, UNWRAP THE TOWEL** and hand out a tasty treat or two. You want your cat to have a positive experience. It may take a few sessions for her to realize that nothing terrible has happened!

1. **WRAP YOUR CAT IN A TOWEL,** then gently pull out one paw at a time from the towel to trim the nails. It might be easier to have a helper hold the cat.

2. **PLACE YOUR THUMB ON TOP OF THE PAW** with your fingers on the pads. Gently press the pads one at a time to expose the claws.

[Adapted from *A Kid's Guide to Cats* by Arden Moore]

Celebrate your cat's birthday or other special occasion not by baking a cake, but by making these tasty cookies. You cat will clamor for more!

MAKE CAT CHOW COOKIES

MAKES 6 TO 8 SERVINGS

INGREDIENTS

Cooking spray, for the baking sheet

1 cup whole-wheat flour, plus more for dusting

⅓ cup powdered milk

¼ cup soy flour

¼ cup milk

1 egg

2 tablespoons butter, melted

2 tablespoons molasses

2 tablespoons wheat germ

1 teaspoon organic catnip

1. Preheat the oven to 350°F/180°C. Lightly coat a baking sheet with cooking spray.

2. Combine all the ingredients in a large bowl and mix well.

3. Dust a rolling pin with flour and use it to roll out the batter on the prepared baking sheet.

4. Cut the rolled-out dough into ½-inch-square pieces.

5. Bake for 20 to 22 minutes, or until lightly browned. Allow to cool before serving. Store the leftovers in an airtight container in a cool place.

[Adapted from *Real Food for Cats* by Patti Delmonte]

TEACH YOUR CAT TO JUMP THROUGH A HOOP

If you have an outgoing feline performer, you can me-WOW your friends by having your cat leap through a hula hoop as you hold it off the ground. Make sure your cat knows how to follow a target stick (or your hand holding a treat) before trying this more advanced trick. You'll need a hula hoop or something similar.

1. Face your cat with the hoop between you. Rest the hoop on the floor.

2. Coax your cat to follow the target stick through the hoop to get the treat. Praise and say "Hoop" each time he walks through, so he starts to associate the word *hoop* with the desired action.

3. Once he is comfortable walking through, start to raise the hoop slightly off the ground. Start at just an inch or two, then slowly increase the height as he learns what to do. You will probably need several training sessions to build up your cat's confidence and willingness.

[Adapted from *A Kid's Guide to Cats* by Arden Moore]

Hay is dried grass or legumes that is used to feed grazing livestock such as cattle, horses, and goats. The basic dilemma for the hay maker is whether to cut early for the highest quality or cut late for the highest volume. The best solution for most is usually somewhere in the middle — if the weather cooperates. In most of the country, that means 4 to 5 days of sunny, warm, moderately breezy weather with relatively low humidity.

CUT HAY

1. **FIRST ROUND.** Cut the outside border, either clockwise (more common) or counterclockwise to "open the field."

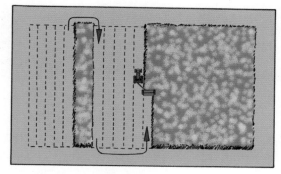

2. **CUT THE HEADLANDS.** Mow the perimeter (the headlands and edges) until there is room to turn around at the ends.

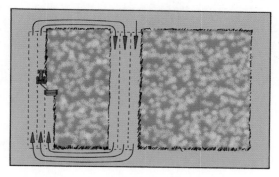

3. **MAKE A CUT STRAIGHT DOWN THE MIDDLE** of the field to create a block, and then mow around the block until it is too tight to turn.

4. **MAKE A WIDER TURN** to cut the first row of the next block.

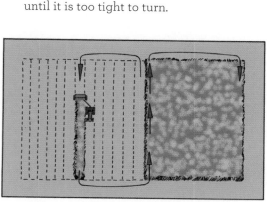

5. **FINISH OFF THE REMAINING ROW(S)** of the first block.

[Adapted from *Making Hay* by Ann Larkin Hansen]

EAT WILD PLANTS

Many edible plants populate our forests, fields, roadsides, and even yards — the key is learning to identify them. For example, you may already know that dandelions (roots, leaves, flowers, and all!) are edible, but there are many others probably growing right outside your door. Just remember, never eat anything unless you are sure you know what it is.

GARLIC MUSTARD is an invasive but highly nutritious plant that pops up everywhere from roadsides to woods to your backyard. Harvest the leaves of first-year plants in early spring and the young flower stalks before flowers have opened. Add them to sandwiches and salads, or make garlic mustard pesto (the garlic mustard replaces both basil and garlic).

ELDERBERRIES AND ELDER-FLOWERS are both edible. The flowers can be used to make fritters or to flavor champagne, liqueur, or even cream for making panna cotta. The berries should be gathered as soon as they ripen to a dark purple-blue. Raw berries are bitter, but when cooked they are sweet and make excellent syrup (which is often used as an immune-boosting tonic), jelly, wine, and pies.

JAPANESE KNOTWEED is an invasive weed best harvested when the stalks are young and tender. Choose unbranched spears between 8 and 16 inches tall. Tart and crunchy, knotweed substitutes well for rhubarb and works well in stir-fries and as a soup.

[Adapted from *Backyard Foraging* by Ellen Zachos]

OSTRICH FERN is considered one of the most delicious fiddleheads (not all fiddlehead ferns are tasty or edible). It has papery sheaths covering the emerging fiddleheads and an obvious deep groove along the inside of the smooth stem. Harvest only tightly furled fronds, and boil them for 10 minutes before sautéing with garlic or adding to pasta.

SUMAC commonly grows on roadsides and produces deep red cones of fluffy berries in mid- to late summer. All sumac bushes with red berries are safe to touch and eat. The berries have a lemony taste and can be cold-brewed to produce a tasty sumac-ade (just strain through fine mesh, a coffee filter, or jelly bag, and add honey as desired). They can also be simmered, juiced, and used to make jelly.

DAYLILIES are popular in gardens and have also spread to wild fields and roadsides. The young shoots, flower buds, petals, and tubers are all edible. The fresh petals add color to salads, while the buds can be added to salads or lightly sautéed in olive oil with salt and pepper. The new shoots make a crisp spring vegetable when sautéed as well, and the tubers are like mini potatoes when harvested in fall or early spring.

CHICKEN-OF-THE-WOODS is a bright orange mushroom that grows on trees (the species that grow on hardwoods are safest), and it is best harvested when young and tender. It doesn't taste much like chicken, but its texture makes it a useful chicken substitute in casseroles, soups, stews, and pastas, and it stands up well to baking and braising.

HOPNISS, or groundnut, is a perennial vine that grows in gardens and on lakesides and riverbanks. The flowers are highly fragrant, and the tubers are tasty and protein-rich. Roast them like potatoes or parboil and sauté in butter.

PRICKLY PEAR CACTUS should be harvested with gloves. The fruits can be twisted off the plant, while the pads (known as *nopales* in Mexican cuisine) should be cut with a sharp knife, leaving about an inch of the bottom of the pad behind. Scrape off the spines and peel the pads before cooking. Chop and cook them with onions and garlic and use them in egg dishes, stews, and soups or on their own as a side dish. The fruits can be sliced and peeled and made into jelly, syrup, or sorbet. When cooked, they turn a bright magenta.

GROW MUSHROOMS ON LOGS

You can easily grow this wild food right in your backyard by inoculating logs with the mycelium of edible mushrooms such as shiitake, reishi, and tree oyster. If you inoculate freshly felled trees, you'll have sufficient moisture content for your spawn. However, if there are more than a few days between felling and inoculating, you'll have to soak the logs overnight before inoculation.

Having a quality drill (with a fresh battery) and a sharp 5⁄16-inch drill bit is essential for cultivating logs. You'll also need to have hardwood spawn plugs (wooden plugs that have been colonized by mycelium, available online), a mallet, melted wax, and, of course, the logs themselves. The standard log length for mushroom cultivation is 40 inches, and each log must be at least 3 to 6 inches in diameter.

Tips: Working on a bench where you can roll the logs is helpful, as is having a measuring stick marked at 6-inch intervals. The larger the log diameter, the more rows you'll be able to have. Be sure to use healthy, living trees for mushroom cultivation logs. Dead or dying logs will have already been colonized by other fungi, drastically reducing or preventing fruiting by your fungi.

1. **DRILL THE HOLES.** Begin your drilling pattern 2 inches from the end of the log, with holes spaced every 6 inches, ending 2 inches before the other end. Drill each hole about ½ inch below the bark; a mark on the drill bit will allow you to consistently drill to the proper depth. Drill the next row 3 inches from the initial row, but with the holes offset by about 1 inch, so that they create a diamond-shaped pattern but still maintain 6-inch spacing between holes in each row. On a 3- to 6-inch log, you'll probably average about four rows. It's a good idea to sterilize the bit with rubbing alcohol between logs to reduce the chance of pathogenic cross-contamination.

2. **TAP IN THE PLUGS.** Once your logs are drilled, tap in the plugs, making sure that they're seated at the bottom of the holes. While you're doing this, you can be warming the wax in preparation for sealing.

[Adapted from *The Woodland Homestead* by Brett McLeod]

3. **WAX THE HOLES.** Warm the wax to 150°F to 155°F/66°C to 68°C, and hold it at that temperature while you work. Dab the wax over the top of each hole, sealing it entirely. If the log you're working on has a branch wound, you can coat it with wax to prevent moisture loss. Some people also coat the ends of the log for moisture retention.

3

4. **SITE YOUR INOCULATED LOGS.** Since mushrooms love moisture, it's best if you can keep the inoculated logs in a shaded, moist area of the woodlot out of the wind. North slopes are optimal. You'll also need to water your mushrooms throughout the season. You can harvest anywhere from 6 months to 2 years after inoculation, depending on the type of mushroom and environmental conditions.

Choosing the Right Mushroom Log

Which tree species are best for cultivating mushrooms? For most mushrooms, it's more about having a proper environment than targeting a specific species. All mushrooms prefer cool, moist, well-shaded areas. Oak, maple, and beech are preferred species for inoculation logs, with aspen, birch, basswood, and alder being alternative choices.

You should always use inoculation logs that have been cut from a live tree. It's tempting to use a dead or dying tree, but chances are good that it's already inoculated with other fungi or pathogens.

It's also important that the bark is intact. This can be a challenge since the best time of the year to cut mushroom logs (spring, when the moisture and sugar content is highest) is also the time at which the bark is most prone to peeling as a result of sap flow. Carrying the logs, instead of dragging them, will go a long way toward preserving the bark.

MAKE AN
INNER TUBE
STOOL

This stool takes the cushy comfort of an inner tube and mounts it to a flat-pack melamine-board base. Held together with nylon straps, the whole thing collapses in seconds. Make a batch and keep them tucked under the couch for unexpected guests, or take them down to a sandbar in the river, cast in a line, and crack a cold one.

MATERIALS

- Two pieces of ¾" melamine board, 16" to 18" square
- Wax, paint, or polyurethane, for the finish
- One 13" ATV inner tube (or similar)
- One ¾"-wide × 96"-long nylon webbing strap

TOOLS

- Tape measure
- Square
- Circular saw (ideally with fine-tooth finish blade)
- Drill and ¾"-spade bit
- File
- Router with roundover bit (optional)
- Sandpaper, 100-grit

[Adapted from *Guerilla Furniture Design* by Will Holman]

1. Draw each half of the base onto a square of melamine board, creating a trapezoid that's 14 inches tall and tapers from 12 inches wide at the top to 16 inches at the bottom. Cut out the base pieces with a circular saw.

2. Draw a centerline, top-to-bottom, on each base piece. Measure ⅜ inch to each side and draw a line parallel to the centerline; the outer lines represent the width of the notch for assembling the base pieces. Measure 6⅝ inches down from the top of one piece (piece A) and drill a ¾-inch hole on the centerline. Measure 6⅝ inches up from the bottom on the other piece (piece B) and drill a ¾-inch hole, again on the centerline. Drill two more ¾-inch holes in each piece, 8 inches up from the bottom and centered between the centerline and the outer edges of the piece.

3. Cut just to the inside of each outer notch line, cutting down from the top of piece A to the ¾-inch hole; do the same to piece B, cutting up from the bottom. Test-fit the notches by fitting the pieces together at the notches, forming a cruciform shape when viewed from above.

4. Disassemble the base and ease the edges of the cut melamine with a file. Use a router with a roundover bit to clean up all the edges, or give them a good sanding. Thoroughly sand all the particleboard visible at the cut edges, then wax, paint, or polyurethane the exposed wood surfaces. Particleboard absorbs moisture and swells, so take care that the edges are well sealed.

5. Assemble the base. Inflate the inner tube and place on top of the assembled base. Secure the base to the inner tube by weaving the nylon strap through the holes in the melamine pieces and up around the inner tube in a figure-eight pattern, as shown below. Tighten the strap until the tube deforms just a little bit.

Piece A

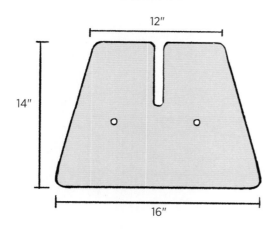

12"

14"

16"

Strapping Diagram

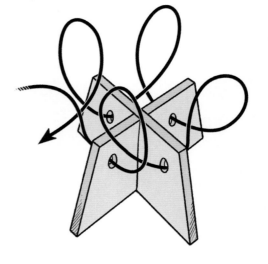

Piece B

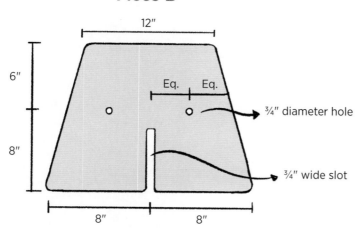

12"

6"

Eq. Eq.

¾" diameter hole

8"

¾" wide slot

8"   8"

BUILD A CLAMP TABLE

This unusual but simple table design uses no fasteners, just physics, and it packs flat in seconds. As weight is applied, each metal frame only clamps down tighter, gaining strength. When on the move, discard the boards and take only the frames. Forage fresh planks once you've arrived at your destination.

MATERIALS

- Two 10-foot lengths of Unistrut metal framing
- Twelve ¼" × 1" hex-head bolts
- Twelve ¼" nuts
- Twenty-four ¼" fender washers
- Two 48" 2×6s
- One 48" 2×4

TOOLS

- Tape measure
- Permanent marker (to mark the cuts on the Unistrut)
- Square
- Angle grinder with metal cut-off blade or metal chop saw
- Metal file
- Locking pliers
- Ratchet set

1. Cut the Unistrut into ten 18-inch lengths, taking care to make the cuts as square as possible. De-burr the cut edges with the grinder and file.

2. Using the existing holes and the ¼-inch bolts, fasten four lengths into an 18-inch square, as shown. Measure 1¾ inches down from the bottom of the top piece of Unistrut and bolt a crossbar into place, using a washer on each side. Use a set of locking pliers to hold the nut and wrench down as tightly as possible on the bolt head The clear space between the crossbar and the top of the structure is critical. If it's too tight, the frames won't cant out and clamp down on the boards; if it's too loose, the frames will cant out too much. A 1⅝- to 1¾-inch clear space is about perfect for use with standard 1½-inch-thick dimensional lumber.

3. Repeat with the other five lengths of Unistrut to make a second frame.

4. To assemble the table, stand the frames up on the floor, upside down, about 3 feet apart. Slide the two 2×6s and one 2×4 through the slot in each frame. With a helper, flip the table over. Press down in the middle of the boards until the frames tilt inward and lock into place.

5. The structure will still have some flex and a tendency to rock from side to side. To secure, tap shims or small wood wedges between the top bar of Unistrut and the boards.

Leg Elevations

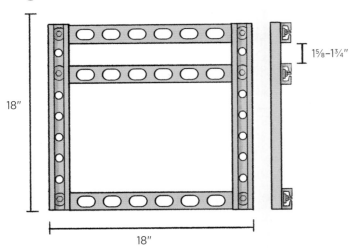

Force Diagram

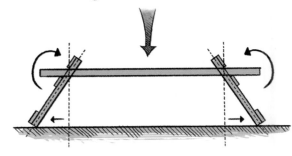

As force is applied, the bottoms of the frames slide outward, clamping the tops down tighter on the boards.

[Adapted from *Guerilla Furniture Design* by Will Holman]

IDENTIFY
AND TAP A
MAPLE TREE

Maple trees grow naturally in the forests of eastern North America, from the coastline of southeastern Canada and the northeastern United States westward through Ontario and Minnesota. To the south they can be found in Georgia, continuing as far west as eastern Kansas and Oklahoma. There are 13 native maple species in North America, all of which can be tapped, but only four of those are commonly tapped: the sugar, black, red, and silver maples, because their sap has a higher sugar content than sap from the other species.

The easiest way to identify a maple tree is by its leaves.

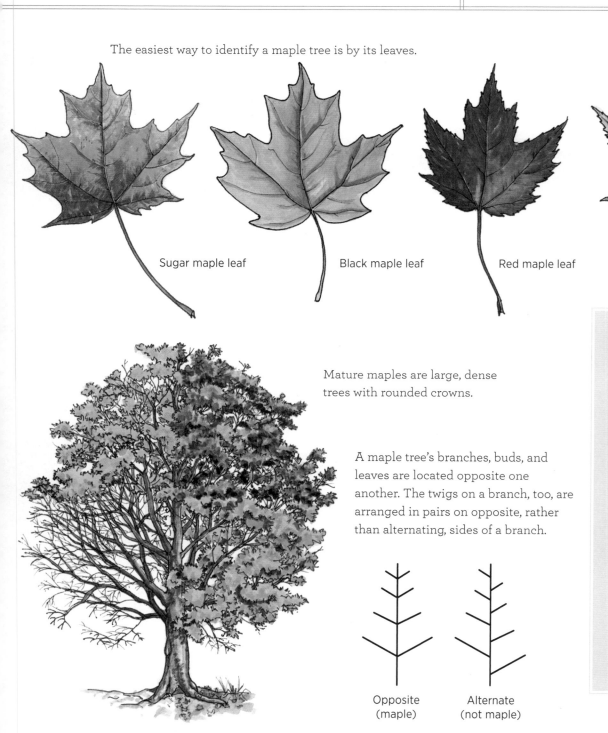

Sugar maple leaf   Black maple leaf   Red maple leaf   Silver maple leaf

Mature maples are large, dense trees with rounded crowns.

A maple tree's branches, buds, and leaves are located opposite one another. The twigs on a branch, too, are arranged in pairs on opposite, rather than alternating, sides of a branch.

Opposite (maple)   Alternate (not maple)

Tips for the New Sugarer

On average, you can get about a quart of syrup from one tapped maple tree. Tap 50 trees and you'll have roughly 12½ gallons of syrup a season. The time to tap maple trees is in late winter or early spring, when the weather is above freezing during the day and below freezing at night. Tapholes begin the process of healing as soon as they are drilled, so if you tap your trees too early, you risk missing out on sap flow later in the season. Trees to be tapped should be at least 10 inches in diameter at chest height. Watch what the experts in your area are doing and tap a "test tree" first.

[Adapted from *How to Make Maple Syrup* by Alison Anderson and Steve Anderson]

1. **PICK YOUR SPOT.** Choose a smooth spot on the tree that doesn't have any visible scarring and is at least 6 inches away, horizontally, from any old visible tapholes. Tree scarring runs mostly vertically within maple trees. You never want to tap directly above or below an old visible taphole.

Hold your drill steady and drill about 2 inches into the tree. Make sure the hole is clear of debris before pounding in your spout.

2. **DRILL AND TAP.** Using a power drill or hand bit and brace, drill a hole that is about 2 inches deep at a slightly upward angle. Place your spout in the hole, and use a hammer to gently tap it in about 1 inch deep, until it is snug. There should be about a 1-inch gap between the back of the drilled hole and the end of the spout once the spout is tapped into place. Be careful not to drive in the spout too far. This could crack the wood, and the crack could leak sap. (If you've cracked the wood, the tree will heal itself, but you'll lose sap.)

Leaving a 1-inch open space inside the taphole, between the back of the drilled hole and the end of the spout, allows for the sap to gather in the hole and create pressure for even sap flow.

3. **COLLECT SAP.** After the spout is in place, hang a bucket on it and wait for the sap to start dripping. It may not flow right away, but when the weather is just right, the sap will drip from the spout. In a season, you'll probably average 10 to 15 days of actual sap collection. On average, one taphole will yield about 1 gallon of sap a day. It takes about 40 gallons of maple sap to make 1 gallon of maple syrup.

Hang your bucket directly from the spout in the tree.

MAKE MAPLE SYRUP

Once you've brought home the sap you collected from your tapped maple trees, you're ready to make maple syrup. It takes about 40 gallons of maple sap to make 1 gallon of maple syrup. Some years all the trees yield sweeter sap than other years, and there is always variation from tree to tree. You can do the initial boil outside or you can make maple syrup entirely in your kitchen, though there are potential problems from the excess moisture — such as ice dams forming on the roof above your kitchen, wallpaper falling off walls, and mold forming on painted surfaces. Consider yourself forewarned. Good ventilation — that is, a ventilation hood over the stove — will go far to prevent problems.

1. **BEGIN THE BOIL.** Line a strainer with a coffee filter, and pour the sap through the filter into a 5-gallon stockpot until it is about three-quarters full. The coffee filter will catch any insects, bark, or other debris that has fallen into the sap bucket. Place the pot over your largest burner, bring to a boil, and maintain the boil. Alternatively, boil outdoors in a large pot, an evaporator, or a turkey fryer over a propane burner or wood fire. When the sap has reduced by about half, add more sap, but try to maintain the boil. Skim off any foam that collects on top of the boiling sap.

2. **TRANSFER TO THE FINISHING POT.** When all of the sap has been added to the large pot and it is reduced to just a few inches of boiling sap, begin monitoring the sap more closely. When the sap begins to take on a golden color, transfer it into a smaller pot.

3. **BOIL UNTIL THE SAP REACHES THE SYRUP POINT.** With the sap in a smaller pot, continue to boil the sap until it has reached the consistency of syrup. As it boils, the syrup may suddenly boil up and threaten to boil over.

You can calm the boil with a drop of fat — butter or cream is traditional, but vegetable oil can be used. Do this sparingly, since it can contribute an off-taste. As the sap comes close to the syrup point, you will begin to get larger, open bubbles. It is syrup when any or all of the following occur:

* The temperature is 7°F/4°C above the boiling point of water on a candy or instant-read thermometer. At sea level, this is usually 219°F/104°C.

* It has reached a density of 36.0 Baumé or 66.9 Brix, depending on how your hydrometer is calibrated.

Boil the filtered sap in the largest pot you own if you're boiling indoors.

Don't fill the finishing pot too full; leave room for the sap to boil up without spilling over.

The sap has become syrup when it reaches 219°F/104°C and will drop off a spoon in sheets rather than single drips.

[Adapted from *The Backyard Homestead Book of Kitchen Know-How* by Andrea Chesman]

* A spoonful dropped on a chilled plate will allow you to leave a trail if you run your finger through it.

* The syrup "aprons" off a spoon in a sheet, rather than forming individual drips.

4. **FILTER THE NITER (OR NOT) AS YOU BOTTLE.** Your syrup will contain a small amount of sediment, known as niter or sugar sand. You can filter the hot syrup through a funnel lined with a felted wool filter, or you can bottle the syrup without filtering and the niter will settle to the bottom of the jar. (Then, when you use the syrup, just don't use every last drop; discard the sediment at the bottom of the jar.) Alternatively, you can let the niter settle, pour off the syrup, again leaving the sediment behind, reheat to 180°F/82°C, and bottle the syrup hot. Don't let the syrup get hotter than 180°F/82°C, or more sediment will precipitate out.

5. **POUR THE HOT SYRUP INTO HOT, STERILIZED CANNING JARS.** Fill the jars to within ¼ inch of the top. Seal with the lids. Let cool on the counter.

6. **STORE.** Store the syrup in the refrigerator or freezer. (If you have an unheated room, you can store the syrup without refrigeration.)

5

Pour the hot syrup into the jars and seal.

MAKE EASY FRUIT WINE

Winemaking doesn't need to be complicated and intimidating, the way it is often presented. You don't need to plant a vineyard to make wines. Many ingredients can be gathered for free or easily grown in a summer garden. This simple recipe for blueberry-apple wine uses mashed and chopped fruits instead of juice and does not contain any sulfites or other preservatives. You can easily substitute other fruits for the blueberries and apples; just be sure to mash or chop them small.

MAKES 1 GALLON

INGREDIENTS

- 3 pounds apples
- 1 pound fresh blueberries
- 1 gallon water
- 2½ pounds sugar
- 1 packet wine yeast

EQUIPMENT

- Star San sanitizer
- 2-gallon fermentation bucket or crock or 1.4-gallon bubbler
- Long-handled spoon
- 2 (1-gallon) glass jugs
- Stopper with hole and solid stopper
- Airlock
- Mini auto-siphon with 3- or 4-foot siphon hose
- Funnels, pint jars, and coffee filters (optional)
- Bottle brush and brush for 1-gallon jugs
- Bottling bucket with spring-tip tube (optional)
- 5 (750 mL) wine bottles and number 8 corks
- Hand corker
- Wine bottle labels

Step 1

1. Clean your equipment. Mix a solution of ¼ ounce Star San per 1 gallon water and use it to sanitize all of your equipment. It's important that you start with clean equipment, so you don't have undesirable yeasts or bacteria ruining your wine.

2. Chop the apples, including the peels, cores, and seeds, into small pieces. Mash the blueberries. Combine the blueberry mash and the apples in the fermentation vessel.

3. Bring the water to a boil in a large pot. Add the sugar and bring back to a boil, stirring to dissolve the sugar. Add the boiling sugar water to the mixture in the fermentation vessel. Cover and let cool.

4. Stir in the yeast and cover. Stir twice a day until fermentation slows, 7 to 10 days.

5. Press out the pulp, pour the wine into your secondary fermentation jug, and secure the airlock, leaving 1 to 2 inches of space between the wine and the airlock.

6. Check the wine the next day; if there is a deep layer of lees (spent yeast), rack the wine and filter the lees through coffee filters to save more of your wine, if desired. Rack again every 2 to 3 months.

7. The wine should be ready to drink in 4 to 6 months. Let it age in the jug for as long as possible before bottling, at least 6 months to 1 year.

8. When you're ready to bottle, fill the wine bottles to just above the bottom of the neck, then cork your wine.

9. Add a nice label for a finishing touch.

Step 2

Step 3

Step 4

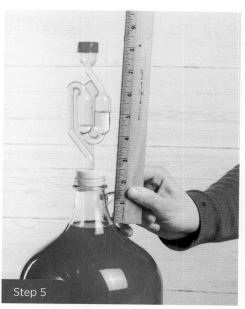

Step 5

Step 6a

Step 6b

Step 7

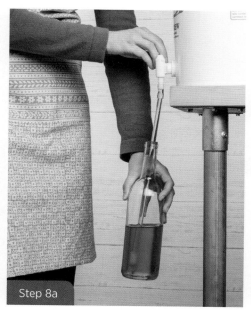

Step 8a

Step 8b

KNOW BIRDS
BY THEIR SONG

The best way to learn birdsongs is to go for a walk with someone who already knows them. But keeping them straight is another matter. To help identify and remember birdsongs, listeners have devised phrases mimicking them. These phrases are known as mnemonics — tricks designed to aid the memory.

YELLOW WARBLER: "Sweet, sweet, little more sweet"

AMERICAN GOLDFINCH: "Potato chip" (often in flight)

HERMIT THRUSH: "Why don't you come to me?"

COMMON YELLOWTHROAT: "Witchety, witchety, witchety"

INDIGO BUNTING: "Fire, fire! Where, where? Here, here."

SONG SPARROW: "Maids, maids, maids, put on the teakettle-ettle-ettle"

AMERICAN ROBIN: "Cheer up, cheerily, cheer up"

BLACK-CAPPED CHICKADEE: "Hey, sweetie" "Chickadee-dee-dee"

RED-WINGED BLACKBIRD: "Konk-la-reee"

NORTHERN CARDINAL: "Purdy, purdy, purdy"

RED-TAILED HAWK: "Ski-errr!" (often in flight)

[Adapted from *100 Skills You'll Need for the End of the World (as We Know It)* by Ana Maria Spagna]

With close observation and a little patience, it is possible to understand something of the language that birds use to communicate. The sounds they make generally fall into one of several categories: song, companion calls, territorial aggression, juvenile begging, and alarm calls.

UNDERSTAND THE LANGUAGE OF CROWS

Crows are known for their cleverness and their complex social lives. They have more than 20 distinct calls, including many variants of the familiar *caw*, differing in quality, duration, and function. Body language also plays a role in communication. Below are just a few examples.

* **A CAWING DISPLAY**, in which the calling crow partly spreads its wings, fans its tail, and swings its head down and up, may be employed during territorial defense.

* **THE ASSEMBLY CALL** is an intense and raucous series of long, drawn-out caws, summoning nearby crows to help drive off a predator (frequently a great horned owl). If you spend time observing crows, you may be able to learn how different alarm calls refer to different sources of danger.

* **A BOWING DISPLAY** is when one crow jerks its head up and down a few times and then bows, clacking its bill. Crows perform this display during courtship and other situations as well. Crows mate for life and stay bonded to their mate throughout the year. This may be why they have few courtship displays.

American crows live in extended families, defending a year-round territory in which they nest and forage. They communicate through a wide variety of calls and body postures.

[Adapted from *Into the Nest* by Laura Erickson and Marie Read]

IDENTIFY
BEEF CUTS

Beef cuts go far beyond ribeye, tenderloin, and strip. A beef side is separated into two unequal halves — the forequarter and the hindquarter. The forequarter includes the neck, shoulder, forelimb, and ribs of the animal. It contains the widest array of muscles and the greatest diversity of cuts. The hindquarter includes the lower spine, flank (or belly), and rear leg of the animal. Aside from the flank, these areas have leaner, and in many cases more tender, muscles than those in the forequarter.

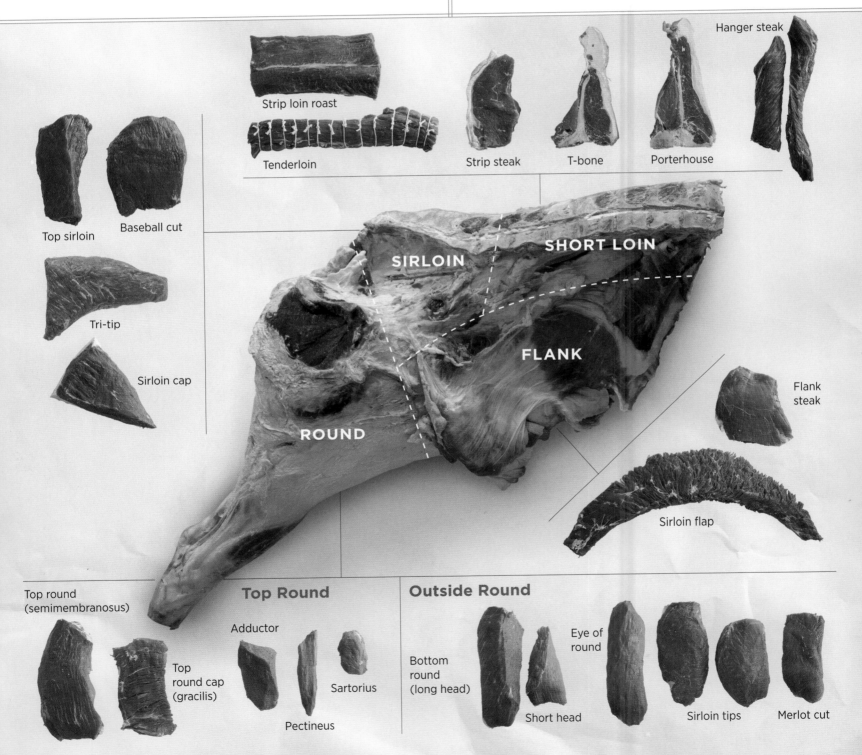

Strip loin roast

Tenderloin

Strip steak

T-bone

Porterhouse

Hanger steak

Top sirloin

Baseball cut

Tri-tip

Sirloin cap

SIRLOIN

SHORT LOIN

FLANK

ROUND

Flank steak

Sirloin flap

Top round (semimembranosus)

Top Round

Adductor

Top round cap (gracilis)

Sartorius

Pectineus

Outside Round

Bottom round (long head)

Short head

Eye of round

Sirloin tips

Merlot cut

[Adapted from *Butchering Beef* by Adam Danforth]

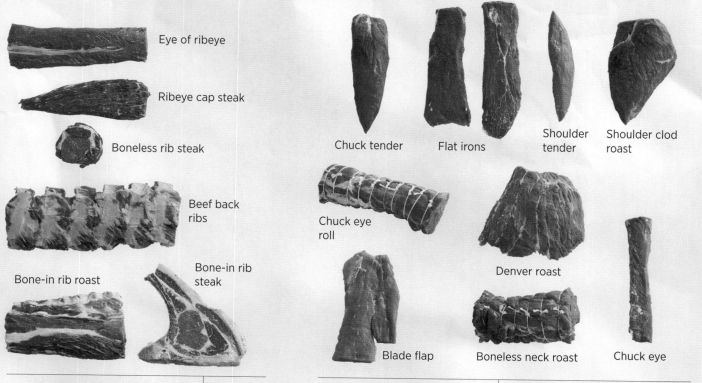

Eye of ribeye

Ribeye cap steak

Boneless rib steak

Beef back ribs

Bone-in rib roast

Bone-in rib steak

Chuck tender

Flat irons

Shoulder tender

Shoulder clod roast

Chuck eye roll

Denver roast

Blade flap

Boneless neck roast

Chuck eye

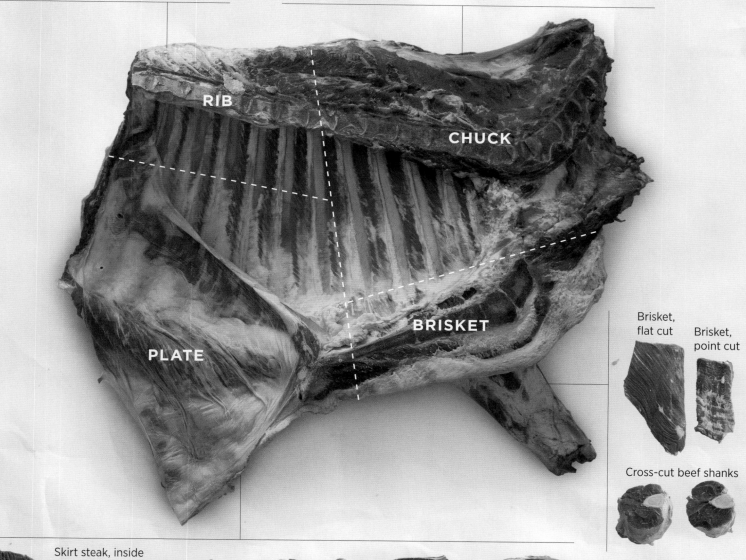

RIB

CHUCK

PLATE

BRISKET

Brisket, flat cut

Brisket, point cut

Cross-cut beef shanks

Skirt steak, inside

Skirt steak, outside

Boned navel

Short ribs

IDENTIFY PORK CUTS

The popular term *nose-to-tail* was derived from the fact that literally everything from the pig — including the viscera — can be used with delicious results, a claim rarely applied to any other animal. Here are the most common cuts of pork.

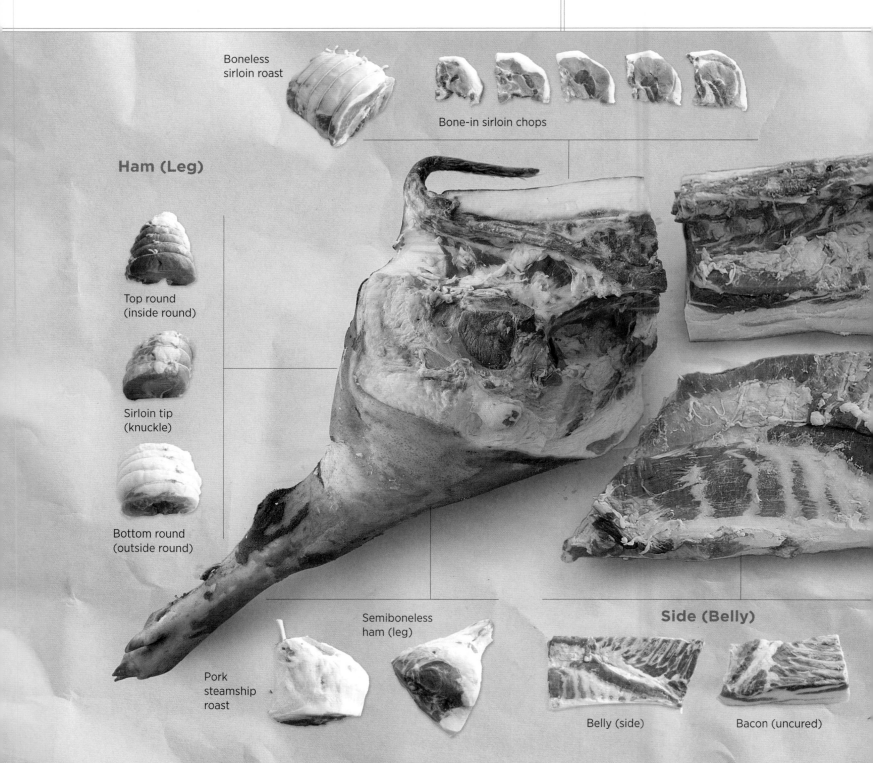

Boneless sirloin roast

Bone-in sirloin chops

Ham (Leg)

Top round (inside round)

Sirloin tip (knuckle)

Bottom round (outside round)

Pork steamship roast

Semiboneless ham (leg)

Side (Belly)

Belly (side)

Bacon (uncured)

[Adapted from *Butchering Poultry, Rabbit, Lamb, Goat, and Pork* by Adam Danforth]

Boneless
sirloin roast
(saddle end)

Tenderloin

Loin

Boston Butt

Baby back ribs

Boneless rib roast

Shoulder eye
(coppa)

Boneless
Boston butt
(shoulder)

Loin

Bone-in rib roast

Boston butt
(shoulder)

Cheeks (masseter)

Jowl

Picnic

Boneless picnic
roast (shoulder)

Spareribs (St. Louis style)

MAKE JERKY

Jerky is an ideal trail food since it's high in protein and can be eaten plain, with no additional preparation. Whole-muscle jerky is made of strips of lean meat that have been marinated in a flavorful liquid or sprinkled with a salt mixture; in some marinades, the salt comes from a condiment such as soy sauce or teriyaki sauce. One pound of raw meat will generally yield about ½ pound of jerky.

1. Choose lean cuts of beef, venison, bison, turkey, or chicken. Trim off any external fat, then freeze the meat until it's firm enough to slice easily. Slice the partially frozen meat or poultry ⅛ to 3/16 inch thick, cutting with or across the grain as you prefer (see the box on opposite page). Cut the slices into strips 1 inch wide and any length you prefer.

2. Pour a little of the marinade into a glass baking dish. Arrange a single layer of meat strips on top of the marinade, then pour a thin layer of marinade over the meat strips. Repeat with the remaining meat strips and marinade, pouring any remaining marinade over the top layer. Cover the dish and refrigerate overnight.

3. Drain the jerky, discarding the marinade. Pat the jerky lightly with paper towels. Arrange the strips on trays or racks in a single layer with a little space between the strips. Place in the dehydrator. If using an oven, place an empty baking sheet on the bottom rack to catch drips.

4. Dehydrate at 140°F/60°C until the jerky is leathery but still flexible. If the surface is oily, blot the meat with paper towels while still warm. Jerky will generally take 3 to 6 hours in a dehydrator or convection oven; jerky dried in a nonconvection oven may be done in the same range or may take close to twice as long. Store in plastic bags or glass jars and keep in the refrigerator. Eat the jerky within 6 months.

Step 1

Step 2

Step 3

Step 4

248   [Adapted from *The Beginner's Guide to Dehydrating Food* by Teresa Marrone]

How Chewy Do You Want It?

By its very nature jerky is chewy, but you can decide how much chewing you want to do. Meat that is cut with the grain before drying will be very chewy when dried because you have to bite and chew through the long muscle fibers, which have been toughened by drying. Meat that is prepared by slicing across the grain will be easier to chew when dried, but it will also be more brittle.

MAKE FRESH SAUSAGE

Making fresh sausage from scratch is simple and straightforward, as demonstrated by the following at-a-glance instruction. This 10-step process will help you visualize what's going to happen before you even get started. Seeing, as they say, is believing.

1. Prepare a natural casing by rinsing, flushing, and soaking. (Do not rinse collagen or vegetarian casings.)

2. Prepare the sausage mixture by cutting the meat (including poultry or seafood) and fat into 1-inch cubes; for vegetarian sausages, prepare all ingredients. Measure all the seasonings. Unless you're planning on using a hand grinder (see step 3), mix together the protein, fat, and seasonings.

3. Grind the meat mixture (once or twice) using your preferred method. (With a hand grinder, grind the sausage ingredients twice, adding the seasoning after the first grinding.)

4. Fry a small amount of the mixture and taste to see if you want to adjust any seasonings. (*Note:* At this point, you could wrap the sausage mixture well and use as bulk sausage.)

5. Gather the sausage casing over the stuffer tube (or nozzle) and pack the ground mixture into the canister of the stuffer until it reaches the opening of the tube. Tie the end of the casing into a knot and begin feeding small amounts of meat mixture through the tube, maintaining an even thickness and filling the entire length of casing, coiling the sausage as you go.

6. Prick any air bubbles with a sausage pricker. (*Note:* If you are making coiled sausages, you can skip steps 7 and 9.)

7. Twist off the sausage links, beginning at the tied end. Grab the desired length of sausage and give it about five twists to form a link. When the entire casing is done, tie off the other end.

8. Refrigerate the sausage overnight, or preferably for 24 hours, to meld the flavors and firm the texture; leave uncovered to allow the surface area to dry for the desired snap.

9. Using kitchen shears, cut the sausages to separate the links.

10. Cook the sausages thoroughly. Enjoy!

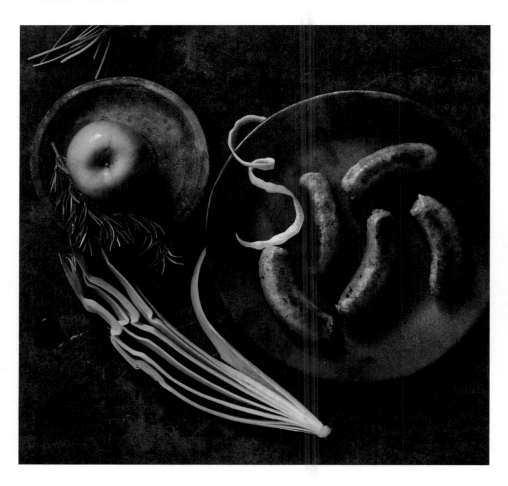

[Adapted from *Home Sausage Making* by Charles G. Reavis and Evelyn Battaglia, with Mary Reilly]

Step 1

Step 2

Step 3

Step 4

Step 5

Step 6

Step 7

Step 8

Step 9

GROW A SPROUT SALAD

Microgreens are the sprouts that first shoot up from seeds. They are packed with nutrients — most notably calcium, potassium, iron, B-complex vitamins, and vitamins A and C. They are also very easy to grow from grocery store staples, like dried peas, lentils, and beans.

1. Soak the dried seeds overnight. After they soak, they grow more quickly. While they're soaking, find something to grow them on: a pie plate or a large, low-sided container from the recycling bin.

2. Put a layer of potting soil on the plate, and sprinkle the soaked seeds thickly over the soil. (You don't even need to cover the seeds with soil.)

3. Put the plate on a sunny counter and wait a few days. If it's warm, you'll sometimes see little roots start to poke out of the seeds within a couple of days. Water the soil if it gets dry, but don't keep it constantly wet — just moist.

4. When the plants are 2 or 3 inches high, cut them off with scissors and eat them.

Lentil seeds

Lentil sprouts

Chickpea seeds

Chickpea sprouts

[Adapted from *Gardening with Emma* by Emma Biggs and Steven Biggs]

Close to 75 percent of the flowering plants on the earth rely to some degree on pollinators to set seed or fruit. You can attract pollinators by choosing diverse plantings. As few as 10 carefully chosen native species will provide a good foundation. The list below makes a good mix for pollinators because it includes a minimum of three blooming plants for each season (spring, summer, and fall) and flowers of different shapes and colors.

CREATE A
POLLINATOR-FRIENDLY
MEADOW

It is especially important to plant flowers that bloom in the very early spring. These flowers are a critical resource for early emerging bees such as bumblebee queens, mining bees, and mason bees. Large wildflower plantings should also include at least one native warm-season bunch grass or sedge adapted to the site. Among other things, they supply potential nesting sites for colonies of bumblebees.

WILDFLOWERS

* Wild lupine (*Lupinus perennis*)
* Beardtongue (*Penstemon digitalis*)
* Ohio spiderwort (*Tradescantia ohiensis*)
* Wild bergamot (*Monarda fistulosa*)
* Purple prairie clover (*Dalea purpurea*)
* Pale purple coneflower (*Echinacea pallida*)
* Culver's root (*Veronicastrum virginicum*)
* Butterfly milkweed (*Asclepias tuberosa*)
* Prairie blazing star (*Liatris pycnostachya*)
* Purple giant hyssop (*Agastache scrophulariifolia*)
* New England aster (*Symphyotrichum novae-angliae*)
* Giant sunflower (*Helianthus giganteus*)
* Showy goldenrod (*Solidago speciosa*)

BUNCH GRASSES

* Little bluestem (*Schizachyrium scoparium*)
* Prairie dropseed (*Sporobolus heterolepis*)

Culver's root
(*Veronicastrum virginicum*)

Purple prairie clover
(*Dalea purpurea*)

Butterfly milkweed
(*Asclepias tuberosa*)

Prairie blazing star
(*Liatris pycnostachya*)

[Adapted from *Attracting Native Pollinators* by The Xerces Society]

BUILD A BUTTERFLY LANDSCAPE

Butterflies have simple needs: food and water and a place to stretch their wings. Still, some details, such as site placement and plant arrangement, generally work better than others. For example, the ideal location for an effective butterfly garden is a site facing south, or whichever direction will offer maximum sun. Also, your winged visitors will appreciate groups of the same variety of plant rather than just one of a kind. Groupings offer easy-to-reach nectar all on the same level, so little energy is wasted.

[Adapted from *The Family Butterfly Book* by Rick Mikula]

Whether or not your chickens are free-range foragers, they will enjoy and benefit from a "chunnel" (chicken tunnel). Made out of 3-foot-tall 14-gauge welded-wire fencing coated in black vinyl, it's a safe and convenient device that lets them hunt for bugs, get exercise and stimulation, and explore their environs. They are safe from predators, and your garden is safe from them. You can also attach the chunnel to another enclosure to give your chickens a convenient and movable passage from one space to another.

MAKE A CHUNNEL (CHICKEN TUNNEL)

1. Using a tape measure and a pair of wire-cutting pliers, cut a section of fence wire to the desired length of your chunnel.

2. Snip off the lowest and highest horizontal strands of wire, which will leave prongs that you'll press into the ground to hold the chunnel in place. Every 12 to 18 inches, snip out a couple of vertical wires between the horizontal wires just above a prong, making a foot space where you can step on the bottom horizontal wire to easily press the prongs into the ground.

3. Bend the fence to shape it into a tunnel. Press the prongs on both sides into the ground.

4. Bend the prongs on the end(s) of the chunnel to attach them to other fencing or to other sections of chunnel.

Step 1

Step 3

Step 2

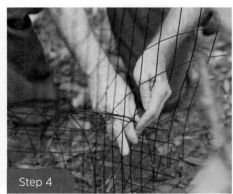

Step 4

[Adapted from *Hentopia* by Frank Hyman]

MILK A COW

It's true that most cows are milked by machine, but small dairy farmers still milk by hand. How long it takes to milk a cow will depend on a number of factors, such as the experience of the milker, the disposition of the cow, the breed, and the size of the cow's teats and orifices — first-fresheners with teeny teats are harder to milk than cows with nice, hand-size versions, and a cow of any age that has extremely small orifices takes forever to milk.

1. Lead the cow to her milking area and secure her. Walk to her side (the right side is traditional), place your milking stool and milking equipment where you want it, and sit down.

2. Wash and dry her udder using paper towels, then massage her udder for at least 30 seconds to facilitate milk letdown.

3. Squirt the first few streams of milk from each teat into your strip cup and examine it for strings, lumps, or a watery consistency that might indicate mastitis.

4. Place the milking pail slightly in front of the cow's udder, lean your head into her flank, and grasp a teat in each hand (or you may wish to grasp the teats and then lean in — any order that feels good to you is okay).

5. Trap milk in each teat by firmly wrapping your thumb and forefinger around the teat (you can feel it if milk slips back up into the udder). Don't include any of the udder itself in your grip (ow!). If the cow has large teats, grasp them close to the bottom; don't let them balloon below your hands. Squeeze with your middle finger, then your ring finger and then your pinky, in one smooth, successive motion to force milk trapped in the teat cistern into your pail (despite what cartoons would lead you to believe, never, ever pull down a cow's teats). Relax your grip to allow the cistern to refill and do it again. Alternate between teats.

6. Gently bump or massage the cow's udder to encourage additional milk letdown as the teats deflate and become increasingly flaccid. Empty each teat as well as you can, but don't finish by stripping the teats between your thumb and first two fingers; this hurts and annoys the cow.

7. When finished with the first two teats, move on to the next set.

8. When you've completely milked out all four teats, dip each teat in the teat dip, then allow the teats to dry before letting your cow to go on her merry way. Alternately, spritz the tip of each teat with an aerosol such as Fight Bac, making sure a bead of liquid forms on the end of each teat.

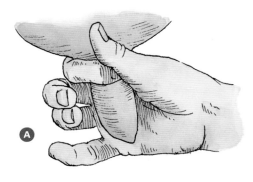

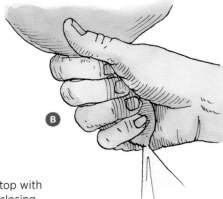

Trap milk inside the teat by firmly circling the top with your thumb and index finger (A). Empty it by closing your middle, ring, and little fingers in turn (B).

Homemade Udder Wash

Most commercial udder washes are iodine- or chlorhexidine-based, and they work very well. If, however, you're a do-it-yourself kind of milker, here is a good udder wash you can make at home.

* 40 drops lavender essential oil
* 16 ounces apple cider vinegar
* 16 ounces water

Combine in a large container and shake well before using. Keep covered between uses.

[Adapted from *The Backyard Cow* by Sue Weaver]

Homemade cream cheese is creamier and more delicious than store-bought, plus it's easy to make! If you make it before you go to bed, it will have plenty of time to set while you sleep. When you wake up, set it up to drain so you can enjoy a delicious afternoon snack. You'll need a dairy thermometer and butter muslin for this recipe.

MAKE CREAM CHEESE

MAKES ABOUT 1½ POUNDS

INGREDIENTS

- 1 gallon whole milk (not ultra-pasteurized)
- 1 pint heavy cream (ultra-pasteurized is fine)
- 1 packet buttermilk culture or ¼ cup cultured buttermilk
- 8 drops single-strength liquid rennet mixed into ¼ cup cool, unchlorinated water

1. Pour the milk and heavy cream into a 5- to 6-quart pot and heat over medium heat to 86°F/30°C.

2. At 86°F/30°C, add the buttermilk culture, and stir slowly for 2 minutes.

3. Add the rennet mixture by pouring it through a slotted spoon while moving the spoon over the pot. Stir gently for 1 minute, moving the spoon from the top to the bottom of the pot.

4. Cover the pot, wrap it with a towel, and let it sit undisturbed on the counter for 8 to 14 hours.

5. Put a colander on a baking sheet or in a bowl. Line the colander with butter muslin, letting the cloth hang over the sides.

6. When the curd (the coagulated milk mixture) has developed a few cracks and is pulling away from the sides, gently ladle it into the lined colander. Fold the ends of the cloth over the curds and let them drain in the fridge for 7 to 14 hours, or until they reach the desired consistency. Store in a covered container in the refrigerator for up to 2 weeks.

Step 3

Step 6

[Adapted from *Say Cheese!* by Ricki Carroll and Sarah Carroll]

MAKE BUTTER

Homemade butter is a rare treat, but making it is a great way to discover the magical properties of milk, and there's nothing that compares to its fresh taste and silky smooth texture. The principle is really quite simple: just agitate cream long enough and it will turn into butter! For best results, the cream should be at about 60°F/16°C when you begin. If it's too warm, your butter will be soft and won't keep well; if it's too cold, your butter will never form.

MAKES ABOUT 2 CUPS

INGREDIENTS

4 cups (2 pints) heavy cream

½ teaspoon salt

1. In a food processor fitted with the metal blade, process the cream until it turns to fine solid pieces about the size of rice grains. It will go through several stages to get to this point, from frothy to soft whipped cream to coarse whipped cream to solid bits, and the color will change from off-white to pale yellow. This will take from 5 to 8 minutes.

2. Let the butter stand for about 5 minutes. The liquid, called buttermilk, will separate from the butter during this time. Set a fine-meshed sieve over a medium bowl. Scrape the butter mixture into the strainer and let the buttermilk drain. Strain the buttermilk again through a fine-meshed sieve, and save for another use if desired.

3. Transfer the buter to a colander and knead it with a wooden spoon, potato masher, or two forks to remove excess water and blend the granules. Pour off the water occasionally, and continue kneading until most of the water has been removed and the butter becomes firmer. This will take about 10 minutes. Mix in the salt; this will help retard spoilage as well as add flavor. Keep working until the butter is dense and creamy and all liquid has been worked out, about another 10 minutes.

4. You can form the butter into any shape you wish at this stage; you might make a simple block or press it into ramekins or molds. When you're done, wrap the butter in wax paper. It will last for several weeks in the fridge or up to 9 months in the freezer.

Drain the butter through a fine-meshed sieve to separate the buttermilk.

Butter Variations

Besides cow's milk, butter can also be produced from the milk of buffalo, camel, goat, sheep, and horse. Sometimes cultures are added to ferment the milk sugars to lactic acid before the milk is churned into butter. These cultures will produce butter that is rich with a fuller, slightly tangy flavor. An easier way to produce a butter with a more complex flavor is to use slightly ripened cream. To ripen cream, simply leave it at room temperature for 12 to 24 hours, or until it starts to look shiny and tastes a bit acidic. Do not let it sit out for longer than 24 hours, or it will become sour-tasting.

[Adapted from *The Home Creamery* by Kathy Farrell-Kingsley]

CROCHET
A PAIR OF
EARRINGS

If you are already familiar with crochet, here's a quick project that yields amazing results — thread crochet over purchased 2-inch hoops. You can make a pair for every color in your wardrobe.

YARN

- Cotton crochet thread size 10

CROCHET HOOK

- Steel US 6 (1.6 mm) or the size you need to obtain the correct gauge

MOTIF GAUGE

- 1¾" in diameter before joining to hoop

OTHER SUPPLIES

- 2" hoop earrings (a front hinge works best)
- Embroidery needle

Pattern Essentials

Puff st (Yo, insert hook into indicated ch-1 space, yo, pull loop through to front of work) five times, yo and pull through all but 1 loop on hook, yo and pull through remaining 2 loops on hook. *Note:* If you have trouble pulling through the puff stitches, make your yarn overs looser by holding your hook a little farther away from the work.

Working into the back of the chain: With the WS of the chain facing, insert hook into the bumps on the back of of the chain. *Note:* The RS of the chain is a series of horizontal Vs.

CROCHETING THE MOTIF

Row 1 (WS): Ch 16; working into the back of the ch, hdc in the 3rd ch from hook (first 2 ch sts count as first hdc), hdc in each ch across, turn. You now have 15 sts.

Row 2 (RS): Ch 5, skip first 7 hdc, (tr, ch 5, tr) in next hdc, ch 5, skip next 6 hdc, slip st into top of ch-2 at end of row, turn.

Row 3 (WS): Ch 4, skip ch-5 space, dc in next tr, ch 1, (dc into next ch, ch 1) five times, dc in next tr, ch 4, slip st in ch st at end of row, turn.

Row 4 (RS): Ch 4, skip (ch-space, dc), (puff st in next space, picot-4) six times, ch 4, slip st ch st at end of row. *Do not fasten off.*

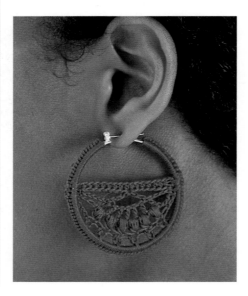

ATTACHING THE MOTIF TO THE HOOP

Place the motif inside the hoop with the working yarn coming out from the back of the hoop. Sc around hoop and motif to join them together as follows: With RS of motif facing, work 3 sc sts into the side of the motif working toward the top of the hoop; work 15 sc sts around hoop, ending at the top of the earring; fasten off.

Starting at top (on other side of hinged post), work 15 sc sts around hoop. Now make 3 sc sts into the other side of motif, work 10 sc around hoop, sc in next picot, (work 5 sc around hoop, sc into next picot) five times, work 10 sc around hoop, slip st to first sc around hoop to join. Fasten off. Weave in the ends.

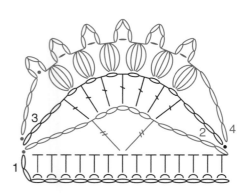

[Adapted from *Crochet One-Skein Wonders*® edited by Judith Durant and Edie Eckman]

Crocheting with your fingers instead of a hook is a good method to start with because it introduces you to the basic process in a simple way. Try finger crocheting shoelaces, a bracelet, or a hair tie. Or tie a length of it into a bow to pretty up a gift! These instructions teach you how to make a finger-crocheted chain, but if you like the process, keep experimenting; you can also make more complicated crochet stitches — and projects — using just your fingers.

FINGER CROCHET

1. Make a slip knot at the end of the yarn, leaving a 6-inch tail.

2. Push your right index finger into the loop formed by the slip knot. Tighten it slightly, but leave enough room to reach your right thumb through as well. Hold the working yarn in your left hand.

3. With your right thumb and index finger, reach through the loop, grab the working yarn, and bring it through the original loop to create a new loop.

4. Adjust the tightness of the chain by gently pulling the new loop and tail in opposite directions.

5. Repeat steps 3 and 4 until the chain is as long as you like, and then snip the yarn, leaving a 6-inch tail. Thread the tail through the last loop and pull it tight.

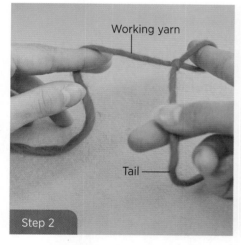
Working yarn
Tail
Step 2

Step 3a

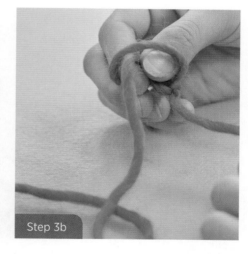
Step 3b

Step 4

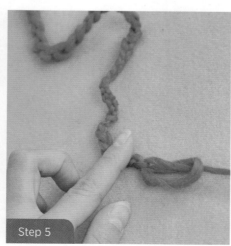
Step 5

[Adapted from *Stitch Camp* by Nicole Blum and Catherine Newman]

SET UP A LOBSTER-CLAMBAKE

Clambakes are primal rituals in New England, big boisterous affairs, usually held in high summer. Like a tailgate picnic, they are best done with a group, for they take a lot of time, but lots of helping hands add to the fun. The hardest part is collecting wet seaweed. It is so worth it — don't be deterred. Look at the tides, and make sure you build your bake at the high-water mark, as you'll need about 7 hours from start to the time you eat. Then, enjoy your feast made even better by your toils!

SERVES 8 TO 10

FOR THE FEAST

- 8 pounds steamers (soft-shell clams), soaked in seawater for several hours
- 10 ears unhusked corn, soaked in seawater for several hours
- 6 medium onions, loose skin removed, with an X cut in the root ends
- 8–10 large potatoes, scrubbed
- 3 pounds spicy sausage (linguica, chorizo, andouille, kielbasa)
- 8–10 lobsters, kept alive under wet seaweed
- 3 sticks unsalted butter

FOR THE FIRE

- Canvas tarp (at least 5 feet square when doubled over)
- Trash can or other container large enough to hold the canvas covered in seawater
- Shovels for digging (the more the merrier)
- Buckets for collecting seaweed
- Seaweed (lots of it!)
- Large stones that haven't been heated before
- Firewood
- Several yards of cheesecloth or wire baskets to hold the clams, corn, onions, potatoes, and sausage
- Iron rake, pitchfork, or boat hook
- Heavy pan or saucepan with lid, for melting the butter

[Adapted from *Fresh Fish* by Jennifer Trainer Thompson]

1. Divide and conquer! Put the canvas in the trash can, cover with seawater, and leave it to soak. Set a group to digging a big hole in the sand near the high-water mark, 2 feet deep by 4 feet wide. Send another crew out to collect enough seaweed to make three heavy layers over the fire. Dried seaweed can be added to the trash can to revive it.

2. Line the bottom and sides of the hole with beach stones the size of footballs.

3. Light a big hardwood fire in the pit and let it burn down.

4. Place more stones on the fire, making sure you don't smother it. Build another fire on top of the second layer of rocks and let it burn down.

5. Place the clams, corn, onions, potatoes, and sausage in wire baskets or tie each up in several layers of cheesecloth. Dampen the cheesecloth with seawater so it doesn't catch on fire. You're now ready to cook.

6. Working quickly, rake the embers away from the rocks, then throw a full 6 inches of wet seaweed over the rocks.

7. Put the potatoes, onions, and sausage on the seaweed and cover them with more wet seaweed. Add the lobsters, corn, and clams. Cover with a final layer of wet seaweed.

8. Cover the mound with the wet canvas.

Continued on next page

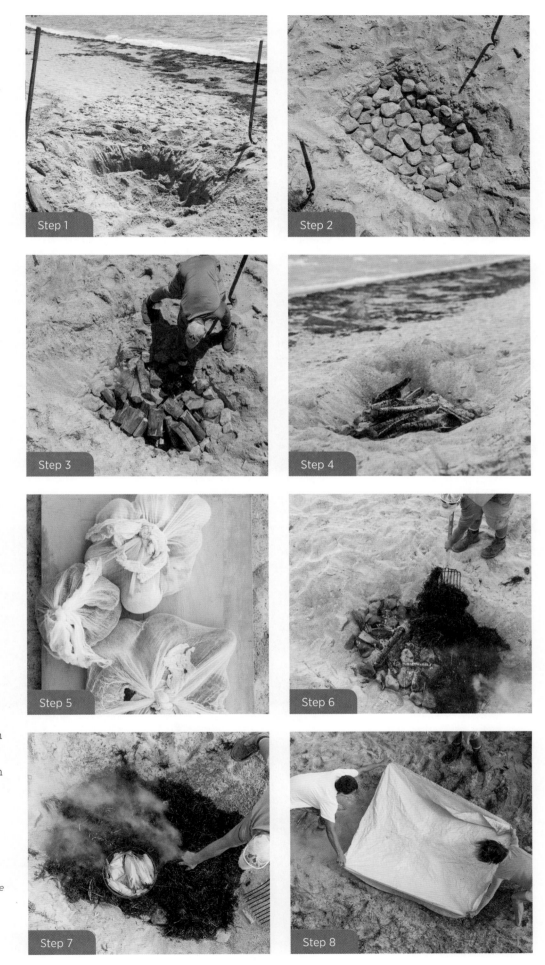

Step 1

Step 2

Step 3

Step 4

Step 5

Step 6

Step 7

Step 8

9. Seal the edges with sand and more seaweed so steam can't escape. Cook for 1½ hours, occasionally dousing the canvas with water. In the last 30 minutes or so, set the butter in a covered pan near the fire to melt.

10. When it's time to eat, dig the sand and seaweed away from the pit.

11. Carefully lift the corners of the canvas and peel it back, making sure sand doesn't get on the food.

12. Rake away the layers of seaweed, lifting out the food as it's exposed. Serve immediately with melted butter.

Step 9

Step 10

Step 11

Step 12

EAT A LOBSTER

Eating a lobster can be a messy (though delicious) ordeal. And to the uninitiated, this strange-looking crustacean can seem intimidating, but it's really quite easy once you get the hang of it. Here's the best way to get the most out of your lobster.

1. Twist off the two large claws where they meet the body. Separate the pincer from the knuckles. Using a nutcracker, crack the claws and the knuckles. The claw meat is easy to get at; sometimes you have to poke out the knuckle meat with a lobster pick or your little finger.

2. For the tail, grasp the lobster with one hand on the body and one hand on the tail and twist to break in two. Expect a gush of liquid on your plate, which you can drain into the shell debris bowl on the table. Remove the flippers at the end and pull each one through your teeth like an artichoke leaf.

3. Then, if the tail hasn't been split, poke the tail meat out with a fork (if the lobster is hard-shell). Split the tail meat lengthwise, and remove and discard the black vein running down the center. Dip the meat into melted butter and eat.

4. Tucked away deep in the body is the soft green tomalley (sometimes referred to as the liver), and, if the lobster is female, the bright pink roe, or coral, reached by separating the shell of the body from the underside. Some consider these morsels, the rich-tasting tomalley in particular, to be the most prized lobster parts of all.

5. For the persistent person, there are still the small legs, again best eaten by pulling them through your teeth to extract the meat. There are also small nuggets of meat in the joints where the legs meet the body.

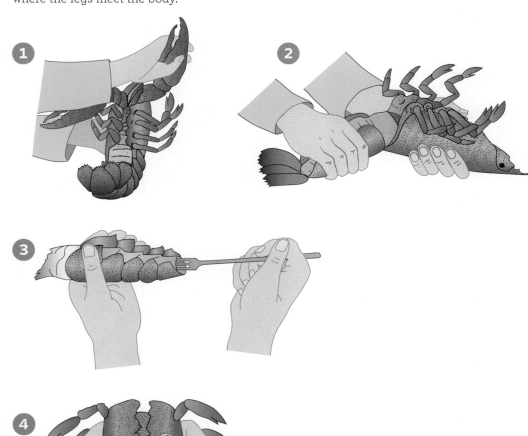

[Adapted from *The New England Clam Shack Cookbook* by Brooke Dojny]

REMOVE A LIMB FROM A LIVING TREE

When removing a branch at the trunk of a tree, make the proper cuts so the health of the tree doesn't suffer. To speed healing, cut just outside the branch collar — the bark swelling at the base of the branch, where it meets the trunk. A cut that is flush to the trunk will callus over more slowly than a cut where the collar is left intact, and it will leave the tree open to infection by wood rot organisms and cankers. Do not apply tree wound dressing to cuts. Such materials can actually slow the development of new bark across wounds.

1. Make your first cut only partway through the branch. Make it on the underside of the branch, about 6 to 12 inches away from the trunk.

2. Cut the branch off outside the first cut.

3. Cut off the branch stub just outside the collar (the swelling) at the base of the branch.

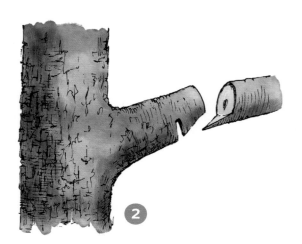

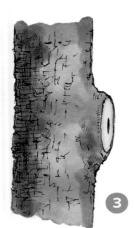

Typical Pruning Tools

The right tools make pruning go faster and produce the best results. Avoid the temptation to buy cheap pruners and saws; they often produce inferior results and make pruning more difficult. Tools that are well designed and constructed will last for many years. Here are some good tools to have on hand.

Bypass hand pruners let you cut off small stems close to the trunk.

Loppers are good for large cuts (up to 1½ inches in diameter)

A folding pruning saw is convenient to carry when pruning many trees.

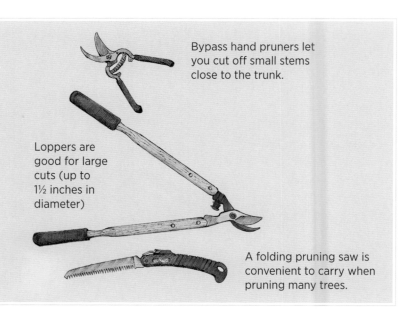

[Adapted from *Storey's Guide to Growing Organic Orchard Fruits* by Danny L. Barney]

A chainsaw chain should be touched up before each use. This can be done at home with a jig made especially for this purpose. Nonetheless, sharpening a chain is tricky and exacting enough that after every five touch-ups or so, it should be done by a professional. The reason is that even with a little jig at home, it is difficult to file down the cutting teeth and depth gauges evenly all the way along the chain.

SHARPEN A CHAINSAW

▲ A good jig costs about the same as a sharpening in a shop, and in 5 minutes you can have a chain that really rips every day.

Cutting edge

▲ The highlighted edges of the cutting teeth shown above are the surfaces that actually bite into the wood — the edges that need sharpening.

▲ The two flat bars on the outside of the jig guide the file and maintain a proper angle during sharpening. The part of the jig that does the actual sharpening is a rounded file that fits into the groove of the cutting tooth.

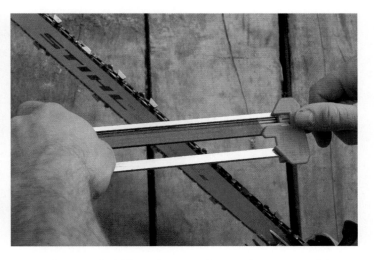

▲ For the rounded file to fit properly into the groove of the cutting tooth, the jig should be held at a 45-degree angle to the chain.

[Adapted from *The Backyard Lumberjack* by Frank Philbrick and Stephen Philbrick]

GO OWLING

You can find owls in just about every habitat, from tropical forest to arctic tundra. Why not start looking for the owls most likely to be living near you? The best time to search for owls is on a calm night with clear or mostly clear skies and some moonlight. Owls are most active during the beginning of mating season. In most of North America this occurs in springtime, while in tropical regions this happens at the end of the dry season.

BARN OWL

Lives in farm buildings, in open fields, along rivers bordering open meadows or fields, in suburbs and towns, and in deserts.

BARRED OWL

Lives in groves of evergreen trees. If disturbed will fly only a few yards to another tree.

NORTHERN SAW-WHET OWL

Lives in dark stands of conifers or thick mixed forests. Roosts in dense evergreen thickets on winter days.

[Adapted from *Raptor!* by Christyna M. Laubach, René Laubach, and Charles W. G. Smith]

EASTERN AND WESTERN SCREECH OWLS

Live in evergreen, mixed, and deciduous forests and along forest edges. In winter they sun themselves by poking their heads out of tree holes.

Eastern
Screech Owl

Western
Screech Owl

GREAT HORNED OWL

Lives in many different types of habitat, such as in forests and woodlands, along rivers, near open fields and meadows, and in both rural and suburban areas.

Learn to Speak "Owl"

The best way to learn to talk with an owl is to imitate the call you hear at night. You can try to attract the birds by calling to them.

GREAT HORNED OWL: "Hoo hoo-hoo, hoo, hoo!" (Sounds like "Who's awake? Me, too!")

BARRED OWL: "Hoo-hoo hoo-hoo, hoo-hoo hoo-hoo-ahh" (Sounds like "Who cooks for you? Who cooks for you all?")

EASTERN SCREECH OWL: A whinny or wail, rising and falling in pitch

ADJUST BINOCULARS TO AVOID EYE STRAIN

Before you try to see birds through your binoculars, you need to make a few adjustments. Virtually all binoculars have several helpful features that allow them to be tailored to different users. Extend the eyecups if you don't wear eyeglasses. Retract the eyecups if you do wear eyeglasses. Next, set the barrels of the binoculars to match the distance between your eyes so that you have a solid image when looking through both eyes.

Virtually all binoculars have center focusing, in which a single knob or lever controls the focus for both eyepieces simultaneously. Our eyes are seldom precisely matched, so to accommodate the difference between our two eyes, binoculars also have a diopter adjustment near the optical lens on one side or the other, or as part of the center focus knob. Diopter adjustments are normally numbered from +2 to -2.

Here's how to adjust your binoculars so you can use them without eyestrain:

1. Find the diopter adjustment and set it at zero.

2. Find an object a good distance away that has clean lines. A sign or something else with letters or numbers is a good choice.

3. Cover the objective lens (the large outside lens) with the lens cap or your hand on the side controlled by the diopter adjustment, and then focus on the sign using the center focus knob. Try to keep both eyes open as you do this.

4. Switch hands, uncovering the lens with the diopter adjustment and covering the other lens. Focus again, this time using the diopter adjustment, not the center focus.

5. Repeat each adjustment a couple of times. After you're done, your sign should be crisply focused through both eyes.

6. Notice the number setting on the diopter adjustment. Sometimes, even during normal use, the adjustment knob may get shifted, so every now and then check to make sure it's set where it should be for your eyes.

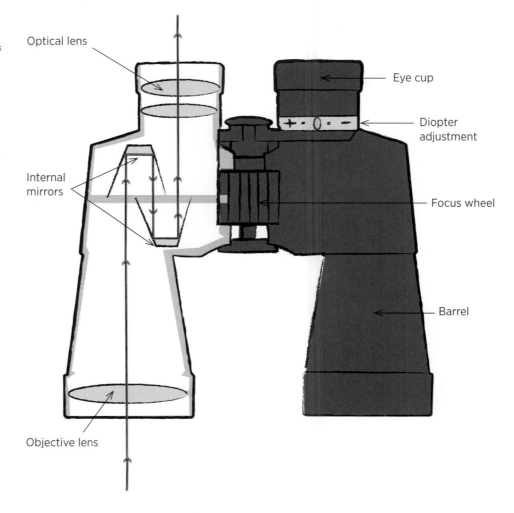

Optical lens

Eye cup

Diopter adjustment

Internal mirrors

Focus wheel

Barrel

Objective lens

[Adapted from *The Bird Watching Answer Book* by Laura Erickson]

A handmade wreath makes a beautiful, low-cost decoration or gift at the holidays. You'll need greens, of course, as well as a wreath ring, lightweight 24-gauge green winding wire, and heavy string or baler twine to tie up the bundles. If you decorate wreaths, you will need supplies like ribbons, cones, wire picks, and berries.

MAKE A
WREATH

1. Wind a few twists of wire around the ring to fasten it securely.

2. Place a bunch of two to four tips of greens on one side of the ring and wire the base of the bunch to the ring with two or three tight wrap-arounds. Select some good bushy greens for this first bunch, because it must hide the base of the last bunch you'll insert. If you are making a double-faced wreath, flip the ring over and wrap a similar bunch onto the back side. Place it almost, but not quite, opposite the first one.

3. Lay another bunch of greens over the base of the first, hiding the wire, and wire this one to the ring. Continue in this fashion, moving around the ring and placing all the greens on one side if it is a single-faced wreath or flipping it for each bunch if it is a double.

4. When you reach the spot where you began, tuck the base of the last bunch underneath the tops of the first that you wired. Wire it in carefully, so neither the stems nor the wire show.

5. Cut or break the wire and fasten it tightly with several twists to one of the wires or to the ring itself.

shears

ring

wire

greens

2

3

4

[Adapted from *Growing Christmas Trees* by Patrick White and Lewis Hill]

CHANGE A FLAT CAR TIRE

If you find yourself driving down the road with a flat tire, pull over and activate your hazard lights so that oncoming traffic will recognize that your car is disabled. Then follow this simple procedure.

1. **SET OUT YOUR WARNINGS.** Set out at least three reflectors or flares. Place one about ten car-lengths behind your car. Place the other reflectors or flares between that flare and your car. If you do not have reflectors or flares, prop open the hood of your car.

2. **SECURE THE THREE TIRES** that are not flat by wedging a block of wood or a rock in front of and behind each wheel.

3. **REMOVE THE HUBCAP.** Using a flathead screwdriver, pry loose the hubcap of the flat tire. Place it near you, upside down.

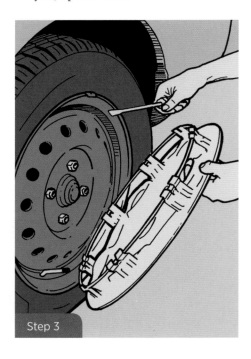
Step 3

4. **LOOSEN THE LUG NUTS.** Using a lug wrench, loosen the wheel's lug nuts by turning them counterclockwise. Move from one lug nut to the other in a crisscross pattern. You'll need to apply some real muscle to this task. Do not fully remove the lug nuts; just get them loose enough that you can remove them by hand once your car has been jacked up.

5. **POSITION THE JACK.** Position the jack under the car, following the instructions in your owner's manual. Most cars have a small notch under their frame that marks the spot where the jack should be positioned. Place the jack exactly as directed.

6. **JACK UP THE CAR.** Using solid, even strokes on the jack, raise your car until the flat tire is suspended. Keeping your feet away from the car, wiggle the jack and its stand to make sure that it and your car are secure. Walk around your car and double-check the wood blocks or rocks. They should be firmly secured against the other three tires.

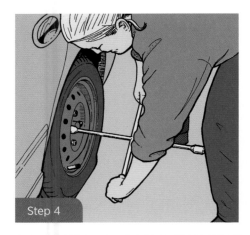
Step 4

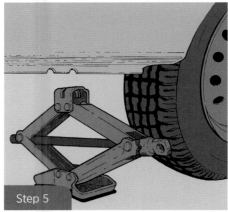
Step 5

Step 6

[Adapted from *Every Woman's Quick & Easy Car Care* by Bridget Kachur]

7. **REMOVE THE WHEEL LUG NUTS.** Remove the lug nuts by hand in a crisscross pattern. Set the lugs in the upside-down hubcap.

8. **REMOVE THE FLAT TIRE.** Crouch or sit so that your chest is even with the sidewall of the tire. Using both hands, wiggle the tire loose from the bolts. Roll the tire to the rear of your car.

9. **INSTALL THE SPARE TIRE.** Roll the spare tire into position. Lift it up, align its notches with the bolts on the wheel rim, and wedge it into place.

10. **REPLACE THE LUG NUTS.** Replace each lug nut, hand-tightening them clockwise and in the crisscross pattern. When all the lugs are hand-tightened, grab the lug wrench and tighten them further, using the same crisscross pattern. When the tire starts to rotate, you've tightened the lug nuts as much as you should.

11. **LOWER THE CAR.** Using solid, even strokes, lower the jack until all four tires are flat on the ground. Remove the jack stand from beneath your car.

12. **TIGHTEN THE LUG NUTS AGAIN.** Using the lug wrench, tighten the lug nuts as much as you can, using the crisscross pattern. If the lugs aren't tight, the tire will wobble.

13. **REPLACE THE HUBCAP.** Hold the hubcap in place with one hand in the middle and tap around the outside of the hubcap with a rag-covered hammer. Don't pound too hard; you might dent the hubcap.

14. **CLEAN UP.** Set the flat tire and all the tools and supplies back inside the vehicle.

Step 9

Step 10

Step 12

MAKE BIODIESEL

Biodiesel is vegetable oil that has been chemically modified to remove the heavy glycerin portion of the oil. Biodiesel can be used in place of diesel fuel, home heating oil, and kerosene for use in diesel engines and oil-fired heating equipment. This is the basic process by which it is made, though you'll need to consult other sources if you intend to give it a try.

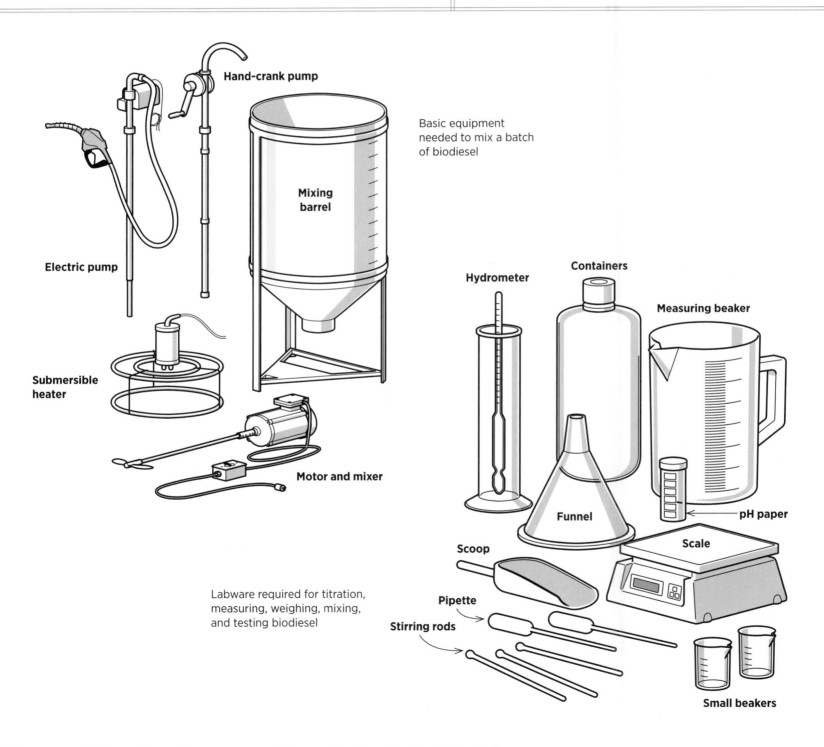

Hand-crank pump

Basic equipment needed to mix a batch of biodiesel

Mixing barrel

Electric pump

Submersible heater

Motor and mixer

Hydrometer

Containers

Measuring beaker

Funnel

pH paper

Scoop

Scale

Pipette

Stirring rods

Labware required for titration, measuring, weighing, mixing, and testing biodiesel

Small beakers

[Adapted from *The Homeowner's Energy Handbook* by Paul Scheckel]

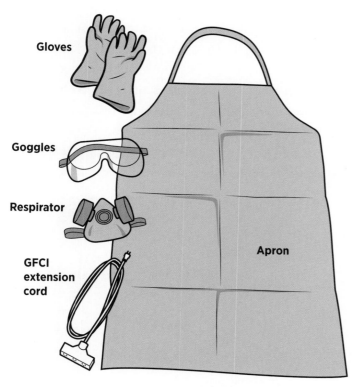

Gloves

Goggles

Respirator

GFCI
extension
cord

Apron

Safety equipment

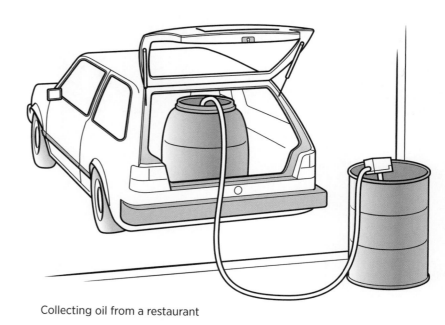

Collecting oil from a restaurant

1. Gather your oil. If using waste oil, strain it to remove bits of food and other debris. Try not to use oil that has been burned or has gone rancid. Do not attempt to use oil that has any water in it — it will ruin the entire batch.

2. Perform a titration if you are using waste fryer oil to determine how much lye to use for a complete reaction.

3. Mix methanol with the correct amount of lye for about 15 minutes to form sodium methoxide. This is an exothermic chemical reaction, meaning heat will be created.

4. Heat the oil to 120°F/49°C. While you can have a successful reaction at temperatures of about 70°F/21°C,

the mixing time will be longer and you may end up with more unreacted by-products, along with lower-quality biodiesel.

5. Add the vegetable oil to the sodium methoxide mixture, and mix for about 1 hour. Avoid splashing the methoxide.

6. After mixing, allow the glycerin to settle to the bottom of the mixing tank (this should take 4 to 8 hours).

7. Pump or drain the glycerin into a waste container after it has settled. If you wait longer than 12 hours, the glycerin will begin to solidify and cleanup will be more difficult because the glycerin will be too thick to be pumped.

8. Pump the biodiesel immediately into a holding tank and let it settle for a week or so, during which time excess methanol will evaporate and smaller particles will fall to the bottom. If necessary, you can "wash" the biodiesel before storing it by mixing it with water to remove impurities. If you're making large amounts of biodiesel, it's a good idea to recapture the methanol by boiling it off the biodiesel and capturing it through distillation for reuse.

JUMP-START A
CAR BATTERY

If your car battery dies, jump-starting it with another car's battery can be quite simple. Before you start, consult the owner's manuals for both cars to be sure that neither recommends against jump-starting. Then have the driver of a "live" vehicle move their car as close to the "dead" car as possible, but make sure the two vehicles do not touch. Before connecting the jumper cables, examine them to make sure no wiring is exposed.

1. **PREPARE THE CARS.** Turn off all electrical accessories in both vehicles. In cars with an automatic transmission, shift into Park; in cars with manual transmissions, shift into Neutral. Set the parking brakes. Turn the ignition key in both cars to the "off" position. (If the live battery has sufficient juice, the live vehicle doesn't need to be running to jump-start the discharged battery.)

2. **ATTACH THE POSITIVE CABLE.** Hook the clamp of the positive (red) booster cable to the positive post on the discharged battery. Then hook the other end of the positive booster cable to the positive post on the live battery.

3. **ATTACH THE NEGATIVE CABLE.** Hook the clamp of the negative (black) booster cable to the negative post in the live battery. Then hook the other end of the negative booster cable to an unpainted metal part of the car. *Do not attach the negative cable to the discharged battery.* Place this clamp as far from the battery as possible.

4. **START UP.** After a couple of minutes, turn the ignition key in the dead car. If it starts up, leave it running and move on to the next step. If it doesn't start up, turn the ignition key back to the "off" position and leave the booster cables where they are. Try again in a few minutes.

5. **DISCONNECT THE NEGATIVE CABLE.** Remove the negative (black) booster cable from the formerly dead car. Then remove the negative cable from the live car.

6. **DISCONNECT THE POSITIVE CABLE.** Remove the positive (red) booster cable from the live car. Then remove the positive cable from the formerly dead car.

7. **LET THE CAR RUN.** Let the engine in the car that has been jump-started run for at least 15 minutes, either idling or as you drive. Running the engine recharges the battery.

To jump-start a battery, connect the booster cables in the order shown. When the battery is up and running, remove the cables in the reverse sequence.

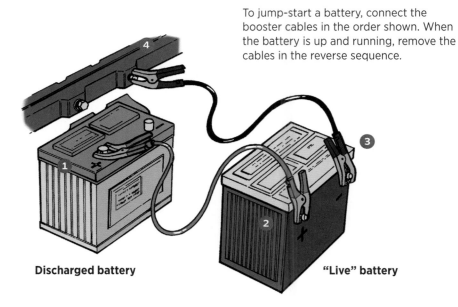

Discharged battery   "Live" battery

[Adapted from *Every Woman's Quick & Easy Car Care* by Bridget Kachur]

Here's a variation of a "candy" that's good for you! This combination of herbs is particularly formulated to give you sustained energy, not from stimulants but from nutrient-dense herbs that nourish and support endocrine gland function.

MAKE HERBAL ENERGY BALLS

INGREDIENTS

- 2 cups nut butter, such as cashew, almond, or peanut
- 2 cups tahini (drain any excess oil from the top)
- 1½ cups honey (or more or less according to your taste)
- 2 ounces maca powder
- 1 ounce ashwagandha powder
- 1 ounce eleuthero powder
- 1 ounce rhodiola powder
- 1 cup finely chopped walnuts or almonds
- 8 ounces unsweetened shredded coconut, lightly toasted
- 1 (12-ounce) package bittersweet chocolate chips
- ½ cup dried cranberries, raisins, or goji berries
- Unsweetened cocoa powder, to thicken
- Unsweetened cocoa powder, unsweetened coconut flakes, or melted chocolate, for coating the balls

1. Combine the nut butter, tahini, and honey in a large bowl and mix until smooth. Stir the herbal powders together in a separate bowl, then add them to the nut butter mixture and mix well. Add the chopped nuts, coconut, chocolate chips, and dried cranberries, and mix well; you may need to use your hands. Work in enough unsweetened cocoa powder to thicken the mixture to a dough-like consistency.

2. Roll the dough into walnut-sized balls.

3. Finish the balls with a coating of your choice: shake them in a baggie filled with cocoa powder or coconut, or dip them into melted chocolate. Store the balls in an airtight container lined with wax paper in a cool spot, where they will keep for several weeks.

TO USE: The suggested dosage is two balls a day.

Step 1

Step 2

Step 3

[Adapted from *Rosemary Gladstar's Herbal Healing for Men* by Rosemary Gladstar]

MAKE NO-KNEAD SOURDOUGH BREAD

Sourdough can be intimidating, but it needn't be. This no-knead recipe is simple — just throw the dough together and wait, then cook in a Dutch oven to steam the bread as it bakes. You'll end up with a loaf that is just as delicious as its kneaded counterparts, one that is worthy of sopping up the juices from your best beef stew or chicken roast. Toasted, with some homemade jam, it is heavenly. Use sourdough starter from a friend or make your own (see page 280).

It's handy to have a flexible plastic tool known as a bowl scraper to coax the wet dough out of the bowl in which it rose, though a silicone spatula will do in a pinch.

MAKES 1 LOAF

INGREDIENTS

- 2 cups sourdough starter (see page 280)
- 2 cups white bread flour
- 2 teaspoons salt
- About ⅓ cup water

1. **MIX THE DOUGH.** Pour the sourdough starter into a large bowl. Add the flour and salt. Stir until all the flour is moistened and incorporated into the dough, adding up to ⅓ cup water, as needed. The amount of water you use won't be the same each time because the sourdough starter will be thinner or thicker depending on ambient temperatures, whether or not you stir in the hooch (the liquid on top; I always do), the moisture content of the flour, and other variables. The mixing should take only a minute or so. The dough is finished when all the flour has been incorporated and the dough is a loose, shaggy ball. Cover with plastic wrap; the long rise will result in a dry skin on the dough if you use a towel instead of plastic wrap.

2. **LET RISE.** Set aside to rise for 12 to 18 hours. The dough should increase in size and may develop bubbles on its surface. You can leave it at this stage to let it develop more flavor, or you can bake it.

3. **SHAPE THE LOAF.** Place a bowl and a sheet of parchment paper on the counter. Spread a few table-spoons of flour on a work surface.

Remove the plastic wrap from the dough and set aside. Using a bowl scraper, turn the dough out onto the floured surface. Make a very rough ball by folding the top of the dough, then the bottom, then one side, then the other side. This should take only a minute; don't handle the dough more than that. If the dough sticks to the work surface, use the bowl scraper to lift it up.

Continued on next page

The dough looks shaggy and wet.

Overnight, the dough relaxes and expands in volume.

Fold in the top, then the bottom.

Fold in the sides.

[Adapted from *The Backyard Homestead Book of Kitchen Know-How* by Andrea Chesman]

4. **PROOF THE DOUGH.** The dough will benefit from another short rise. Place the dough on the parchment paper, seam side down. Lift up the paper and ease it into a bowl. Cover with the plastic wrap and let rise for about 30 minutes.

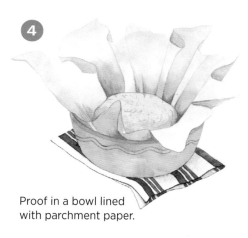

Proof in a bowl lined with parchment paper.

5. **PREHEAT THE OVEN AND PAN.** When you are ready to bake, put a cast-iron Dutch oven in the oven and preheat to 500°F/260°C.

6. **TRANSFER THE DOUGH TO THE PAN.** When the oven is preheated, remove the Dutch oven. Remove the plastic wrap from the dough. Lift up the parchment paper that holds the dough and gently ease it into the preheated Dutch oven. With a very sharp knife, score a deep X in the top of the loaf. If you like, spray the dough with water to make the crust crisper. Cover the Dutch oven with the lid.

7. **BAKE.** Bake for 30 minutes. Then reduce the oven temperature to 400°F/200°C and remove the lid from the Dutch oven. Continue baking for another 20 minutes, until the bread is browned; it should register 190°F/88°C on an instant-read thermometer.

8. **COOL.** Turn the bread out of the Dutch oven and let cool completely on a wire rack before slicing. (If you slice the bread while it is still warm, it will develop a gummy texture.)

The loaf is moved on the parchment paper into the preheated Dutch oven.

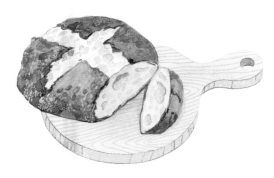

A good crumb means lots of large air holes.

Sourdough Starter

Keeping a sourdough starter alive is not that demanding, though it does take up refrigerator space. If you bake with the sourdough starter at least every 2 weeks, you can keep it alive indefinitely.

    2 cups all-purpose flour
    2 teaspoons sugar
    1 packet (2¼ teaspoons) active
        dry yeast
    2 cups warm water
        (105°F–115°F/41°C–46°C)

1. Mix the flour, sugar, and yeast together in a clean 2-quart canning jar. Gradually stir in the water and mix until it forms a thick, fairly smooth batter.

2. Cover the container with a kitchen towel and set it in a warm, draft-free place, preferably at around 70°F/21°C. Temperatures above 100°F/38°C will kill the yeast. Let sit for 2 to 5 days, stirring it once a day. The mixture should bubble as it ferments. (This will foam up quite a bit, hence the large canning jar.) The starter is ready when it develops a pleasant sour smell and looks bubbly.

3. Your starter is now ready to use. Store it in the refrigerator with the lid screwed on just lightly, so developing gases can escape. You will need to feed the starter at least every 2 weeks to keep it alive. The more frequently you feed it, the more active it will be and the shorter the time it will need to rise in a dough. Every time you remove starter to make bread, replace what you take with equal amounts of flour and water.

Charcoal is nearly pure carbon. By "cooking" wood in a low-oxygen environment, you release water, hydrogen, methane, and even tar (in the case of softwoods). What's left after the cooking process are lumps of coal that weigh about 25 percent as much as the original material but are more energy-dense than the original "raw" wood. The quality of the charcoal produced is superior to store-bought briquettes that are made of compressed sawdust and burn quickly.

MAKE CHARCOAL IN A HOMEMADE CRUCIBLE

This can be done with a 55-gallon metal drum (the still) and a 5-gallon metal paint can with lid (the crucible). Smaller batches can be made using a 1-gallon paint can. You'll need about 40 pieces of dry wood to fire the oven. For the charcoal, use dry firewood 1 to 3 inches in diameter, debarked and cut into uniform pieces; you'll need enough to fill the can.

1. **MAKE THE OVEN.** Convert the metal drum to a charcoal oven by punching holes in the lower third of the barrel. These holes can be punched randomly, as their only purpose is to provide oxygen to the fire inside.

2. **CONSTRUCT THE CRUCIBLE.** The crucible, which holds the charcoal, can be constructed from the metal paint can. It's important that the can be clean. Layer the small, debarked firewood in the can, packing it as tightly as possible. The goal is to minimize the chance of combustion by minimizing air space. Drill a ⅝-inch hole in the lid of the can, and secure the lid using the metal clenching tabs. If your can doesn't have tabs or a closure band, place a weight on the top.

3. **BUILD THE FIRE.** Place the crucible inside the barrel. Because a fire will have trouble drafting well inside the barrel, you'll need to start a small fire and build it up slowly. Be sure to use untreated wood. Continue to build the fire so that it covers the sides and the top of the crucible, though you'll want to make sure that the hole in the crucible's lid is unobstructed and visible. It is very important to keep the fire hot! You may need to split your firewood into smaller pieces that will burn faster but hotter.

4. **COOK THE MOISTURE OUT OF THE WOOD.** After 30 minutes or so, you will likely see steam wisping from the hole in the top of the crucible. This is the remaining moisture being cooked out of the wood. As your charcoal nears completion, a small flame will appear from the hole in the top of the crucible. As this last little bit of hydrogen and oxygen burns, you'll want to pay attention to the crucible flame. Once it goes out, carefully remove the crucible using long tongs, and immediately cover the hole in the top with a damp rag.

5. **REMOVE YOUR CHARCOAL.** Once the crucible has cooled, it's time for the moment of truth. If you have tended your fire carefully and removed the crucible as soon as the flame burned out, you'll be rewarded with your own harvest of genuine lump charcoal.

[Adapted from *The Woodland Homestead* by Brett McLeod]

BAKE BREAD
over COALS

Baking over coals is a fun and rustic way to make bread. If you are lucky, you may find a bake kettle at a junk shop or yard sale. Snatch it up and marvel at your good fortune if it still has its original snug-fitting cover. New bake kettles are also still available, squat legs, straight sides, ember-holding lid, and all. This classic white bread bakes perfectly in a 10-inch bake kettle.

MAKES ONE 2¼-POUND LOAF

INGREDIENTS

- 18 ounces bread flour
- ¾ ounce (⅓ cup) dry milk powder
- 2 teaspoons sugar
- 1½ teaspoons kosher salt
- 1½ teaspoons active dry yeast
- ¾ ounce (1½ tablespoons) butter, softened
- 3 ounces leavening culture (whole wheat or white), optional
- 1½ cups lukewarm water

1. Mix all the ingredients in a stand mixer with the dough hook, or by hand. (If you mix by hand, work the butter into the dry ingredients first, then stir in the leaven, in bits, and water.) Add a few drops more water as necessary. Once everything is combined, mix for 3 minutes. Scrape down the bowl and stir up from the bottom. Cover tightly.

2. Allow to ferment for 2 hours, interrupting it halfway through to stretch and fold the dough on a lightly floured counter. If you don't already have a cooking fire going for another purpose, start a lazy fire now. Small dry hardwood sticks (about 1 to 2 inches in diameter) are great for this.

3. When the bulk fermentation time is up, line a round medium basket with a floured cloth. Turn the dough out onto a lightly floured counter and knead it gently for a few seconds, gathering it up into a nice smooth ball with good surface tension. Flour the good side, and put it, good side down, in the basket to rise. Cover well with plastic or put the whole thing inside a plastic bag.

4. Allow the loaf to rise for about 40 minutes.

5. Preheat the bake kettle on a bed of coals for 5 to 10 minutes.

6. Nestle the proofed dough in the kettle.

7. Cover the pot securely.

8. Shovel more coals onto the lid than are under the kettle.

9. Bake the bread for about 50 minutes, or until golden brown, rotating the pot 180 degrees halfway through the baking time.

10. Brush most of the coals and ashes from the lid.

11. Lift the lid carefully with a pothook.

The result can be as delicious and crusty as bread baked in a wood-fired oven.

[Adapted from *Cooking with Fire* by Paula Marcoux]

Step 5

Step 6

Step 7

Step 8

Step 9

Step 10

Step 11

MAKE
MEDICINAL
BASIL PESTO

A pesto is simply an herb paste. Though few rival the flavor of a classic pesto made with all the yummy goodness of fresh basil, pine nuts, Parmesan, garlic, and olive oil, pestos can combine basil with other medicinal herbs. Depending on the herbs you use, you can pack a powerful punch of nutrients and healing factors into a delicious and nutritious pesto without your family ever suspecting they are "taking their medicine." This recipe is good for cleansing heavy metals and toxicity from the body.

INGREDIENTS

½–1 cup olive oil

1–3 garlic cloves

1 cup fresh cilantro leaves and stems

½ cup fresh basil leaves

½ cup fresh dandelion leaves

½–1 cup pine nuts or walnuts

¼ cup freshly grated Parmesan, Pecorino, or other hard cheese

1. Combine the oil, garlic, and fresh greens in a blender or food processor. Pulse until smooth.

2. Add the nuts and cheese and pulse again, until the mixture reaches the desired consistency (some like pesto chunky, others like it creamy smooth).

3. Use immediately, and freeze any extra in ice cube trays, then place the frozen cubes in ziplock bags so you'll have them available through the winter months.

Medicinal Herb Pesto Variations

You can use this basic recipe to make any number of medicinal herb pestos. The proportions will vary, depending on personal taste and intention (the desired effect). Try mixing 1 cup wild herbs with 1 cup common culinary herbs. Taste as you go — some of these herbs are surprisingly strong, but good! Some good pesto herbs are the following:

WILD HERBS	CULINARY HERBS
Amaranth	
Chickweed	Marjoram
Lamb's-quarter	Mint
Nettle	Oregano
Plantain	Sage
	Thyme

[Adapted from *Rosemary Gladstar's Medicinal Herbs* by Rosemary Gladstar]

Don't let the name throw you. While bitters may taste truly bitter on their own, in a cocktail they don't take center stage. That doesn't mean they're not essential. You wouldn't serve most food without a little salt, and bitters work a similar magic, pulling everything together, accenting a cocktail without stealing the show. It's best to start with a neutral grain spirit (like Everclear or vodka) so as not to interfere with the flavors of the plants.

MAKE BITTERS

1. **MACERATE IN ALCOHOL.** Put your plant parts in a glass jar, then pour in the base spirit. Seal tightly. Store the mixture out of direct light and give it a shake at least once a day. After 3 weeks, taste the spirit. If it's strongly flavored, strain out the solids and set them aside. If the flavor is still weak, continue to macerate for another week.

2. **DECOCT IN WATER.** Measure the strained alcohol solution and hold it in reserve. Measure out twice as much water as you have alcohol. Combine that water in a saucepan with the solids you strained from the alcohol. Bring this mixture to a boil, then reduce the heat and simmer for 10 minutes. Remove from the heat and let the liquid sit, covered, overnight.

   The next morning, strain out and discard the solids. Measure the infused liquid, return it to the saucepan over medium heat, and for each ½ cup of liquid, add 1 teaspoon of sugar. Whisk to combine, then remove from the heat and let the liquid cool.

3. **COMBINE AND TASTE.** Combine your alcohol maceration and your water decoction in the proportions needed to bring the ABV to between 35 and 45 percent. Taste the result. Remember, you're not aiming for something that is palatable on its own. Straight bitters will be herbal, highly alcoholic, and, well, bitter. If you need a signpost, something to show you what you're aiming for, try a drop or two of straight Angostura bitters.

Wild Bitters

LICORICE FERN BITTERS

✳ 8 ounces Everclear 151
✳ 1 ounce dried devil's club root
✳ 1 ounce fresh or frozen licorice root
✳ 1 ounce fresh or frozen Oregon grapes

SUMAC BITTERS

✳ 8 ounces Everclear 151
✳ 1 ounce chopped dried dandelion root
✳ 1 ounce fresh or frozen crab apples
✳ ½ ounce dried sumac berries

READ A **RABBIT'S** BODY LANGUAGE

Rabbits are prey animals. They are surrounded by their food, delicious greenery, but their lives are hardly a walk in the park. Rabbits must skulk secretively, tiptoe quietly, and hide constantly. So what are rabbits thinking? Watch their ears, nose, and body position to learn what a rabbit is thinking about you or another rabbit.

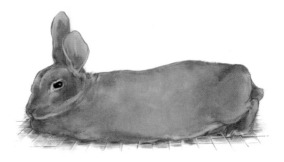

INTERESTED/ALERT: Both ears reach forward, with the neck outstretched slightly and the tail relaxed. The faster the nose wiggles, the more interested the rabbit is. If the rabbit stops wiggling its nose, it may be anticipating the need to flee.

ANGRY/AGGRESSIVE: Its ears are laid flat, with the opening pressed against its back. The rabbit's rump is in the air, with a lifted tail, while its front end crouches like a sprinter in the blocks. Growling is associated with rising anger and portends an impending attack.

RELAXED/CALM: The ears flop loosely as the rabbit lounges in a stretched-out position, on its stomach or its side, with its nose wiggling slowly or not at all.

HAPPY: A rabbit in a good mood lets you know it with its whole body. It jumps straight up in the air either from a standstill or in a full run, twists its body at both ends, and flicks its ears. This is known as a "binky" or "happy dance."

[Adapted from *The Rabbit-Raising Problem Solver* by Karen Patry]

When handling a rabbit, always support the hind end. A rabbit that struggles and kicks could wind up with a broken back. Never pick up a rabbit by the ears alone! It is terribly painful and can cause serious injury.

PICK UP AND CARRY a RABBIT

1. Place one hand under the chest and the other under the rump and scoop the rabbit into your arms.

2. Tuck its head under your elbow and carry the rabbit close to your side like a football. Carried this way, rabbits typically feel safe.

Tip: Cover the Eyes

Rabbits are like ostriches in that what they cannot see won't frighten them. Covering their eyes increases their sense of safety in all but the most inquisitive rabbits. This is why they tend to settle down comfortably when you tuck their heads under your arm in a football hold.

[Adapted from *The Rabbit-Raising Problem Solver* by Karen Patry]

TELL IF A RABBIT IS PREGNANT

The only way to know if a doe is pregnant, aside from a blood test, is to palpate her belly. As the kits grow, they form bulges along the twin horns of the rabbit's uterus. With a little practice, you can distinctly feel these bulges by the time the rabbit is 10 to 12 days along. Here's how to palpate.

1. Place the doe on a flat surface in front of you with her head closest to you.

2. Secure her rump with one hand (so she can't back up) and reach under her with your other hand, palm up.

3. The backbone line divides the abdomen into two halves and marks the inside boundary of both halves.

4. Using your fingertips on one side and the tip of your thumb on the other, you can examine, or palpate, both halves of the lower abdomen at once.

5. With enough pressure to lift the doe's hind end partly off the table, move the tips of your fingers and thumb cautiously and gently along the length of her belly. You are looking for grape-sized lumps, not along the center but toward both sides of the abdomen. Small, hard lumps along the center line of the rabbit's belly are fecal pellets lined up single file on their way out of the rabbit. A tiny tangle of soft "spaghetti" right in front of the pelvis is usually an empty uterus.

How Do I Know When She's Due?

The gestation period for rabbits is almost exactly 31 days. A careful palpation may help reveal the size of the fetuses and hence give you a ballpark idea of about when she might kindle (give birth).

* Marble-sized at day 8
* Olive- or grape-sized at day 10
* Quarter- or half-dollar-sized at day 14
* Small-egg-sized at day 21

[Adapted from *The Rabbit-Raising Problem Solver* by Karen Patry]

Division is a simple form of pruning. It is as essential to good perennial gardening as the pruning of a fruit tree is to a productive orchard.

DIVIDE PERENNIALS

Propagate **shallow-rooted perennials** by gently pulling apart the clump.

Keep **clumping plants** healthy by occasionally cutting away sections of the exterior and replanting them elsewhere.

Bulbs can be propagated by separating and replanting them, or by removing the bulblets and setting them out in a transplant bed.

When plants have **carrot-like roots**, it is necessary to dig up the entire plant and use a knife to cut it into a number of smaller plants.

[Adapted from *Successful Perennial Gardening* by Lewis and Nancy Hill]

POLLINATE BY HAND

Pollinating plants by hand is generally a simple process in which you collect pollen or entire male flowers and rub, brush, or pour the pollen onto stigmas of your seed-stock plants. It's a skill that all seed savers will want to develop, and it's easy and fun to do. The details of how to hand-pollinate vary from plant to plant. The directions below show you how to hand-pollinate squash.

1. Bag or tape shut male and female flowers in the evening, and mark them well for ease of location in the morning.

3. Working with just one female flower at a time, remove the bag or tape from the flower and quickly "paint" pollen from the anthers to the stigma, distributing pollen evenly. Use more than one male to pollinate each female.

2. Early the next morning, clip the male flowers from the plant and remove the corolla to reveal the anthers.

4. Re-bag or re-tape and flag the flower so that you know you have pollinated it. If any bees land on the female while you're working, do not save seed from that flower.

[Adapted from *The Complete Guide to Saving Seeds* by Robert Gough and Cheryl Moore-Gough]

When held, all farm birds need to be firmly supported underneath, but how you accomplish that will vary slightly depending on the type of bird you are holding. Birds that are handled frequently are familiar and comfortable with human contact and so are calmer and more relaxed around people.

HOLD A FARM BIRD

▲CHICKEN

Support the feet and lower body to give the chicken a better feeling of security.

▲DUCK

Place your hand and arm under the body at the base of the feet to give support.

◄TURKEY

A firm hold on the wings and feet will prevent injury to both the bird and the person holding it.

►GUINEA

Care must be taken to secure the legs and wings.

▲GOOSE

Hold the bird against your body with one hand, and hold the outside wing with the other hand.

[Adapted from *Showing Poultry* by Glenn Drowns]

DETERMINE WHETHER A CHICKEN IS HEALTHY

If you're in the market for chickens, you'll want to be sure that you know what healthy birds look like. Although most sellers won't try to palm off unhealthy chickens, the occasional unscrupulous seller sees the wonderstruck novice buyer as an opportunity to turn unwanted birds into cash.

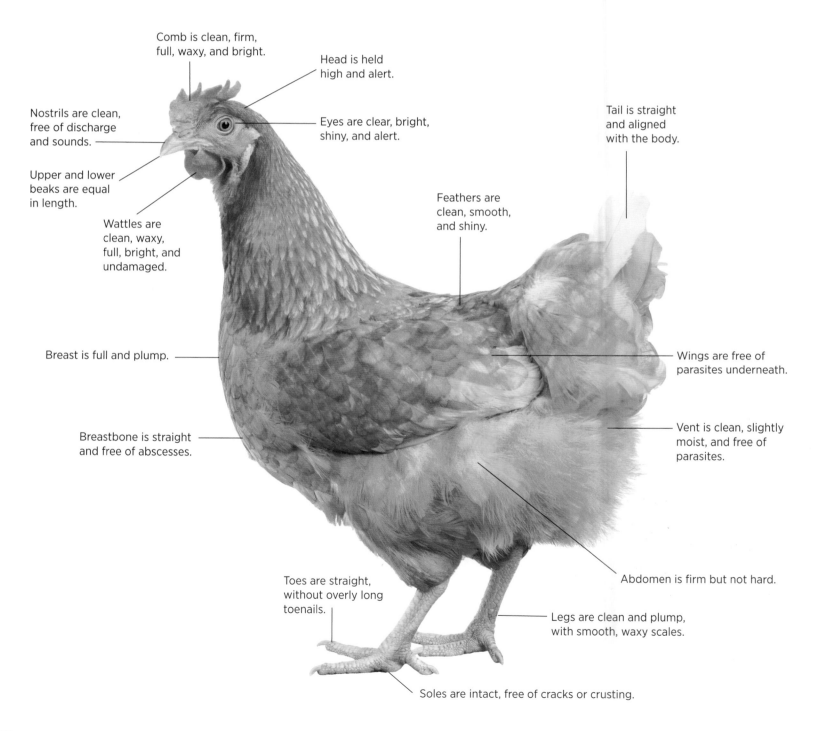

Comb is clean, firm, full, waxy, and bright.

Head is held high and alert.

Nostrils are clean, free of discharge and sounds.

Eyes are clear, bright, shiny, and alert.

Upper and lower beaks are equal in length.

Tail is straight and aligned with the body.

Wattles are clean, waxy, full, bright, and undamaged.

Feathers are clean, smooth, and shiny.

Breast is full and plump.

Wings are free of parasites underneath.

Breastbone is straight and free of abscesses.

Vent is clean, slightly moist, and free of parasites.

Abdomen is firm but not hard.

Toes are straight, without overly long toenails.

Legs are clean and plump, with smooth, waxy scales.

Soles are intact, free of cracks or crusting.

[Adapted from *Storey's Guide to Raising Chickens* by Gail Damerow]

Whether you are trying to figure out what killed your chickens or goats or just interested in the animals that live near you, scat can be an especially useful clue when combined with other signs.

IDENTIFY THE SCAT OF PREDATORS

COYOTE

Twisted and ropelike, tips tapered, 3–4 inches long, ½–1 inch in diameter. May be left on rocks, logs, and trails. Varies according to diet. May contain hair, feathers, bones, fruit, or seeds.

GRAY WOLF

Similar in size to large dog scat, cylindrical, tapered ends, about 6–8 inches long, 1 inch in diameter, black to brown in color. Contains hair and bone fragments. Do not handle, as it may contain tapeworm eggs or other parasites.

BOBCAT

Blunt, dry, 3 inches long, and ¾ inch wide. Kittens cover their feces, but adults leave feces uncovered.

MOUNTAIN LION

Blunt ends, 4–6 inches long, and about 1¼ inches in diameter (size of the scat may indicate the relative size of the mountain lion). Usually covered; may contain bone fragments and hair.

AMERICAN BLACK BEAR

Cylindrical, thick, blunt ends, 7 inches long, 1 inch in diameter, usually coiled, black to brown in color. Can resemble human feces except the contents may reveal hair, bone, and plant fibers. Scat will be looser and softer if the bear was feeding on berries. Left uncovered at the site of a kill.

FISHER

Long, slender, tapered at ends, 3½ inches long, and ½ inch in diameter. Often left on logs or high sites; may contain porcupine quills.

RACCOON

Blunt, 3–5 inches long, and ¾ inch in diameter. Often contains fruit seeds. Due to potentially fatal parasite contamination, do not handle any raccoon feces without protection.

STRIPED SKUNK

Blunt, 5 inches long, and ¾ inch in diameter. Contains insect pieces.

[Adapted from *The Encyclopedia of Animal Predators* by Janet Vorwald Dohner]

SPLIT FIREWOOD

Splitting is different from chopping: with splitting, you're bisecting the wood along the grain, instead of diagonally cutting it. Therefore, to effectively split wood, you'll need an ax that works less like a knife and more like a wedge. You can use a well-worn felling ax filed at a 40-degree angle on each side to create a blunt wedge, or you can use a splitting maul. When splitting, be sure you are wearing steel-toe boots.

1. Place the log to be split on a splitting block. Your splitting block should be a minimum of 15 inches in diameter and 12 to 16 inches high. By using a block, you're preserving your ax by avoiding rocks, giving the blade a safe landing spot well away from your feet, and saving your back from bending over too far.

2. Raise the ax directly over your head. Keep the ax in a perfect line with the center of your body for greater accuracy and precision. Space your legs wide enough so that they're free and clear of the ax should you miss, and make sure you're far enough away that you don't strike the handle of the ax on the log.

3. As you bring the ax down, aim for the near edge of the log. It's always easier to start a split at the edge than in the center. If the log shows no sign of splitting after a couple of blows, rotate it 90 degrees and try from that side. If you still can't manage to pop open the log, consider "slabbing" the log by removing inch-thick slabs from the edges. Once the slabs are removed, you can resume your regular splitting pattern.

And old tire bolted to your splitting block will hold your wood securely as you split it. No more standing up fallen pieces or chasing runaway firewood!

[Adapted from *The Woodland Homestead* by Brett McLeod]

The three basics of stacking wood are *off the ground*, *under cover*, and *safe*. The goal is to keep the wood dry, with air circulating through the pile. So if you can't keep your wood indoors, put a tarp or some old sheet-metal roofing on top. If you use a tarp, cover the top of the pile only. Many is the newcomer to the country who has wrapped up his or her woodpile in plastic, and great is their dismay when they later find the wood dripping wet from condensation. The wood's like you: it's gotta breathe.

STACK FIREWOOD AND KEEP IT STABLE

Here are some other key pointers:

* Keep the wood off the wet ground. If you can stack on top of wood pallets, that's fine. Otherwise "stringers" work well; stringers are two boards or saplings laid out parallel to each other and closer together than the piles of firewood are wide. You lay the firewood across the stringers, which boost the wood off the ground, encouraging that vital circulation of air.

* For the same reason, don't obsess about stacking perfectly tight. You want to be able to see a little bit of daylight through the pile. Mark Twain wrote about some wood dealers, "Those crooks had it stacked so you could throw a dog through it anywhere." That's a little too loose.

* Finally, safety: the woodpile should not fall on you. Keep it level, and brace the ends. If possible, build your woodpile against a post, a tree, or something else vertical and strong. If none is available, you'll have to "crib" the ends. Cribbing is making a freestanding tower of wood at the end of the row by alternating the directions of the layers of wood. The first layer is placed at right angles to the direction of the row; the next layer in the same direction as the pile; the third layer at right angles, and so on. Cribbing will steady the pile surprisingly well.

* To diminish the risk of avalanche, it is important not to stack too high. Of course, the more convenient to the stove or fireplace (but at least 3 feet away!) the better.

This backyard woodpile uses old pallets in lieu of stringers. Notice the cribbing on the left end.

[Adapted from *The Backyard Lumberjack* by Stephen Philbrick and Frank Philbrick]

BUILD A WALL
WITH
CORDWOOD

While it's hard to deny the value of a cord of wood for keeping you warm, cordwood can also be used as a simple and efficient alternative building material. Cordwood building is simple: debarked firewood-length logs (8 to 24 inches long) are stacked with an insulated mortar to create a wind- and watertight wall.

1. **SOURCE AND CUT YOUR LOGS.** It's imperative that the wood be completely dry before you begin, so start this process at least a year in advance of construction. Softwoods are generally preferred over hardwoods (which are prone to greater expansion/contraction); cedar is among the most desirable woods since it's rot resistant. You can use either rounds or split wood; just make sure all pieces are cut to the same length.

2. **MIX THE MORTAR.** Once your wood is dry and you've built a solid foundation above grade, you're ready to mix your mortar. Like cooks, most cordwood builders have their own recipe, but this one is the most common: 9 parts sand to 3 parts sawdust to 3 parts builder's lime (not agricultural) to 2 parts Portland cement by volume.

3. **LAY UP THE WALL.** With the mortar mixed to the consistency of thick mud, you're ready to begin building, or "laying up" the wall. Start with a layer of mortar at the base (about 2 inches thick), and press the cordwood into it until the wood is firmly bedded. The logs shouldn't touch one another, and mortar should fill all the air gaps. When you have your first course in place, you can continue building layer by layer. Make sure that the wall doesn't bow in or out, and that the areas around door and window frames are completely chinked with mortar. Before the mortar dries you'll want to smooth, or "point," both the inside and outside of the wall using a butter knife with a slightly upturned blade.

4. **LET IT DRY.** It can take up to 3 weeks for the mortar to completely dry. It's best if it dries slowly. You can control the rate by misting the wall daily with water.

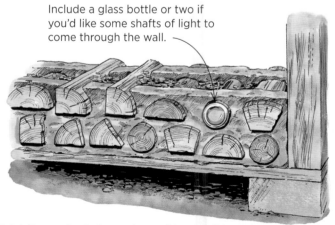

Include a glass bottle or two if you'd like some shafts of light to come through the wall.

Point the mortar between logs with a small trowel or a butter knife that has an upturned blade. Individual logs should not touch; they should be separated by a thick layer of mortar.

[Adapted from *The Woodland Homestead* by Brett McLeod]

Ask two woodsmen how to sharpen an ax, and you're liable to get three answers. Some swear by a filed edge, while others believe in only using a whetstone. Still others use bench grinders or belt sanders. The condition of the bit and the quality of the steel are the two factors that ultimately determine which tool is best for sharpening.

SHARPEN AN AX

SHARPENING WITH A BELT GRINDER

An effective tool for sharpening dull and damaged axes is a narrow-gauge (1⅛ by 21 inches) belt sander. To begin, use 180-grit sandpaper belts. Before you even plug the sander in, practice drawing the sander back and forth, following the radius of the ax. The sander should point toward the poll of the ax as you do this, and it should be angled upward at approximately 20 to 25 degrees.

Be sure to mark the center of the arc on the poll of the ax and use a punch to create a small divot. This will create a reference point for sharpening in the future.

Once you are comfortable with the motion, you can begin grinding by using light strokes. Be sure to count the number of strokes so that you maintain an even bit angle on both sides. Check the bit regularly to make sure it's not too hot to touch. If it is, you're either going too fast or applying too much pressure.

As you flip the ax from side to side, use a small piece of hardwood to drive off the metal burr that forms as the bit of the ax is thinned to an apex. If you don't drive the burr off, you'll end up with a brittle edge that will break off. Once you've removed the major imperfections, you're ready to hone the ax using a whetstone.

Continued on next page

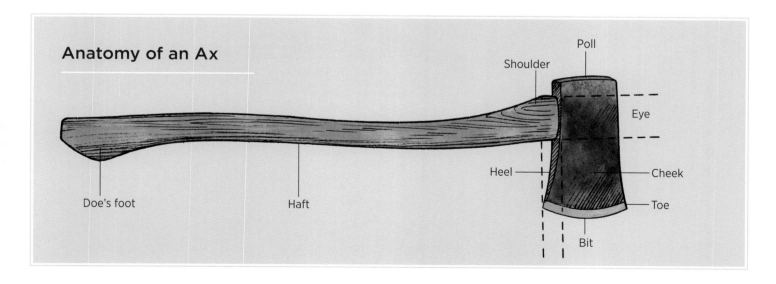

Anatomy of an Ax

Poll

Shoulder

Eye

Heel

Cheek

Doe's foot

Haft

Toe

Bit

SHARPENING WITH A BASTARD FILE

An alternative to the belt sander is the single-cut bastard file, preferable for axes with soft steel or only minor dings. The file can be used freehand or with a jig.

This simple jig is made from a C-clamp, part of an old yardstick, and a bastard file. The angle can be measured using a compass and adjusted by adding or subtracting metal washers on the C-clamp. A 20-degree angle is ideal for chopping most wood.

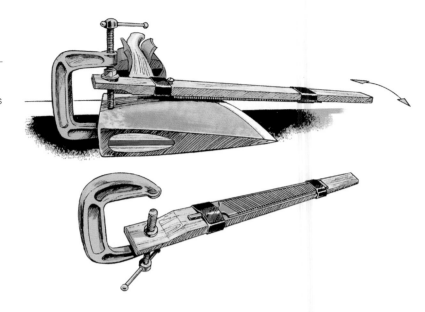

HONING WITH A WHETSTONE

The last step in sharpening an ax is to use a whetstone on the cutting edge. This final cutting edge is about 10 degrees stouter than the grinding or filing angle. You can use either a hard Arkansas stone or a long-lasting but expensive diamond stone. As with grinding and filing, it is important to maintain a constant angle and to do an equal number of strokes on each side.

Use long, even strokes from heel to toe. For a more durable final edge, you can increase the honing angle up to 30 degrees.

If your old ax haft, or handle, shows any signs of deterioration (cracks, a loose head, or a rotted eye), it's time to fit on a new handle. Woodsmen often call the process of fitting a handle "hanging an ax." It requires both patience and practice, and it is as much of a skill as swinging or sharpening an ax.

HANG AN AX

1. File the eye of the handle with a rasp until the ax head fits on the shoulder of the handle. Aligning your eye with the ax head, look down the handle and check for trueness. You may have to fine-tune the fit to get it to hang perfectly straight, but this is time well spent.

2. Mark the head location with a pencil and extend the wedge slit with a thin-bladed handsaw, if necessary. The slit should extend to within ½ inch of the bottom of the ax head. Cut off any excess handle above the ax head.

3. Slide the ax handle into the head and use a rubber or wooden mallet to pound the doe's foot. This will drive the head onto the handle.

4. When you're happy with the hang of the ax, drive the wooden wedge in with your mallet. Saw off the top of the seated wedge with a coping saw.

5. If your new handle is untreated, rub linseed oil into it. This will help prevent it from becoming brittle and/or cracked. If the new handle is varnished, consider using medium-grit sandpaper to remove the varnish, and then treat the wood with linseed oil. Varnish can make for an impossibly slick ax handle in wet conditions.

[Adapted from *The Woodland Homestead* by Brett McLeod]

MAKE KOMBUCHA

Put simply, kombucha is fermented tea. A SCOBY (symbiotic culture of bacteria and yeast) and starter liquid are added to sweet tea. This dynamic health duo — tea and fermentation — packs a nutritional punch that improves digestion and boosts immunity in one tasty quaff. It's easy, and making your own will save you a *lot* of money. Ask a friend who makes kombucha for a SCOBY (they will most likely have extra) or buy one online. Each time you start a new batch, you will grow a new SCOBY.

MAKES 1 GALLON

INGREDIENTS

- 1 gallon cool, unchlorinated water
- 4-6 tea bags or 1-2 tablespoons loose-leaf tea
- 1 cup sugar
- 1 full-size kombucha SCOBY (4-5 ounces)
- 1-2 cups mature kombucha, for starter liquid

1. Heat 1 quart of the water to just below boiling. Combine the tea and hot water in the pot, a separate bowl, or the brewing vessel. Let steep for 5 to 15 minutes, then remove the tea leaves.

2. Add the sugar to the hot tea, and stir until completely dissolved.

3. Pour the remaining 3 quarts cool water into the brewing vessel. If you prepared it separately, add the sweet tea. Dip a clean finger into the mixture to gauge its temperature. If it's warmer than body temperature (about 100°F/38°C), cover with a clean cloth and set aside until lukewarm.

4. Once the sweet tea solution is cooler than body temperature, use clean hands to place the SCOBY in it.

Pour the starter liquid on top of the SCOBY; this acidifies the pH of the tea near the top of the vessel, where the culture is most vulnerable, offering a layer of protection from potential pathogens.

5. Cover the vessel with breathable cloth, secured with a rubber band if necessary. Set it in a warm location (ideally 75°F to 85°F/24°C to 29°C), out of direct sunlight, unless you are brewing in an opaque vessel. (At this stage you have the option to say a prayer, send good vibes, or otherwise commune with your new brew. It is a culture of living organisms and responds to energy — positive and negative.)

6. Allow the sweet tea to ferment for 7 to 21 days. After 5 days (or sooner, if you're curious), it's okay to begin tasting once a day. To taste, remove the cloth cover, gently insert a straw beneath the SCOBY, and take a sip. Or dip a shot glass or other small cup past the new layer of SCOBY into the brew.

7. Once the brew reaches the flavor you prefer, it is ready to harvest. Before bottling or flavoring, collect at least 1 cup of starter liquid for the next batch from the top of the brew (2 cups if you can spare it or

if the brew is young) and pour it into a clean bowl. Then remove the SCOBYs to the bowl, cover with a clean towel, and set aside.

8. The rest of the kombucha is now available for drinking, either straight from the vessel, or, more commonly, after bottling with or without flavors.

9. To start the next batch, use one or both of the SCOBYs, either the original and/or the new one, with the starter liquid. (If you use only one, the extra culture may be placed in a large jar with mature kombucha, covered with a cloth, and stored at room temperature.) Enjoy the first batch while the second brew is in progress!

[Adapted from *The Big Book of Kombucha* by Hannah Crum and Alex LaGory]

Step 1

Step 2

Step 3

Step 4

Step 5

Step 6

Step 7

Step 8

Step 9

Flavor Inspirations

From mildly astringent to lip puckering, sweet to savory, and mild to wild, you can achieve nearly any flavor of kombucha with a little imagination. Try adding these flavors during secondary fermentation, after you've removed the SCOBY, or add them at bottling time. Measurements are for a 1-gallon batch of kombucha.

BERRY MEDLEY

½ cup blackberries, quartered
¼ cup raspberries, lightly mashed
¼ cup strawberries, chopped

COLD FIGHTER

1 tablespoon dried elderberries
1 tablespoon diced fresh ginger
1 teaspoon grated lemon zest

DREAMY ORANGE

¼ cup fresh orange juice
1 whole vanilla bean, sliced
1 tablespoon honey

VANILLA CHAI

1 tablespoon hand-ground chai spice blend
¾ whole vanilla bean, sliced

FIRE CARROT

¼ cup carrot juice
½ teaspoon ground cayenne

IDENTIFY A HORSE'S GAIT

How do horses get where they're going? Most often, they do one of four standard gaits: walk, trot, canter, or gallop. Gaits describe the sequence of movements of a horse's legs. Some breeds have a natural gait, such as the running walk of Missouri Fox Trotters and Tennessee Walking Horses.

THE WALK is a four-beat gait with each foot striking the ground at a separate interval.

THE TROT is a two-beat gait with diagonal pairs striking the ground simultaneously — left front with right rear and right front with left rear.

THE CANTER is a three-beat gait with three feet in contact with the ground during each stride. At one point in each canter stride, the horse's weight is borne for a split second on one front leg.

THE GALLOP is a four-beat gait very much like the canter but faster and with a longer stride.

[Adapted from *Knowing Horses* by Les Sellnow and Carol A. Butler]

Horses communicate their feelings and intentions quite well, and you can tell what a horse is thinking by watching his body language. Tail swishing means irritation and sometimes anger — a prelude to a kick. Tenseness or relaxation of the body can also be a clue to a horse's mood. Ears forward means alert interest; ears flat back signals a threat that could be followed by a bite or kick; ears to the side means boredom or sleepiness. Remember, though, that each horse is unique, and the meaning of these ear positions may vary from horse to horse and from circumstance to circumstance.

READ A HORSE'S BODY LANGUAGE

ANGRY. A horse with ears pinned back and folded flat to his neck may be afraid or annoyed, but this threatening gesture clearly says *stay away*.

ATTENTIVE. While being ridden or driven, he will often turn one ear backward to concentrate on what the handler wants and point the other one forward to be alert to his surroundings.

FEARFUL/WORRIED. A horse with extremely pricked ears, wide eyes, and head held high is frightened or worried.

RELAXED/SLEEPY. A relaxed head and shoulders and both ears turned backward in a relaxed manner indicate that the horse feels safe. A bored or sleepy horse may let his ears flop almost to his neck.

ALERT. Head up and ears pricked indicate that something's up.

UNHAPPY/IN PAIN. A head held down and tense with the ears up and toward the side indicates unhappiness or pain.

[Adapted from *Knowing Horses* by Les Sellnow and Carol A. Butler and *Storey's Guide to Training Horses* by Heather Smith Thomas]

303

FRENCH-BRAID A HORSE'S TAIL

The French braid is similar to the familiar three-strand braid, but the altered technique creates a unique look. This "overhand" braid is used for English and dressage shows. Start with a dampened, combed tail.

1. At the top of the tail, separate a small portion of tail hair from the left (A) and one from the right (B), then cross the right over the left in the middle of the tail.

2. Hold these two pieces in your right hand. Take another small portion from the left (C) and cross it over the middle (B) so that there are three pieces.

3. Twist the right section (A) over the middle (C) so that the right becomes the new middle. Separate another portion from the right (D) and add it to the middle. Pull all braid pieces very tightly.

4. Twist the left piece (B) over the middle (A) so that the left becomes the new middle. Add another portion from the left (E) to the middle. Continue braiding, adding hair from alternate sides.

5. About one-third of the way down the tailbone, make a regular three-strand braid with the end hairs from the French braid (see facing page). Finish with yarn or a rubber band.

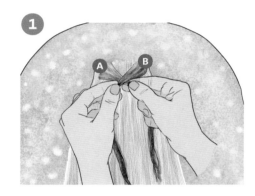

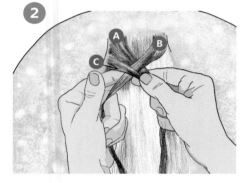

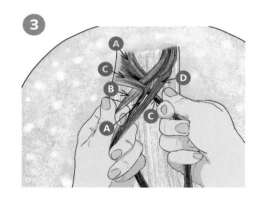

Don't Forget the Forelock!

Following steps 1 to 4, French-braid the top of the forelock. Continue adding sections from each side until you reach the end of the scalp. Use the remaining long hairs to complete a three-strand braid. Braid in yarn and tie off or finish with a rubber band.

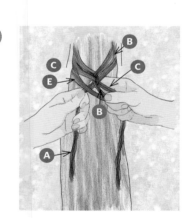

[Adapted from *Braiding Manes and Tails* by Charni Lewis]

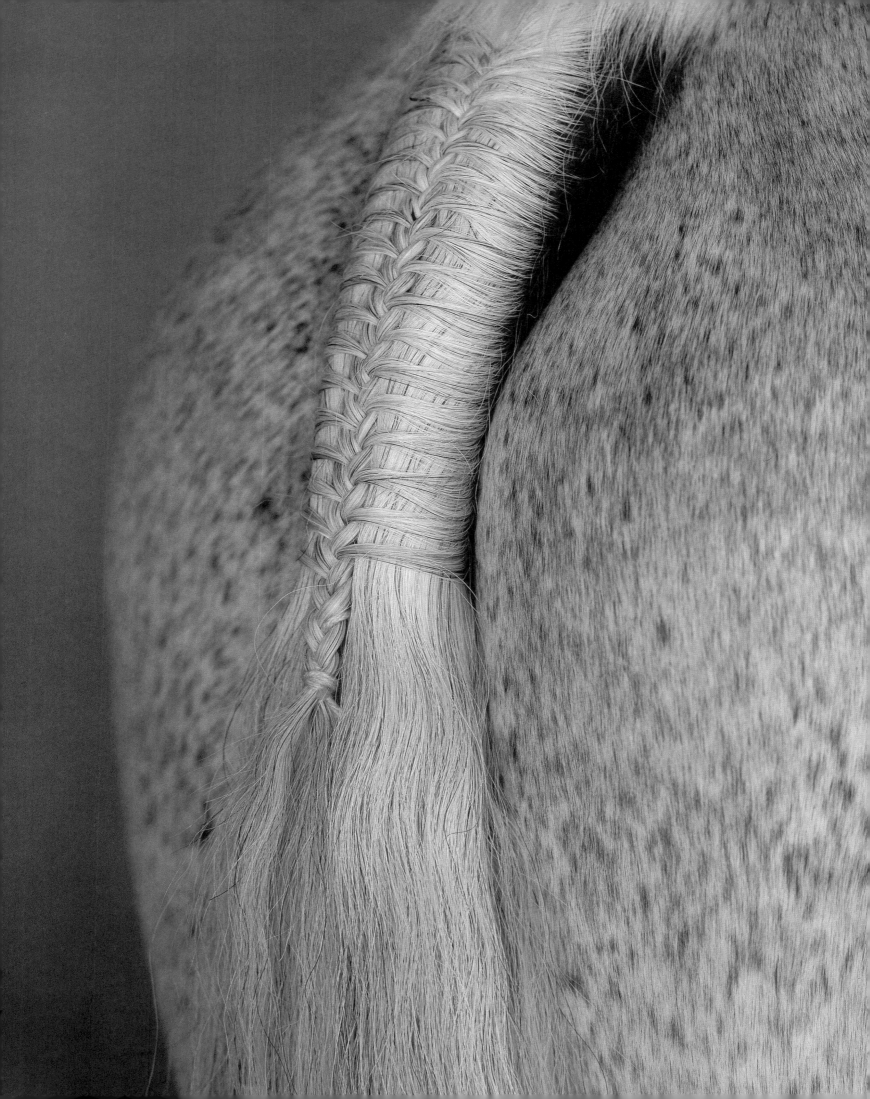

FIX A TOILET
THAT RUNS CONSTANTLY

Toilets that continually run in between flushes waste a lot of water. You can tell if a toilet is using water in between flushes by the sound in the tank and the ripples of running water in the toilet bowl. Lift the lid off the tank to see what is going on.

ADJUSTING THE WATER LEVEL

Inside the tank, you will notice an overflow tube and water. If the water level is too high, the water spills into the tube, creating the problem. The water level is regulated by the large ball that floats in the tank. A brass arm connects the ball to a shut-off valve. As the water in the tank rises and the ball floats upward, it creates downward pressure on the shut-off valve, which eventually closes. To make the shut-off valve close more quickly, you need to increase the downward angle of the brass arm.

1. Screw the ball in a little on the connecting arm so that the distance between the shut-off valve and the ball is reduced.

2. If the ball is completely screwed in, gently bend the connecting arm so that the ball is lower in the water.

3. Flush the toilet and see how high the water rises in the tank. If it still rises above the mouth of the tube, gently bend the float arm further so that the ball sits even lower in the water.

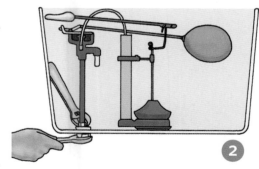
Overflow tube

REPLACING THE SHUT-OFF VALVE

Occasionally a toilet runs because it has a defective shut-off valve. If the water won't shut off as you pull up on the ball in the tank, replace the old valve mechanism with a new self-contained plastic mechanism that can be purchased at any hardware or plumbing supply store.

1. Close the water intake valve under the toilet. Then flush the toilet. This should mostly empty out the tank and toilet.

2. Place a pan or bucket under the tank to catch any water that remains in the tank. Place an adjustable wrench onto the nut of the old valve mechanism and use another wrench to loosen the nut under the tank that holds the old mechanism in place. Now remove the old mechanism.

3. To install the new plastic mechanism, follow the instructions on the package. This new plastic mechanism regulates the water level according to the pressure in the tank. To increase the water level, turn the knob at the base of the regulator mechanism clockwise. To decrease the water level, turn the knob counterclockwise. Start with one turn at a time and check the water level.

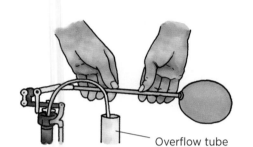
2

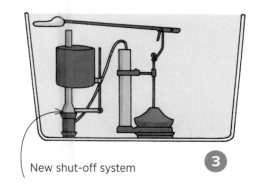
New shut-off system
3

[Adapted from *The Woman's Hands-On Home Repair Guide* by Lyn Herrick]

The conventional flush toilet is one of the largest water users in the home, accounting for up to one-third of all indoor water use. Depending on your toilet and flushing habits, switching to a composting toilet can give you a savings of 18 to 30 percent of total indoor water consumption.

CONSIDER A COMPOSTING TOILET

PROS OF COMPOSTING TOILETS

✳ Save water, up to one-third of indoor use
✳ Prevent pollution of waterways by keeping nutrients like nitrogen and phosphorus on land and out of the water
✳ Function anywhere
✳ Prevent infections by keeping water-borne pathogens out of water where people swim

CONS OF COMPOSTING TOILETS

✳ There are limited options if there are space restraints in the home
✳ Some designs require space outside for a composting area
✳ They require maintenance by someone comfortable managing excreta
✳ Visitors and guests may not be accustomed to a waterless toilet and need education

Vent

Compost chamber

Leachate drain

[Adapted from *The Water-Wise Home* by Laura Allen]

BUILD A WATTLE FENCE

The wattle fence is probably one of the oldest forms of fence construction. Basically, it involves a row of upright posts with limbs woven between them. The upright posts give the fence its primary strength. The "weaving" material can be any moderately flexible material, including limbs, reeds, vines, or anything else that can be woven. The resulting fence offers a barrier to animals and some privacy.

This design is for a fence with a height of up to 4 feet. If you want to build a taller fence, simply use longer uprights and plan on doing more weaving. For taller fences, set a post in the ground every 4 feet, with about 18 inches driven into the ground. This gives the fence greater stability.

1. **PREPARE THE UPRIGHT POSTS.** Measure, in inches, the length of the area where you want your fence to run and divide it by 24. This gives you the approximate number of upright posts you need. Cut limbs to use as posts. These should be about 1¾ inches in diameter on the thicker end and the height of your finished fence plus 12 inches. For example, for a 24-inch-high fence, cut 36-inch posts. Don't worry about cutting the posts exactly to length, as you will trim off the excess when the fence is finished.

2. **DRIVE THE POSTS.** Set out the posts along the fence line, spacing them approximately 24 inches apart. Drive each post about 12 inches into the ground.

3. **SET THE SPACER UPRIGHTS.** Cut enough spacer uprights to place between each pair of upright posts. The spacers should be about 24 inches long and slightly smaller in diameter than the posts. Push the end of a spacer into the ground halfway between the first two posts. It doesn't have to be firmly in the ground, just enough so that you can weave around it. Place the other spacers between the remaining posts.

4. **CUT THE WEAVERS.** Cut bundles of any green or nearly green wood for the weavers. These should be about the thickness of your index finger at the large end and 36 to 48 inches long.

5. **WEAVE THE WATTLE.** Lay out one weaver at ground level with a tail end of several inches extending beyond the first post. Direct the weaver in front of the first post, then behind the spacer and in front of the next post. Continue weaving in and out of the uprights for the length of your fence, adding weavers by overlapping them as needed. Leave the ends extending beyond the final post.

   To start the next row, alternate the weave, beginning behind the first post, coming in front of the spacer, and continuing on.

   Continue adding rows, pushing the weavers down as you complete each row to make the fence firm and tight. Add rows until you reach the tops of the posts.

6. **FINISH THE FENCE.** Trim the ends extending beyond the posts to 1 to 2 inches. Trim off any loose overlapping pieces that are sticking out of the weave. Wire the ends of the weavers on the top row, at each post, if desired.

[Adapted from *Making Bentwood Trellises, Arbors, Gates & Fences* by Jim Long]

Stepping-stones give focus to paths. This project surrounds the stones with pea-sized gravel to accent them, and the border stones contain the gravel so it doesn't disappear into the grass. The stones give a solid surface to walk on; a path of plain gravel, in contrast, can shift underfoot. Grass will sprout in the gravel, which means you'll need to trim it or apply an herbicide.

BUILD A
STEPPING-STONE
PATH

To build a 36-inch-wide, 35-foot-long woodland or garden path, you'll need 1 ton of fieldstone, as near to 6 by 6 inches as possible, with a length of 6 inches or longer, for use as border stones; 1 ton of flat, irregular flagstones, each 2 inches or so thick and no smaller than 18 inches across, for use as stepping-stones; and 1 ton of pea gravel, in any color you prefer.

1. Lay out your path in any course you like, remembering that turnings should come at natural obstacles (trees, bushes, stone groupings).

2. Dig a trench about 3 inches deep and 6 inches wide along both borders of the path. Spread the soil to even out rough places in the path.

3. Set border stones, shaping where necessary, end to end in the trenches, so that about 3 inches stand out of the ground. Vary the lengths, but avoid stones shorter than 6 inches; they won't stay in place. Tamp the soil around the stones to hold them.

4. Arrange the stepping-stones in the path. Leave about 6 inches of space between stones. To create the effect of stone floating in a stream of gravel, alternate large and medium stones, avoiding any under 18 inches across, and leave at least 6 inches of space at the sides of the path. Dig out a base for each stone so that approximately 1 inch will stand up from the surface.

5. Spread 1 inch of gravel along the path, sweeping the excess off the stepping-stones. Where you've loosened the soil in digging out roots or stumps and where you've spread loose soil to level it, tamp before graveling. After a few weeks, spots will settle in the path. Add gravel here as needed.

[Adapted from *Stonework* by Charles McRaven]

BUILD A DRYSTONE WALL

A freestanding drystone wall is the simplest and most attractive structure you can build of stone. There's no footing, no mortar, no cracking with freezing. If you use stones gathered from the top of the ground, they'll have lichens and an aged appearance. So a new drystone wall will look as if it's centuries old.

TOOLS

- Pick
- Shovel
- Tape
- Wheelbarrow
- Four-foot level
- Stone chisel
- Striking hammer
- Mason's hammer
- Pry bar (straight or crowbar)

1. Dig a shallow trench to the subsoil. The trench should be 24 inches wide with a slight V slope, and about 2 inches deeper in the center than at the edges.

2. Place stones along the bottom of the trench in pairs, with each sloping toward the center. Use stones that have a relatively even outside edge and that reach near the center of the trench. If a stone extends 2 to 3 inches past the center, adjust the soil for it, and use a narrower one opposite it. If both stones are short, fill the center space with broken stones. Place uneven surfaces down on this first course, digging out as necessary. Leave as smooth a top surface as possible, matching stone heights.

3. Begin the next course with similar stones, taking care to cover the cracks between the first-layer stones. If you have spanned the 24-inch trench with one 15-inch stone on, say, the right side and a 9-inch one on the left, reverse this now. If the stones were 12 inches long (along the length of the wall), use shorter or larger ones on this second layer to avoid vertical running joints. Try to use stones of uniform thickness (height) in each course. Where this is impossible, use two thin ones alongside a thick one for an even height.

4. Wedge wherever necessary for solidity, using nontapered shims so that they won't be worked out as the wall flexes.

5. Use a 4-foot level to keep the wall vertical. Place a 24-inch stone every third or fourth layer as a tie stone. Since the tie stone will be seen on both wall faces, it should have relatively straight ends. Use a hammer and chisel if necessary to shape these faces. The wall should have a tie stone about every 4 feet along its length. Reestablish your V slope after each course, as necessary.

6. Use as many tie stones as possible for the top layer. These are called capstones, and they are easily dislodged unless large and heavy. The best stones should be saved for capstones, since piecing this top layer will make it unstable.

7. Begin and end the wall vertically (A), or step it down to the ground (B). If the ground rises, keep the wall top level until it fades into the grade (C).

How Much Stone?

One ton of stone makes about 3 running feet of stone wall, 3 feet high and 2 feet thick. You can buy a ton of stone at a stone and gravel yard or some home and garden centers. If you gather stone in the field, a ton of stone is about 17.5 cubic feet (3.5 × 5 × 1 foot), or a full-size pickup truck load about 6 inches deep.

[Adapted from *Stonework* by Charles McRaven]

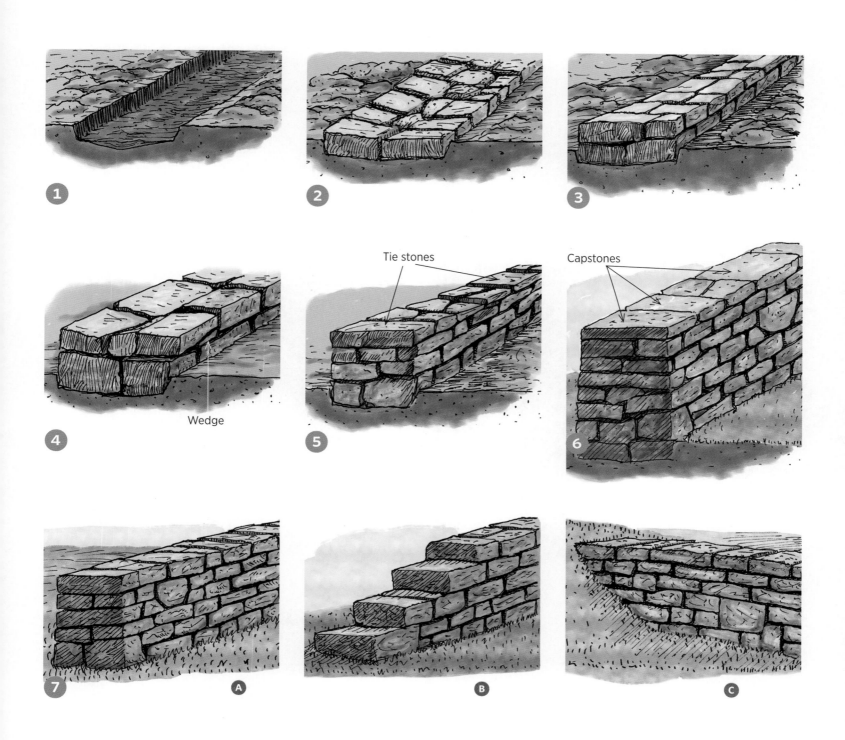

Tie stones

Wedge

Capstones

HARVEST RAINWATER

Collecting rainwater for irrigation or indoor use reduces home water consumption, prevents water pollution, and utilizes a free source of pure water delivered right to the house. There are two main ways to harvest rainwater: in a tank and in the ground. Roofwater collection directs rainwater or snowmelt into a tank or a barrel. Harvesting rain in the landscape, with rain gardens, directly irrigates plants and recharges the groundwater table.

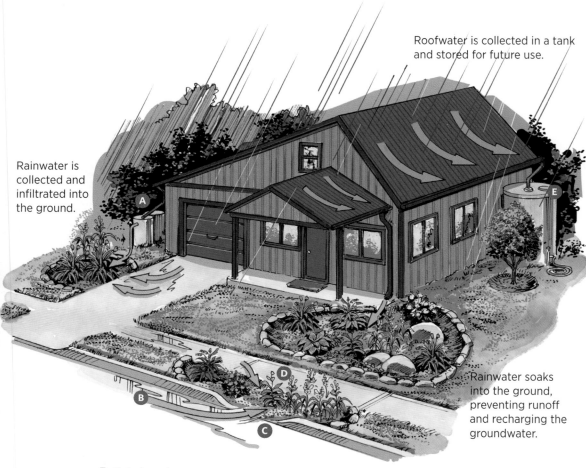

Roofwater is collected in a tank and stored for future use.

Rainwater is collected and infiltrated into the ground.

Rainwater soaks into the ground, preventing runoff and recharging the groundwater.

A. Rain barrel
B. Street runoff
C. Curb cut
D. Rain gardens
E. Cistern

Gutters and Downspouts

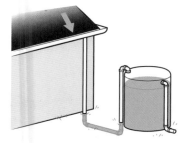

Water remains in the pipe in a "wet" system and should be drained/cleaned out with annual maintenance and in freezing conditions.

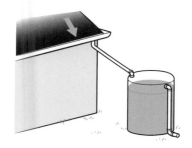

Rainwater drains out of pipe in a "dry system."

Catchment Surface (the Roof)

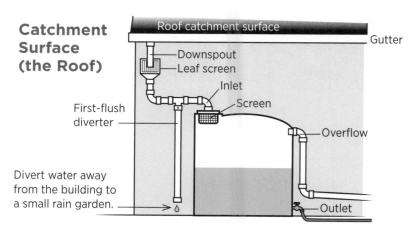

Roof catchment surface

Gutter

Downspout
Leaf screen
Inlet
Screen
Overflow

First-flush diverter

Divert water away from the building to a small rain garden.

Outlet

[Adapted from *The Water-Wise Home* by Laura Allen]

Kitchen sinks usually produce a plentiful supply of water that can be diverted from the sink drain inside the house. Kitchen graywater tends to contain food scraps and grease, so it takes more effort to maintain the system than with those for other graywater sources.

DIVERT
KITCHEN SINK
GRAYWATER
TO THE LANDSCAPE

Divert kitchen water directly below the sink for easy access to the pipes and diverter valve. The graywater pipe needs a route to the landscape, and you can send it below the floor or directly out of the house, depending on your situation and climate. Local code may require the diverter valve be located downstream of the vent connection.

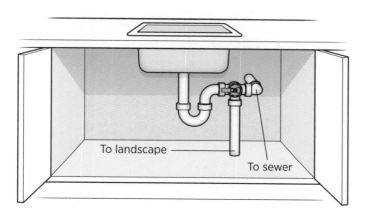

Single sink basin with diverter valve

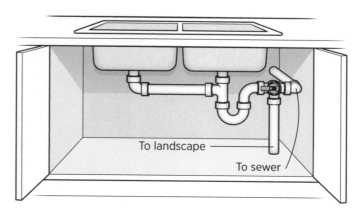

Double sink basin with diverter valve

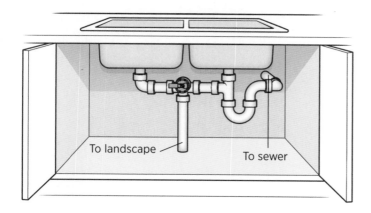

Double sink basin with one side of the sink connected to the graywater system

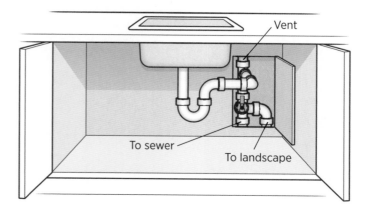

Installation of the diverter valve after the vent connection

[Adapted from *Greywater, Green Landscape* by Laura Allen]

313

CREATE A LAUNDRY-TO-LANDSCAPE GRAYWATER SYSTEM

A laundry-to-landscape system captures graywater from the drain hose of the washing machine, connects to a diverter valve so you can easily switch the system on or off, and then distributes the graywater into the landscape to feed specific plants. It can be built with off-the-shelf parts, doesn't alter the household plumbing, and doesn't require a permit in many states. It is one of the easiest systems to construct, and it is very easy to change.

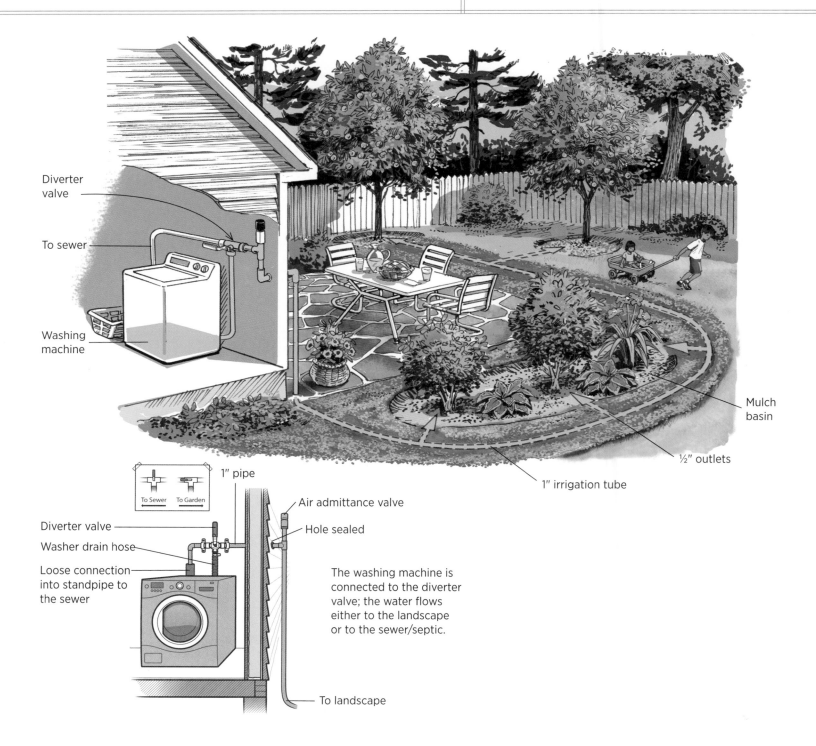

Diverter valve

To sewer

Washing machine

Mulch basin

½" outlets

1" irrigation tube

1" pipe

To Sewer   To Garden

Diverter valve

Washer drain hose

Loose connection into standpipe to the sewer

Air admittance valve

Hole sealed

The washing machine is connected to the diverter valve; the water flows either to the landscape or to the sewer/septic.

To landscape

[Adapted from *Greywater, Green Landscape* by Laura Allen]

Whole roasting is a wonderfully low-labor method of cooking an entire chicken, but it takes a while, and whole roasted birds run the risk of overcooked breasts or undercooked thighs. Spatchcocking (also called butterflying) to the rescue. By simply removing the bird's backbone and cracking the keel bone, you transform the carcass into one that cooks more quickly and evenly and offers a better surface for seasoning. It's best to use shears for this process.

SPATCHCOCK A CHICKEN

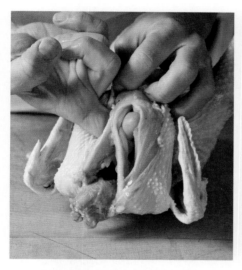

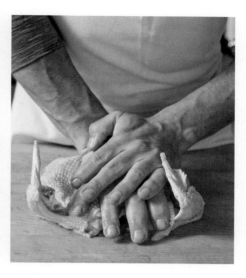

1. **EXTRACT THE WISHBONE.** Peel the skin away from the front of the breasts, exposing the area where the wishbone is located. Follow its shape with the tip of a knife, without plunging too deeply. Then pull the bone away, using your knife or taking hold of the bone with a towel (to help with grip and protect your hand, as the bone can be sharp if broken).

2. **REMOVE THE BACKBONE.** Place the carcass breast side down on the table. Starting at the rear, use shears to cut through the pelvis, leaving a portion (the ilium) attached to the leg (femur). Moving parallel to the spine, continue cutting through the ribs and other bones until you have fully separated one side. Repeat on the other side. Save the backbone and neck for stock.

3. **CRACK THE KEEL.** Lay the spineless carcass skin side up. It will lie flat except for the keel bone, which is situated between the breasts. Press down on the keel bone until you feel it crack and the carcass sits flat on the table.

RENDER
ANIMAL FAT

There are many reasons to cook with animal fats — among them, they are healthier than many processed oils, more economical, and a great deal tastier. With a few exceptions, the fat that is removed from the carcass of an animal must be rendered or cured before you can cook with it. Rendering is a process by which fat is melted and then strained to remove impurities and nonfat solids, greatly extending its shelf life. This fat should be from pasture-raised animals because it is healthier for you and has different characteristics than fat from factory-farmed animals.

1. Chop the fat, if necessary. When you're working with tallow (beef fat) or lard (fat from a pig), it's helpful if the fat is very cold — even frozen. To get even smaller pieces, use a well-chilled meat grinder or the grating disk of a food processor.

2. Transfer the chopped or ground fat to a heavy pot, adding just enough water to cover the bottom of the pot to prevent scorching. Set the pot over low heat.

3. Ladle off the fat as it melts and strain it through fine mesh. Do not let the rendered fat sit on the browning bits, where it will pick up meaty flavors.

4. Discard the cracklings from tallow or feed them to pets. The cracklings from chicken and pork are delicious and can be crisped in a skillet, seasoned with salt, and eaten.

Step 1

Step 2

Step 3

Step 4

[Adapted from *The Fat Kitchen* by Andrea Chesman]

Cook with Animal Fats

Any recipe or technique that requires oil can be adapted to use animal fats as long as the dish is baked or served hot. Here are a few ideas.

ROASTED VEGETABLES: Heat the sheet pan in a 425°F/220°C oven, then add three-quarters of the amount of fat you'd normally use, rotating the pan to coat it. Add the vegetables, tossing to coat, then roast.

FRIED VEGETABLE CHIPS: Slice veggies thinly, then deep-fry at 350°F/180°C.

ANY POTATO RECIPES: Try in mashed or roasted potatoes, hash browns, home fries, or Potatoes Anna (shown above).

SAUTÉED VEGETABLES: Sauté vegetables in poultry fat over high heat, using three-quarters of the amount of fat you normally would.

EGGS ANY WHICH WAY: Poultry fats give the richest flavor.

RICE PILAFS AND RISOTTOS: Poultry fat is a good complement to any recipe that uses chicken broth; Mexican (or Spanish) rice should be made with lard.

STIR-FRIES: Lard and tallow withstand the high heat of wok cooking and make dishes that are not greasy.

PAN-SEARED MEATS AND FISH: Match the meat with the animal fat (use any animal fat for fish).

PIE PASTRY: Short-crust pastry can be made with any animal fat.

QUICK BREADS: Substitute melted fat for the oil the recipe calls for.

MAKE A MEDICINAL INFUSION

An infusion is simply a tea made by steeping herbs in hot water. Infusions are made from the more delicate parts of the plant, such as the leaves, flowers, buds, some berries and seeds, and other aromatic plant parts. Highly aromatic roots such as valerian, ginger, and goldenseal are often steeped rather than decocted, though they are effective either way. After, add the spent herbs to your compost.

1. Put 4 to 6 tablespoons of dried herb (or 6 to 8 tablespoons of fresh herb) into a glass quart jar.

2. Pour boiling water over the herbs, filling the jar. Let steep for 30 to 45 minutes. (The length of steeping time and the amount of herb you use will affect the strength of the tea.)

3. Strain and drink.

Allergy Tea

The herbs in this blend reduce springtime pollen sensitivity and allergy symptoms such as sneezing, runny nose, congestion, inflamed sinuses, and watery eyes. For best results, start taking this tea early in the season (a few weeks before you typically start feeling spring allergies).

* 3 parts nettle leaf
* 1.5 parts catnip
* 1.5 parts peppermint
* 1.5 parts anise seeds
* 1 part eye bright
* 1 part elderflower
* 1 part marshmallow root
* 1 part local bee pollen or 1 teaspoon local honey (optional)
* 0.5 part red clover blossoms

Pour 1.5 cups hot water over 1 tablespoon tea. Cover and steep for 10 to 15 minutes. Add a touch of local honey for a sweeter taste.

[Adapted from *Rosemary Gladstar's Medicinal Herbs* by Rosemary Gladstar and *Healing Herbal Teas* by Sarah Farr (Allergy Tea recipe)]

Decoctions are teas made from the more fibrous or woody plant parts, such as the roots and bark, twiggy parts, and some seeds and nuts. It's a little harder to extract the constituents from these tough parts, so a slow simmer is often required. After, add the spent herbs to your compost. Here are the basic steps.

MAKE A MEDICINAL DECOCTION

1. Place 4 to 6 tablespoons of dried herb (or 6 to 8 tablespoons of fresh herb) in a small saucepan. Add 1 quart of cold water.

2. With the heat on low, bring the mixture to a slow simmer, cover, and let simmer for 25 to 45 minutes. (The length of simmering time and the amount of herb you use will affect the strength of the tea.) For a stronger decoction, simmer the herbs for 20 to 30 minutes, then pour the mixture into a quart jar and set it aside to infuse overnight.

3. Strain and drink.

Dandelion Mocha

This delicious roasted dandelion mocha blend helps you cut back on caffeine consumption. It's delicious and satisfying, with none of the irritating properties of caffeine.

* 3 tablespoons roasted dandelion root
* 1 tablespoon raw cocoa nibs (or raw chocolate)
* ½ cup milk or almond milk
* 1 tablespoon maple syrup or honey
* ½ teaspoon cinnamon powder
* ½ teaspoon vanilla extract
* A dash of nutmeg or clove powder

TO MAKE: Decoct the roasted dandelion root and cocoa nibs in 3 cups water, letting the mixture simmer for 30 minutes. Strain, then add the milk, maple syrup, cinnamon, vanilla, and nutmeg. Stir to combine and reheat if necessary.

TO USE: Drink as you please. If you want to cut down on your coffee consumption, try drinking this in place of coffee, perhaps mixing in a small amount of coffee so that you get a little of the buzz.

[Adapted from *Rosemary Gladstar's Medicinal Herbs* by Rosemary Gladstar]

MAKE ROSEMARY'S ORIGINAL FIRE CIDER

Fire cider is used to prevent colds and flus, to stimulate immune function, and to aid in circulation. This is one of herbalist Rosemary Gladstar's favorite and most famous recipes. She started making it at the herb school she founded, the California School of Herbal Studies, around 1980, and it quickly became a popular and well-known recipe. Made from common kitchen ingredients that are easy to find and inexpensive, fire cider is also simple and fun to make. And it tastes darn good.

INGREDIENTS

- ½ cup grated fresh horseradish root
- ½ cup or more chopped onions
- ¼ cup or more chopped garlic
- ¼ cup or more grated ginger
- Cayenne pepper, fresh (chop it up) or dried (flaked or ground), to taste
- Apple cider vinegar (preferably raw and organic)
- Honey

1. Place the herbs in a half-gallon mason jar and add enough vinegar to cover them by 3 to 4 inches. Seal the jar with a tight-fitting lid. Place the jar in a warm spot and let sit for 3 to 4 weeks. Shake the jar every day to help in the maceration process.

2. After 3 to 4 weeks, strain out the herbs, reserving the liquid. Warm the honey (so that it will mix in well) and add it to the vinegar, to taste. "To taste" means your fire cider should be hot, spicy, and sweet. "A little bit of honey helps the medicine go down . . ." The honey also helps cool the heat, moistens, and balances all the fiery ingredients.

3. Bottle, label, and enjoy! Fire cider will keep for several months if stored in a cool pantry. But it's better to store it in the refrigerator if you have the room.

A small shot glass daily serves as an excellent tonic. Or take fire cider by the teaspoon throughout the day if you feel a cold coming on. Take it more frequently, if necessary, to help your immune system do battle.

[Adapted from *Fire Cider!* by Rosemary Gladstar]

Herbal honey pills are really not much different from electuaries (see page 71); they are simply mixed with more powdered herb and less honey. Instead of blending to a spreadable consistency, the goal is to create a kneadable dough. These soft pills are a convenient way to take an electuary with you while you're on the go.

MAKE HERBAL PILLS

1. Combine powered herbs and a small amount of honey in a bowl and blend until you have a slightly sticky dough. It is better to add your honey just a tablespoon at a time rather than to add a big dollop. You'll be surprised by how little honey this takes. Stir well after each addition because it takes a minute or so for the herbs to absorb the honey.

2. Roll a pinch or two of the sticky dough in your palm to form a small round ball about the size of a pea.

3. In a separate bowl, measure out a few tablespoons of a sweet powder for coating the pills. Cocoa powder, marshmallow root powder, or cinnamon would work well.

4. Roll or toss the pills in the coating powder. Store the finished pills in the refrigerator. A standard serving is three or four pills two or three times per day.

Step 1

Step 2

Step 3

Step 4

Herbal Headache Pill

3 parts hops powder
2 parts lemon balm powder
1 part rosemary powder
1 part skullcap powder
½ part ginger powder
2–3 teaspoons raw honey

½ teaspoon cocoa powder (for rolling)
½ teaspoon guarana powder (for rolling)

TO USE: Eat 1 or 2 pea-sized balls every 30 minutes until symptoms subside.

[Adapted from *Sweet Remedies* by Dawn Combs]

MAKE SEVEN TENTS FROM TARPS

From a rectangle of cloth, canvas, or plastic, you can erect many different shelters. Each sketch shows an elevation along with a view of the material laid flat. Dashed lines indicated folds, dots indicate fasteners, and circles show a ring, needed for suspension or pole support.

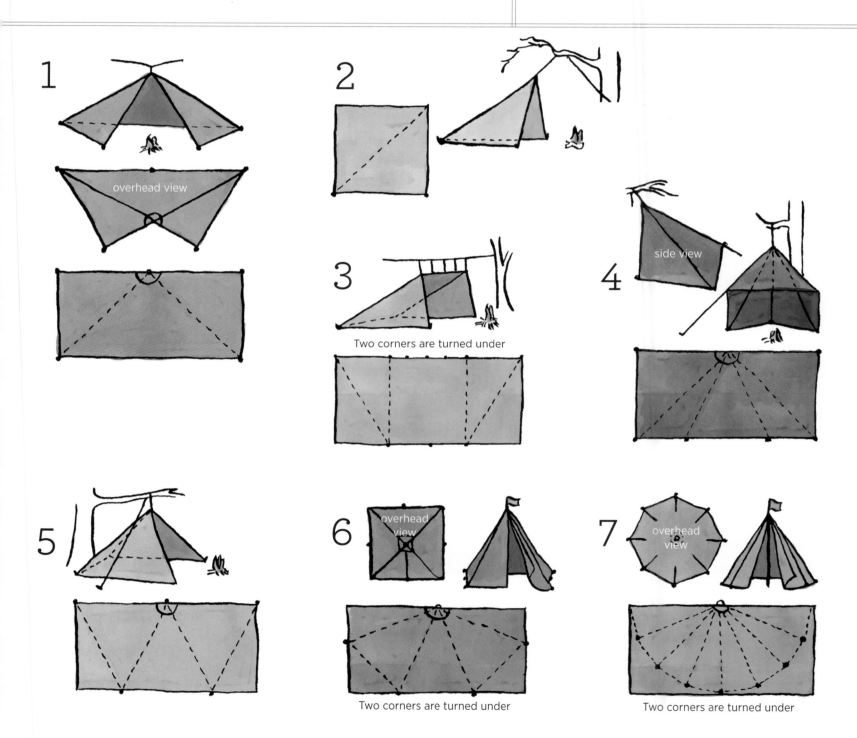

1

overhead view

2

3

Two corners are turned under

4

side view

5

6

overhead view

Two corners are turned under

7

overhead view

Two corners are turned under

322   [Adapted from *100 Skills You'll Need for the End of the World (as We Know It)* by Ana Maria Spagna]

This "Woodsy Waggon," as its original builder Sage Rad likes to call it, is designed to be a smaller version of the traditional gypsy wagons of old Europe. It's a 32-square-foot pullable, lightweight wagon with a small sleep space, counter space for food prep, and storage. It also has a hinged stoop/seat over the front handlebars, which makes a great campfire seat and can flip up to help secure the cabin door.

BUILD A TINY SHELTER ON WHEELS

Base

Roof and Stoop Details

Sides

Optional Built-ins

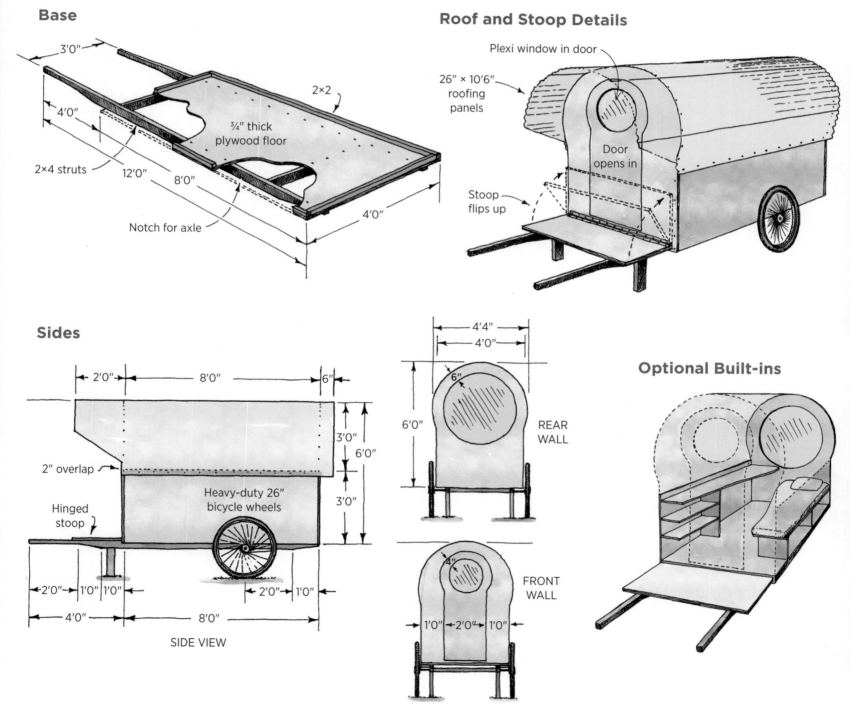

Base:
3'0"
4'0"
2×4 struts
12'0"
8'0"
Notch for axle
4'0"
2×2
¾" thick plywood floor

Roof and Stoop Details:
Plexi window in door
26" × 10'6" roofing panels
Door opens in
Stoop flips up

Sides:
2'0"
8'0"
6"
2" overlap
Hinged stoop
3'0"
6'0"
3'0"
Heavy-duty 26" bicycle wheels
2'0" 1'0" 1'0"
4'0"
2'0" 1'0"
8'0"
SIDE VIEW

4'4"
4'0"
6"
6'0"
REAR WALL

4"
FRONT WALL
1'0" 2'0" 1'0"

[Adapted from *Microshelters* by Derek "Deek" Diedricksen]

REUPHOLSTER A SEAT

Have an old chair or bench that would be perfect except for that stained or ugly upholstery? Reupholstering a seat is a simple process and a great way to give an old piece of furniture a fresh, personal touch. The example pictured here is an old "telephone table," a fun find at an antique shop. The finished size of the seat is 15 by 25 inches.

MATERIALS

- Chair, bench, or stool with a drop-in seat
- 1½"-thick batting or foam
- 1 yard of cotton batting
- 1 yard of fabric, depending on seat size
- Spray adhesive

TOOLS

- Staple remover, flathead screwdriver, or pliers
- Electric kitchen knife or serrated knife (if using foam)
- Staple gun or upholstery tacks

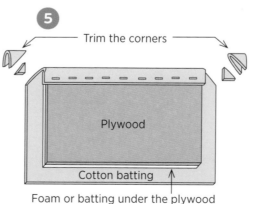

1. Unscrew or pop out the seat of your chair, bench, or stool. Carefully strip off the fabric by removing the tacks or staples on the underside. If you're short on time or everything is in great shape, you might just want to cover the entire seat without stripping off the old fabric.

2. Cut a piece of thick batting or foam to fit the top of the plywood seat. If you are using batting, cut two or three layers to fit the top exactly and affix them to the seat one layer at a time. If you are using foam, cut it to fit the seat with an electric kitchen knife or serrated knife.

3. Use the fabric you removed as a template to cut a piece of cotton batting and a piece of the new fabric, adding 2 inches on all sides.

4. Spray the plywood seat with adhesive, following the manufacturer's directions, and place the cut-to-fit batting or foam on top of it. Let the adhesive set.

5. Flip the padded seat facedown and center it on the large piece of cotton batting. Pull the top edge over to the back of the plywood and staple it in place, starting at the center and moving out to the corners. Do the same for the bottom and sides. Be sure to smooth out any wrinkles as you go. Trim any excess lumps, especially around corners, to reduce bulk.

6. Center the padded seat facedown on the fabric, and attach the fabric in the same way as the batting. Tuck in the corners as you fold, as if you were wrapping a package, and trim away excess, being careful not to cut too close to the sides.

7. Drop the seat back into the frame. Screw it into place, if needed.

5
Trim the corners

Plywood

Cotton batting

Foam or batting under the plywood

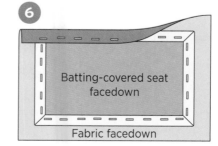

6

Batting-covered seat facedown

Fabric facedown

[Adapted from *Sew Up a Home Makeover* by Lexie Barnes]

Once you've whipped up your first pillowcase, you'll quickly realize that certain items aren't worth buying when they can be made at home with very little time and effort. Create a set from a favorite fabric, or repurpose an old white top sheet, which will be silky soft after many washings, providing the perfect blank canvas for stitching decorative lines.

SEW
A PRETTY
PILLOWCASE

MATERIALS
- 1 yard of cotton fabric (woven or jersey)
- 1 spool of contrasting thread

1. **MEASURE, MARK, AND CUT.** Fold the fabric in half with the right sides together and selvages aligned. Mark and measure a 19- by 34-inch piece, then cut along the lines through both thicknesses of fabric (do not cut along the fold).

2. **HEM AND STITCH THE LINES.** Unfold the fabric. Along one 38-inch edge, press under ½ inch, and then press under another 3½ inches. Stitch the hem close to the inside folded edge with contrasting thread. Then add meandering lines and decorative utility stiches.

3. **CLOSE THE SEAMS.** Fold the fabric in half with the right sides facing, bringing the short edges together. Using a straight stitch, sew a ½-inch seam along the raw edges to close the case. Finish the seam allowances with an overcast stitch, such as a zigzag. Turn the pillowcase right side out.

BUILD A
MANUALLY OPERATED
OUTDOOR SHOWER

What could be better than a hot shower surrounded by the great outdoors? Outdoor showers don't have to be complicated. This design is easy to assemble and requires only minimal materials. The flow of water is controlled by the bather with a foot-operated nautical bilge pump. For privacy, a tarp or other material can be wrapped around the outside of the tripod.

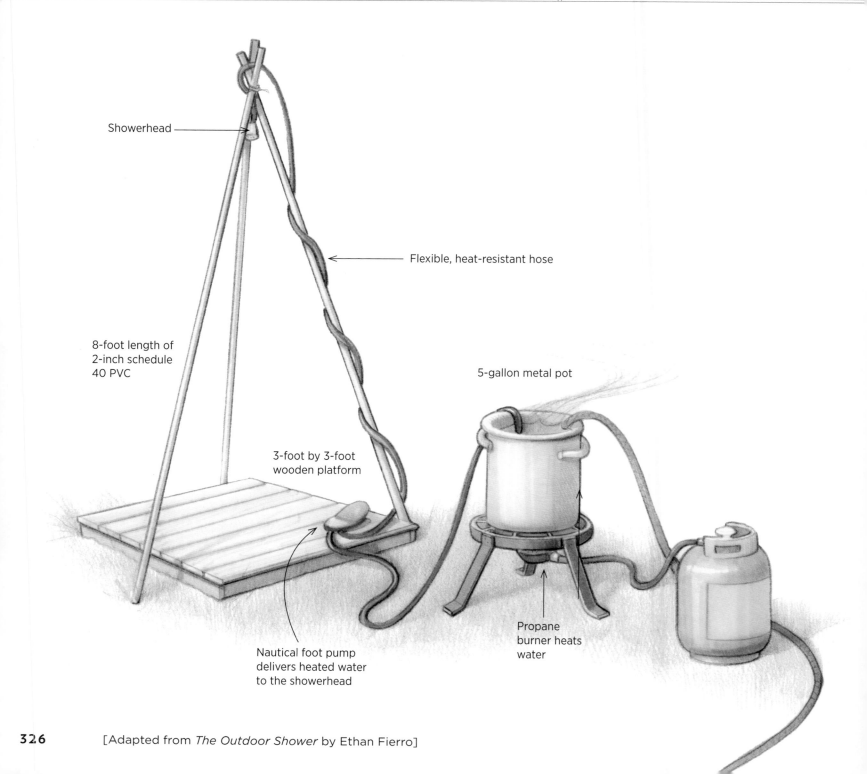

Showerhead

Flexible, heat-resistant hose

8-foot length of 2-inch schedule 40 PVC

5-gallon metal pot

3-foot by 3-foot wooden platform

Nautical foot pump delivers heated water to the showerhead

Propane burner heats water

[Adapted from *The Outdoor Shower* by Ethan Fierro]

There are many different types of windows. Some are wood and some are aluminum. There are double-hung windows, casement windows, horizontal sliding windows, awning, and jalousie windows . . . but no matter what kind of window you have, one of the most common problems is a broken pane.

FIX A BROKEN WINDOWPANE

Replacing a broken pane of glass is not a difficult task and it can save you lots of money. The project varies slightly with each type of window. First the broken glass must be carefully removed. In a wooden window it is often held in place by a layer of putty (a claylike substance) and glazier's points (small metal triangles with sharp points).

1. Scrape away the old putty with a kitchen knife or putty knife.

2. Next, pull away the broken pieces of glass. Make sure to wear protective gloves so you don't cut yourself.

3. You will probably see three or four glazier's points inserted into the wood; pull them out with pliers. Some windowpanes are held in place by small wooden slats that are nailed into place; pry them out.

4. Clean around the lip of the wooden frame and then take an exact measurement of the frame. Write down the length and width so you don't forget the dimensions. At a hardware store or glass company, purchase a new glass pane. Have it cut to fit ⅛ inch smaller than each dimension of your frame. You will also need to buy a small can of putty and some glazier's points.

5. Thinly layer the window frame with putty.

6. Gently push the new glass into place. It should fit snugly up against the lip of the frame.

7. To hold the glass in place, insert a glazier's point along each side of the window frame. Hold the glazier's point right next to the glass and push it into the frame with a straight-slot screwdriver or a putty knife. The point is sharp and should go in easily.

8. Now you need to seal the window tight with an additional layer of putty. The best way to do this is to take a handful of putty and shape it into a ball. Rub the putty ball between your hands until the putty takes the shape of a snake. Press the snake along the edges of the glass, which forms the seal. Finally, smooth over the putty with your putty knife, removing any excess putty from the glass.

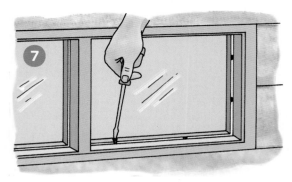

[Adapted from *The Woman's Hands-On Home Repair Guide* by Lyn Herrick]   **327**

SKILLS BY TOPIC

METRIC CONVERSION CHARTS

WEIGHT

TO CONVERT	TO	MULTIPLY
ounces	grams	ounces by 28.35
pounds	grams	pounds by 453.5
pounds	kilograms	pounds by 0.45

US	METRIC
0.035 ounce	1 gram
¼ ounce	7 grams
½ ounce	14 grams
1 ounce	28 grams
1¼ ounces	35 grams
1½ ounces	40 grams
1¾ ounces	50 grams
2½ ounces	70 grams
3½ ounces	100 grams
4 ounces	112 grams
5 ounces	140 grams
8 ounces	228 grams
8¾ ounces	250 grams
10 ounces	280 grams
15 ounces	425 grams
16 ounces (1 pound)	454 grams

VOLUME

TO CONVERT	TO	MULTIPLY
teaspoons	milliliters	teaspoons by 4.93
tablespoons	milliliters	tablespoons by 14.79
fluid ounces	milliliters	fluid ounces by 29.57
cups	milliliters	cups by 236.59
cups	liters	cups by 0.24
pints	milliliters	pints by 473.18
pints	liters	pints by 0.473
quarts	milliliters	quarts by 946.36
quarts	liters	quarts by 0.946
gallons	liters	gallons by 3.785

US	METRIC
1 teaspoon	5 milliliters
1 tablespoon	15 milliliters
¼ cup	60 milliliters
½ cup	120 milliliters
1 cup	240 milliliters
1¼ cups	300 milliliters
1½ cups	355 milliliters
2 cups	480 milliliters
2½ cups	600 milliliters
3 cups	710 milliliters
4 cups (1 quart)	0.95 liter
4 quarts (1 gallon)	3.8 liters

LENGTH

TO CONVERT	TO	MULTIPLY
inches	millimeters	inches by 25.4
inches	centimeters	inches by 2.54
inches	meters	inches by 0.0254
feet	meters	feet by 0.3048
feet	kilometers	feet by 0.0003048
yards	centimeters	yards by 91.44
yards	meters	yards by 0.9144
yards	kilometers	yards by 0.0009144
miles	meters	miles by 1,609.344
miles	kilometers	miles by 1.609344

US	METRIC
0.5 inch	1.27 cm
1 inch	2.54 cm
1.5 inches	3.81 cm
2 inches	5.08 cm
2.5 inches	6.35 cm
3 inches	7.62 cm
3.5 inches	8.89 cm
4 inches	10.16 cm
4.5 inches	11.43 cm
5 inches	12.70 cm
5.5 inches	13.97 cm
6 inches	15.24 cm
6.5 inches	16.51 cm
7 inches	17.78 cm
7.5 inches	19.05 cm
8 inches	20.32 cm
8.5 inches	21.59 cm
9 inches	22.86 cm
9.5 inches	24.13 cm
10 inches	25.40 cm
11 inches	27.94 cm
12 inches	30.48 cm
13 inches	33.02 cm
14 inches	35.56 cm
15 inches	38.10 cm
16 inches	40.64 cm
17 inches	43.18 cm
18 inches	45.72 cm

US	METRIC
19 inches	48.26 cm
20 inches	50.80 cm
21 inches	53.34 cm
22 inches	55.88 cm
23 inches	58.42 cm
24 inches	60.96 cm
25 inches	63.50 cm
26 inches	66.04 cm
27 inches	68.58 cm
28 inches	71.12 cm
29 inches	73.66 cm
30 inches	76.20 cm
31 inches	78.74 cm
32 inches	81.28 cm
33 inches	83.82 cm
34 inches	86.36 cm
35 inches	88.90 cm
36 inches	91.44 cm

US	METRIC
⅛ inch	3.2 mm
¼ inch	6.35 mm
⅜ inch	9.5 mm
½ inch	1.27 cm
⅝ inch	1.59 cm
¾ inch	1.91 cm
⅞ inch	2.22 cm
1 inch	2.54 cm

INDEX

BOOK CREDITS

GARDENING

Adolph, Jonathan. *Mason Jar Science*. 2018. Excerpts on pages 15 and 222.

Bainbridge, David A. *Gardening with Less Water*. 2015. Excerpt on page 14.

Barney, Danny L. *Storey's Guide to Growing Organic Orchard Fruits*. 2012. Excerpt on page 85.

Biggs, Emma and Steven Biggs. *Gardening with Emma*. 2018. Excerpts on pages 219 and 252.

Gough, Robert and Cheryl Moore-Gough. *The Complete Guide to Saving Seeds*. 2011. Excerpt on page 290.

Groves, Maria Noël. *Grow Your Own Herbal Remedies.* 2018. Excerpt on page 76.

Hansen, Anne Larkin, Mike Severson, and Dennis L. Waterman. *A Landowner's Guide to Managing Your Woods*. 2011. Excerpt on page 129.

Hansen, Ann Larkin. *Making Hay*. 2014. Excerpt on page 227.

Hart, Rhonda Massingham. *Vertical Vegetables & Fruit*. 2011. Excerpts on pages 35 and 202.

Hill, Lewis and Nancy. *The Flower Gardener's Bible*. 2012. Excerpt on page 220.

—. *Successful Perennial Gardening*. 1988. Excerpt on pages 289.

LeHoullier, Craig. *Epic Tomatoes*. 2014. Excerpt on page 200.

—. *Growing Vegetables in Straw Bales*. 2015. Excerpt on page 30.

Lizotte, Mike. *Mini Meadows*. 2019. Excerpt on page 177.

Madigan, Carleen. *The Backyard Homestead*. 2009. Excerpt on page 148.

Martin, Byron E. and Laurelynn G. Martin. *Growing Tasty Tropical Plants in Any Home, Anywhere*. 2010. Excerpt on page 190.

McCrate, Colin and Brad Halm. *High-Yield Vegetable Gardening*. 2015. Excerpt on page 143.

O'Sullivan, Penelope. *The Homeowner's Complete Tree and Shrub Handbook*. 2007. Excerpts on pages 62, 186, 188, and 189.

Pleasant, Barbara. *The Complete Houseplant Survival Manual*. 2005. Excerpt on page 12.

—. *Homegrown Pantry*. 2016. Excerpts on pages 86, 146, and 162.

—. *Starter Vegetable Gardens*. 2010. Excerpt on page 32.

Pleasant, Barbara and Deborah L. Martin. *The Complete Compost Gardening Guide*. 2007. Excerpt on page 126.

Reich, Lee. *Landscaping with Fruit*. 2008. Excerpt on page 178.

Smith, Edward C. *The Vegetable Gardener's Bible*. 2009. Excerpts on pages 87 and 123.

Tukey, Paul. *The Organic Lawn Care Manual*. 2006. Excerpt on page 179.

White, Patrick and Lewis Hill. *Growing Christmas Trees*. 2014. Excerpt on page 271.

WELL-BEING

Breedlove, Greta. *The Herbal Home Spa*. 1998. Excerpt on page 88.

Combs, Dawn. *Sweet Remedies*. 2019. Excerpts on pages 71 and 321.

Farr, Sarah. *Healing Herbal Teas*. 2016 Excerpt on page 318.

Gladstar, Rosemary. *Fire Cider!*. 2019. Excerpt on page 320.

—. *Rosemary Gladstar's Herbal Healing for Men*. 2017. Excerpt on page 277.

—. *Rosemary Gladstar's Medicinal Herbs: A Beginner's Guide*. 2012. Excerpts on pages 284, 318, and 319.

Groves, Maria Noël. *Grow Your Own Herbal Remedies*. 2018. Excerpts on pages 76, 78, 82, 137, 138, and 149.

Pagán, Maya. *Girls' Home Spa Lab*. 2018. Excerpts on pages 84 and 184.

Shahin, Christine. *Natural Hair Coloring*. 2016. Excerpt on page 36.

Tourles, Stephanie. *Natural Foot Care*. 1998. Excerpt on page 89.

—. *Pure Skin Care*. 2018. Excerpts on pages 134 and 185.

—. *Stephanie Tourles's Essential Oils: A Beginner's Guide*. 2018. Excerpt on page 79.

Tremayne, Wendy Jehanara. *The Good Life Lab*. 2013. Excerpt on page 38.

Weinberg, Norma Pasekoff. *Natural Hand Care*. 1998. Excerpt on page 91.

NATURE

Erickson, Laura. *The Bird Watching Answer Book*. 2009. Excerpt on page 270.

Erickson, Laura and Marie Read. *Into the Nest*. 2014. Excerpt on page 243.

Harrison, Kathy. *Prepping 101*. 2018. Excerpt on page 74.

Landers, Jackson. *The Beginner's Guide to Hunting Deer for Food*. 2011. Excerpt on page 168.

Laubach, Christyna M., René Laubach, and Charles W.G. Smith. *Raptor!* 2002. Excerpt on page 268.

Leslie, Clare Walker. *The Curious Nature Guide*. 2015. Excerpt on pages 22.

—. *Keeping a Nature Journal*. 2003. Excerpt on page 39.

Mars, Brigitte. *The Natural First Aid Handbook*. 2017. Excerpt on page 75.

McLeod, Brett. *The Woodland Homestead*. 2015. Excerpts on pages 61, 142, 230, 281, 294, 296, 297, and 299.

Mikula, Rick. *The Family Butterfly Book*. 2000. Excerpt on page 254.

Philbrick, Frank and Stephen Philbrick. *The Backyard Lumberjack*. 2006. Excerpts on pages 267 and 295.

Spagna, Ana Maria. *100 Skills You'll Need for the End of the World (as We Know It)*. 2015. Excerpts on pages 23, 128, 242, and 322.

Thacher, Meg. *Sky Gazing*. 2020. Excerpt on page 182.

Zachos, Ellen. *Backyard Foraging*. 2013. Excerpt on page 228.

FOOD AND DRINK

Anderson, Alison and Steve Anderson. *How to Make Maple Syrup*. 2014. Excerpt on page 236.

Bender, Richard W. *Wild Winemaking*. 2017. Excerpt on page 240.

Billis, Stacie. *Winner! Winner! Chicken Dinner*. 2020. Excerpt on page 196.

Caldwell, Gianaclis. *Homemade Yogurt & Kefir*. 2020. Excerpt on page 56.

Carroll, Ricki. *Home Cheese Making*. 2018. Excerpts on pages 10 and 58.

Carroll, Ricki and Sarah Carroll. *Say Cheese!* 2017. Excerpt on page 257.

Chesman, Andrea. *The Backyard Homestead Book of Kitchen Know-How*. 2015. Excerpts on page 70, 195, 238, and 279.

—. *The Fat Kitchen*. 2018. Excerpt on page 316.

Crum, Hannah and Alex LaGory. *The Big Book of Kombucha*. 2015. Excerpt on page 300.

Dojny, Brooke. *The New England Clam Shack Cookbook*. 2008. Excerpt on page 265.

Farrell-Kingsley, Kathy. *The Home Creamery*. 2008. Excerpt on page 258.

Fisher, Dennis and Joe Fisher. *Brewing Made Easy*. 2012. Excerpt on page 102.

Groves, Maria Noël. *Grow Your Own Herbal Remedies*. 2018. Excerpts on pages 138 and 149.

Haedrich, Ken. *The Harvest Baker*. 2017. Excerpts on pages 52 and 199.

—. *Pie Academy*. 2020. Excerpts on pages 204 and 206.

Levin, Jake. *Smokehouse Handbook*. 2019. Excerpt on page 10.

Madigan, Carleen. *The Backyard Homestead*. 2009. Excerpt on page 198.

Manikowski, John. *Fish Grilled & Smoked*. 2004. Excerpt on page 169.

Marcoux, Paula. *Cooking with Fire*. 2014. Excerpts on pages 8 and 282.

Marrone, Teresa. *The Beginner's Guide to Dehydrating Food*. 2018. Excerpt on page 248.

Mosher, Randy. *Tasting Beer*. 2017. Excerpt on page 104.

Pleasant, Barbara. *Homegrown Pantry*. 2016. Excerpts on pages 146 and 162.

Reavis, Charles G. and Evelyn Battaglia, with Mary Reilly. *Home Sausage Making*. 2017. Excerpt on page 250.

Shockey, Kirsten K. and Christopher Shockey. *Fermented Vegetables*. 2014. Excerpts on pages 24 and 26.

—. *Miso, Tempeh, Natto & Other Tasty Ferments*. 2019. Excerpt on page 28.

Thompson, Jennifer Trainer. *Fresh Fish*. 2016. Excerpts on pages 170, 171, and 262.

Vinton, Sherri Brooks. *Put 'em Up!* 2010. Excerpt on page 160.

—. *Put 'em Up! Fruit*. 2013. Excerpt on page 144.

Zachos, Ellen. *The Wildcrafted Cocktail*. 2017. Excerpt on page 285.

CRAFTS

Bethmann, Laura. *Hand Printing from Nature*. 2011. Excerpt on page 40.

Blum, Nicole and Debra Immergut. *Improv Sewing*. 2012. Excerpts on pages 85, 158, and 325.

Blum, Nicole and Catherine Newman. *Stitch Camp*. 2017. Excerpt on page 261.

Bubel, Nancy. *Braiding Rugs*. 1977. Excerpt on page 66.

Durant, Judith and Edie Eckman. *Crochet One-Skein Wonders®*. 2013. Excerpt on page 260.

ffrench, Crispina. *The Sweater Chop Shop*. 2009. Excerpts on pages 94 and 96.

Grindrod, Frank. *Wilderness Adventure Camp*. 2021. Excerpt on page 64.

Grummer, Arnold E. *Trash-to-Treasure Papermaking*. 2010. Excerpt on page 45.

Hiebert, Helen. *Paper Illuminated*. 2001. Excerpt on page 48.

Hobson, Phyllis. *Tan Your Hide!* 1977. Excerpts on pages 16 and 18.

Jarchow, Deborah and Gwen W. Steege. *The Weaving Explorer*. 2019. Excerpt on page 43.

Oppenheimer, Betty. *Sew & Stow*. 2008. Excerpt on page 192.

Pearl-McPhee, Stephanie. *Knitting Rules!* 2006. Excerpt on page 172.

Plumley, Amie Petronis and Andria Lisle. *Sewing School® Quilts*. 2018. Excerpt on page 154.

Redmond, Lea. *Knit the Sky*. 2015. Excerpt on page 174.

Steege, Gwen W. *The Knitter's Life List*. 2011. Excerpt on page 175.

ANIMALS

Belanger, Jerry and Sara Thomson Bredesen. *Storey's Guide to Raising Dairy Goats*. 2017. Excerpt on page 55.

Caughey, Melissa. *A Kid's Guide to Keeping Chickens*. 2015. Excerpt on page 133.

—. *How to Speak Chicken*. 2017. Excerpt on page 130.

Conroy, Drew. *Oxen*. 2007. Excerpt on page 150.

Damerow, Gail. *Storey's Guide to Raising Chickens*. 2017. Excerpts on pages 132, 163, and 292.

Danforth, Adam. *Butchering Beef*. 2014. Excerpt on page 244.

—. *Butchering Chickens*. 2020. Excerpt on page 315.

—. *Butchering Poultry, Rabbit, Lamb, Goat, and Pork*. 2013. Excerpt on page 246.

Delmonte, Patti. *Real Food for Cats*. 2001. Excerpt on page 225.

Dohner, Janet Vorwald. *The Encyclopedia of Animal Predators*. 2017. Excerpt on page 293.

Drowns, Glenn. *Showing Poultry*. 2015. Excerpt on page 291.

Ekarius, Carol. *Storey's Illustrated Guide to Poultry Breeds*. 2007. Excerpt on page 164.

Grandin, Temple. *Temple Grandin's Guide to Working with Farm Animals*. 2017. Excerpt on page 152.

Hyman, Frank. *Hentopia*. 2018. Excerpt on page 255.

Klober, Kelly. *Storey's Guide to Raising Pigs*. 2018. Excerpt on page 152.

Lewis, Charni. *Braiding Manes and Tails*. 2007. Excerpt on page 304.

McElroy, Kevin and Mathew Wolpe. *Reinventing the Chicken Coop*. 2012. Excerpt on page 208.

Mehus-Roe, Kristin. *Canine Sports & Games*. 2008. Excerpt on page 112.

Mettler, John J. Jr., DVM. *Basic Butchering of Livestock & Game*. 2003. Excerpt on page 166.

Moore, Arden. *A Kid's Guide to Cats*. 2020. Excerpts on pages 224 and 226.

—. *A Kid's Guide to Dogs*. 2020. Excerpts on pages 109 and 110.

Morrison, Alethea. *Homegrown Honey Bees*. 2012. Excerpts on pages 68, 69, and 212.

Patry, Karen. *The Rabbit-Raising Problem Solver*. 2014. Excerpts on pages 286, 287, and 288.

Ruechel, Julius. *Grass-Fed Cattle*. 2005. Excerpt on page 80.

Sanford, Malcolm T. and Richard E. Bonney. *Storey's Guide to Keeping Honey Bees*. 2018. Excerpts on pages 68 and 215.

Sellnow, Les and Carol A. Butler. *Knowing Horses*. 2012. Excerpts on pages 302 and 303.

Simmons, Paula and Carol Ekarius. *Storey's Guide to Raising Sheep*. 2019. Excerpt on page 92.

Thomas, Heather Smith. *Storey's Guide to Training Horses*. 2019. Excerpts on pages 21 and 303.

Weaver, Sue. *The Backyard Cow*. 2012. Excerpts on pages 153 and 256.

—. *The Backyard Goat*. 2011. Excerpt on page 223.

—. *The Backyard Sheep*. 2013. Excerpt on page 54.

The Xerces Society. *Attracting Native Pollinators*. 2010. Excerpts on pages 210 and 253.

SUSTAINABLE LIVING

Allen, Laura. *Greywater, Green Landscape*. 2017. Excerpts on pages 313 and 314.

—. *The Water-Wise Home*. 2014. Excerpts on pages 307 and 312.

Barnes, Lexie. *Sew Up a Home Makeover*. 2011. Excerpt on page 324.

Bibbins, Neil. *Bikes, Scooters, Skates & Boards*. 2002. Excerpts on pages 216 and 217.

Herrick, Lyn. *The Woman's Hands-On Home Repair Guide*. Excerpts on pages 118, 121, 306, and 327.

Kachur, Bridget. *Every Woman's Quick & Easy Car Care*. 1997. Excerpts on pages 272 and 276.

McKenzie, James W. *Antiques on the Cheap*. 1998. Excerpts on pages 98 and 100.

Roach, Kristin M. *Mend It Better*. 2011. Excerpts on pages 115 and 116.

Scheckel, Paul. *The Homeowner's Energy Handbook*. 2013. Excerpts on pages 194 and 274.

Twitchell, Mary. *What to Do When the Power Fails*. 1999. Excerpt on page 120.

BUILDING

Bradley, Fern Marshall. *Building Raised Beds*. 2015. Excerpt on page 106.

Carlsen, Spike. *The Backyard Homestead Book of Building Projects*. 2014. Excerpts on pages 50 and 108.

Diedricksen, Derek "Deek". *Microshelters*. 2015. Excerpt on page 323.

Editors of Storey Publishing. *The Vegetable Gardener's Book of Building Projects*. 2010. Excerpt on page 124.

Fierro, Ethan. *The Outdoor Shower*. 2005. Excerpt on page 326.

Holman, Will. *Guerilla Furniture Design*. 2015. Excerpts on pages 232 and 234.

Long, Jim. *Making Bentwood Trellises, Arbors, Gates & Fences*. 1998. Excerpt on page 308.

McRaven, Charles. *Stonework*. 1997. Excerpts on pages 309 and 310.

Sobon, Jack. *Hand Hewn*. 2019. Excerpt on page 141.

Thomsen, Amanda. *Backyard Adventure*. 2019. Excerpt on page 191.

ART CREDITS

COVER PHOTOGRAPHY CREDITS

Front, top to bottom, left to right

Row 1: © Erin Kunkel, © Jared Leeds Photography, Mars Vilaubi, © Joshua McCullough, Phytophoto, © Emulsion Studio

Row 2: © Winky Lewis, © Emulsion Studio, © Keller + Keller Photography, © Keller + Keller Photography, © Erin Kunkel

Row 3: © Evi Abeler Photography, © Stacey Cramp, © Jason Houston, © Joe St.Pierre, © Melinda DiMauro

Row 4: © Tom Thulen, Mars Vilaubi, © Stacey Cramp, © Erin Kunkel, © Carl Tremblay

Row 5: © Emulsion Studio, Mars Vilaubi, © Jared Leeds Photography, © Michael Piazza Photography, © John Polak

Row 6: © Margaret Lampert, © Evi Abeler Photography, © Keller + Keller Photography, © Stacey Cramp, © Jennifer May Photography, Inc.

Row 7: © Mars Vilaubi, © Keller + Keller Photography, © Kip Dawkins Photography, © pingpao/stock.adobe.com, © Adam DeTour

Back, top to bottom, left to right

Row 1: Mars Vilaubi, © Alexandra Grablewski, © Lynn Stone, © Rob Cardillo

Row 2: © Winky Lewis, © Jared Leeds Photography, © Joe St.Pierre, © Keller + Keller Photography

Row 3: Mars Vilaubi, © Erin Kunkel

INTERIOR PHOTOGRAPHY CREDITS

© AardLumens/stock.adobe.com, 253 r. 3rd from t.

© Adam DeTour, 4 l., 248

© Adam Mastoon, 41, 151, 267

© age fotostock/Alamy Stock Photo, 177 row 2 c.l.

© Alan Shadow/USDA-NRCS, 253 b.r.

© Alexandra Grablewski, 83, 158 c., 159, 325

© alexmak72427/iStock.com, 81 b.r.

© AntiMartina/iStock.com, 319 b.

© Arco Images GmbH/Alamy Stock Photo, 150

© Arunee/stock.adobe.com, 181 t.l.

© Aubrie Pick, 249

© Ben Fink, 48

© beres/stock.adobe.com, 179 t.

© Blade kostas/iStock.com, 45 b.r.

© Bruce Newhouse/Salix Associates, 210 t.c.

© Bryan Reynolds/Alamy Stock Photo, 211 t.r.

© Carl Tremblay, 15, 222

© Carmen Troesser, 56, 57 ex. t.c., 315

Carolyn Eckert, 158 r.

© Chokniti Khongchum/ Shutterstock.com, 131

© Daniil/stock.adobe.com, 180 t.

© David W. Inouye, 211 b.r.

© DGFOTO/stock.adobe.com, 179 b.

© Dina Avila, 29

© Dirk/stock.adobe.com, 181 t.c.

© Dominic Perri, 197

© Donna Chiarelli, 126, 127 b.

© Donna Griffith, 218, 219

© Ellen Zachos, 229 b.c.

© Emulsion Studio, 4 c.r., 52, 53, 199, 204–207

© Erin Kunkel, 24, 25, 27, 208, 209

© Eric Lee-Mäder/The Xerces Society, 253 r. 2nd from t.

© Evi Abeler Photography, 58–60, 259

© fottoo/stock.adobe.com, 63 b.r.

© Gina Kelly/Alamy Stock Photo, 180 b.r.

ILLUSTRATION CREDITS

Alethea Morrison, 23, 128, 322

Alison Kolesar, 32, 118, 119, 121, 254, 258, 290, 306, 327

© annalisa e marina durante/Shutterstock.com, 68

© Bethany Caskey, 164, 165

Bethany Caskey, 132, 163

Betty Oppenheimer, 192 r. (all), 193

© Beverly Duncan, 4 c.l., 190, 236 ex. b.r.

Beverly Duncan, 87, 289

Brigita Fuhrmann, 148 t., 192 l.

Bruce Kieffer, 50, 108 l.

Carl Fitzpatrick, 309, 311

Christine Erickson, 12, 13, 62, 63, 188, 324

© Clare Walker Leslie, 22, 39

© Crispina ffrench, 95, 97

© Elara Tanguy, 55, 92, 93, 152 t.

© Elayne Sears, 5 r., 69, 106, 107, 108 r., 152 b. (all), 153, 178, 198, 215, 237 b. (all), 256, 291, 293

Elayne Sears, 48, 49, 166, 167, 266, 271 #2 & #3

© Elena Bulay, 5 c.l., 6 c.l., 70, 195, 238, 239, 279, 280

Ilona Sherratt, 74, 182, 183, 191, 271 #1 & #4, 302 row 4; 160, 161, 286–288 based on illustrations by © Elara Tanguy; 236 b.r. based on illustration by © Elayne Sears; 265 based on illustrations from Maine Lobster Producers Council; 270 based on illustration by © P. Fernandez

© Jack Sobon, 141

© Jada Fitch, 268 t. (all), 269 t. (all)

Joanna Rissanen, 4 r., 21, 302 rows 1–3, 303

© John Burgoyne, 11, 14

© John Manikowski, 169

© John Provost, 194, 274, 275

Judy Sitz, 268 b. (all), 269 b. (all)

© Julia Rothman, 38

© Karen Bussolini, 187, 189

Karen Manthey, design by Brenda K. B. Anderson, 260

© Kathryn Rathke, 35, 112–114, 202, 203

Kathy Bray, 89–91

Kimberlee Knauf, 242

© Koren Shadmi, 233, 234

Laura Tedeschi, 88

Lee Mothes, 323

© Lauren Nassef, 174

Melanie Powell, 304

© Michael Gellatly, 30, 31, 124, 125

Randy Mosher, 104, 148 b.

Rick Daskam, 308

© Robert LaPointe, 326

© Robert Smith, 168

Robert Strimban, 6 r., 98–101

© Ryan McMenamy, 158

© Ryan Wheatcroft, 110, 111, 224, 226

© Scotty Reifsnyder, 103

Steven Edwards, 16–19

© Steve Sanford, 61, 129, 142, 143, 227, 230, 231 b., 281, 294–299, 307, 312–314

Steve Sanford, 75

Storey Publishing, 66, 67, 120

Terry Dovaston, 216, 217, 272, 273, 276

© Veronica B. Lilja/peppercookies.com, 243